WRITING AND POLITICAL ENGAGEMENT IN SEVENTEENTH-CENTURY ENGLAND

EDITED BY

DEREK HIRST

Washington University, St. Louis

and

RICHARD STRIER

University of Chicago

CAMBRIDGE
UNIVERSITY PRESS

CAMBRIDGE UNIVERSITY PRESS
Cambridge, New York, Melbourne, Madrid, Cape Town, Singapore, São Paulo, Delhi

Cambridge University Press
The Edinburgh Building, Cambridge CB2 8RU, UK

Published in the United States of America by Cambridge University Press, New York

www.cambridge.org
Information on this title: www.cambridge.org/9780521661751

First published 1999
This digitally printed version 2008

A catalogue record for this publication is available from the British Library

Library of Congress Cataloguing in Publication data

Writing and political engagement in seventeenth-century England /
edited by Derek Hirst and Richard Strier.
p.   cm.
Includes bibliographical references and index.
ISBN 0 521 66175 7
1. English literature – Early modern, 1500–1700 – History and
criticism. 2. Politics and literature – Great Britain – History – 17th
century. 3. Authors, English – early modern, 1500–1700 – Political
and social views. 4. Great Britain – Politics and
government – 1603–1714. 5. England – Intellectual life – 17th century.
I. Hirst, Derek. II. Strier, Richard.
PR438.P65W76   1999
828'.40809358 – dc21   98-56018
CIP

ISBN 978-0-521-66175-1 hardback
ISBN 978-0-521-10030-4 paperback

Contents

Notes on contributors

JACKSON I. COPE is Leo S. Bing Professor Emeritus of English and Comparative Literature at the University of Southern California. He has written extensively on Renaissance literature in such books as *Theatre and the Dream: From Metaphor to Form in Renaissance Drama* (1973), *Dramaturgy of the Daemonic: Studies in Antigeneric Theater from Ruzante to Grimaldi* (1984), and *Secret Sharers in Italian Comedy: From Machiavelli to Goldoni* (1996).

BARBARA DONAGAN is Research Fellow at the Huntington Library, San Marino, California. She is the author of articles on legal, moral, and material aspects of the English Civil War, and on ways in which seventeenth-century men and women tried to negotiate a way between their religious beliefs and the demands of practical life. She is currently at work on a book on the codes, conditions, and conduct of the English Civil War.

STANLEY FISH, whose thirtieth anniversary edition of *Surprised by Sin* was awarded the 1998 Hanford Book Prize by the Milton Society, is Dean of the College of Liberal Arts and Sciences at the University of Illinois at Chicago. In the next year, Harvard University Press will publish two new books by Professor Fish, *How Milton Works* and *The Trouble with Principle*.

DEREK HIRST is William Eliot Smith Professor of History at Washington University in St. Louis. The interdisciplinary concerns that intermittently surface in his *England in Conflict 1603–1660* (1999) have been more fully vented in a series of essays on Marvell as well as on the 1650s.

J. G. A. POCOCK is Professor Emeritus at the Johns Hopkins University. He has been interested in the history and politics of historiography for over forty years, and is now at work on a series of volumes studying

Edward Gibbon and his age. He is a director of the Folger Institute Center for the History of British Political Thought.

VICTORIA SILVER is Associate Professor of English at the University of California at Irvine. She has written on Hobbes, Ben Jonson, Milton, Marvell, and Thomas Browne. Her book, *The Predicament of Milton's Irony*, is forthcoming from Princeton University Press.

QUENTIN SKINNER is Regius Professor of Modern History at the University of Cambridge and a Fellow of Christ's College, Cambridge. His most recent books are *Reason and Rhetoric in the Philosophy of Hobbes* (1996), and *Liberty before Liberalism* (1998), both published by Cambridge University Press.

RICHARD STRIER is Frank L. Sulzberger Professor in the College and in the Department of English at the University of Chicago. He has published *Love Known: Theology and Experience in George Herbert's Poetry* (1983) and *Resistant Structures: Particularity, Radicalism, and Renaissance Texts* (1995). He is currently working on Shakespeare, on Donne, and on seventeenth-century women poets.

This volume is dedicated
to the memory and the example of
John M. Wallace
1928–1993

Introduction

Derek Hirst and Richard Strier

Festschrifts are suspect. They are often motivated more by personal affection than by intellectual kinship, and they are therefore often mere miscellanies. This volume is and is not a tribute to John Wallace. Although the contributors were all friends of Wallace's, their intention is to pay tribute to work they continue to admire rather than to the man whose loss they have mourned. There is accordingly a true intellectual kinship among the contributors in their sense of kinship with Wallace's work, especially his book, *Destiny His Choice: The Loyalism of Andrew Marvell* (1968).[1] That book demonstrated the inadequacy of the (mostly) discipline-bound scholarship that then flourished in Departments of History and English on both sides of the Atlantic; it represented a virtuoso integration of texts and contexts. These features will inevitably seem less remarkable now that a whole generation since has added rich examples and approaches to contextual and historical reading. Even more important, however, than an interdisciplinary method that showed how the timeless and the time-bound could be held in balance and made to illuminate each other is the example of Wallace's reconstruction of an intellectual and political world from the point of view of a recognizable person. Wallace took as his subject a poet and a polemicist, Andrew Marvell, who had the fortune to live through interesting times. By dint of broad imaginative sympathy – together with broad and thoughtful reading in the pamphlet literature of the time – Wallace was able to show with rigor and plausibility how Marvell had coped with questions of value and allegiance in a revolution. Wallace's Marvell was neither a martyr nor a timeserver. He was an engaged and deeply thoughtful observer and participant in his times, one who maintained his principles (and his head) from the days of army radicalism and regicide through the period of restoration and reaction. Thoughtful historical engagement was both the topic and the mode of Wallace's book.

The essays in this volume are united by a shared concern with the relationship between ideas and events, and by a shared geographical and chronological focus: England in the seventeenth century. Their authors may take some encouragement from recent developments in ethical and political theory that have resurrected a case for a life of virtue that seemed lost in the 1980s, with that decade's exaltation of the market.[2] They are certainly convinced that such a case has merit for seventeenth-century England, for in that time and place, perhaps more than most others, the relationship of virtue and principle to public life became an issue of particular urgency.

The claims of seventeenth-century public life on individual virtue are perhaps easiest to demonstrate by contrast with what came after. The rise of politeness and the cult of domesticity by the end of the century were accompanied by the novelists' assertions of a purely private virtue inconceivable a century earlier; indeed, Bernard Mandeville was soon to argue the irrelevance of virtue, conventionally measured, to the public weal.[3] The development of a prudential, and even probabilistic, moral calculus in the same period may have made more widespread, and certainly more respectable, the kind of guarded public commitment that an earlier age dismissed as "politique," or questioned as "trimming."[4] And on the other hand, the growth of party encouraged public commitments that were not necessarily or largely principled.

The seventeenth century stands out for the sensitivity and complexity of its scruples and commitments against the period that preceded as well as that followed it. By the end of the sixteenth century, the Ciceronian civic humanism that had a brief heyday in the England of Sir Thomas Elyot, Roger Ascham, and Sir Thomas Smith had been complicated and challenged by the rise of a darker Tacitean vision.[5] But though the Tacitists' fascination with reason of state and self-preservation might argue the submergence of conscience, in fact it is clear that Tacitism did not triumph over Ciceronianism, either within individuals – Francis Bacon, for example, has been characterized as engaged in a life-long interrogation of Tacitean principles[6] – or in the wider polity, where Milton's *Of Education* provides a reminder of the vitality of the civic humanist tradition of education for moral involvement in the world. Hobbes's pupil and patron, William Cavendish, the second Earl of Devonshire, was an heir to that tradition, as was Algernon Sidney.[7] What was characteristic of the seventeenth century was a heightened awareness of the complexities of the relation of virtue and the public life as a result of the divergence of the two main strands of humanism; we might turn for a typically thoughtful and provocative example to the deep disagreements in 1659 between Milton and James Harrington over the potential of individuals versus institutions as vehicles for reform.[8]

The seventeenth century brought other pressures, both on the polity and the individual. Not only did increasing political, and ultimately constitutional, dissension require the attention of and even redress from superiors and inferiors alike, but religious controversy subjected ordinary consciences to a call to action in defense of God's truths. But of course the religious history of the period cannot be told only as a story of confrontation. The long-term transition from the Seven Deadly Sins to the Ten Commandments may have been at its height in this period of deep and widespread awareness of the Calvinists' God. That shift may have made the application of doctrine to daily life more urgent; it also made it more complicated. Both complexity and urgency are evident in the godly moralism that arose at the end of Elizabeth's reign, overlying an increasingly rigid predestinarian orthodoxy, and bringing to the fore the troubling subject of the relation of the individual to God's purposes.[9] Further, the development of an overtly contestatory Arminianism gave additional polemical charge to the role of human will and human actions. The determination to expunge the self in George Herbert reflects, no less than does Oliver Cromwell's famous hostility to "self-ends," the pressure of the dilemma of selfhood in this culture.[10]

It was for such reasons that the probity of the individual became the qualification for participation in public life in a way that it had not been before and perhaps was not to be again until the modern age of the media blitz and its attendant cult of personality.[11] Indeed, this volume helps us to see how little the "private/public" distinction captures of the texts and (as far as we can reconstruct it) the experience of persons in seventeenth-century England. The denial of the "private/public" distinction is insisted on by contemporary theoretically informed scholars, by Althusserian Marxists and Foucauldian new historicists who find common ground with feminist scholars and queer theorists in an insistence that all relations are structured by power, and that all human life is in an important sense political. Such structuring and such politicization did not go unremarked in early modern England. In this period, with its governing metaphor of the "body politic," it was difficult to ignore the politics of the body, physical and sexual as well as civic. Recent work has reminded us of the interconnectedness of the political, conventionally understood, and the personal: royal favorites, local worthies, and unruly women alike were often the targets of prodigious, and unfailingly sexual, slander and ridicule.[12] Many of the figures and texts that have long held the interest of seventeenth-century scholars reinforce and embody the perception that the personal is also political. The preoccupations of satire, that seventeenth-century delight, are not far from those of the charivari. The vivid characterization of the rogues gallery in *Absalom and Achitophel* helps to explain why that poem should have been the most successful of all seventeenth-century political writings after that other literary masterpiece, *Eikon Basilike.* Conversely, the *Eikon*'s construction of the king as the Virtuous Man was surely more central to its success than were its historical reflections.

The pressure to vindicate the uprightness of the self could extract some surprisingly revelatory and sustained performances from those who would engage in public life in seventeenth-century England. John Milton often appears singular in the insistence with which he trails the intimate and the sexual before the reader in a progress that took him to some quite radical religious and political places. Yet others were moved by similar assumptions about the relation of the personal and the political. To Milton's fury, Charles I's happy marriage became part of the political argument of *Eikon Basilike.*[13] In our non-theoretical moments, we tend to conceive of and experience sexuality, like conscience, as an intensely private matter, but the "fantasies" of a major Caroline courtier, revolving around his own and his wife's sexuality, were a consciously contrived rhetorical work meant as an act of public vindication and self-representation.[14] Such vindication may have been particularly necessary in a court whose rather prudish tone was set by the extravagantly married king and queen, yet Sir Kenelm Digby's readiness to circulate his manuscript account, a form (as Jackson I. Cope insists) of "publication," speaks to Digby's concern to establish the "inner" self on a wider stage. Digby's use of the form of the "meditation," moreover, itself points us to the ways in which the most intense and private emotional experiences were, and were seen to be, guided by and part of public norms.

No less self-consciously, another "gentleman" later in the century, Algernon Sidney, was to hold out personal virtue as his defense in the court of Judge Jeffreys as well as in the court of opinion when he was charged with treason. But, as Victoria Silver shows, Sidney's business with virtue went further than simple self-representation. He manifested and theorized a highly developed ideology of the politics of reason, volition, and character, and an equally developed critique of a contrary politics. Proper judgment of political structures hinged on how one conceived and represented oneself as a person. Like Milton in 1659, Sidney was intrigued by the relation of political forms to personality types – what sort of person does a particular political structure or theory imply or create? Algernon Sidney saw the tyrant and the courtier as precisely the figures that Sir Robert Filmer's patriarchal absolutism created, in theory and in practice; and he saw implicit in his own existence as English gentleman, rational agent, and user of a properly demythologized language the need for a very different civic polity.

Sidney's republican critique obviously took him further than most of his contemporaries (other than, for instance, John Milton and Sir Henry Vane, Jr.) would have gone in the predication of public life on personally embodied virtue. This political distance serves to alert us to how easily the "organic" world of the "body politic," with its apparent implications of hierarchy and place, could give way to something much less stable when the overlap of personal and public was tested. Yet however unusual the outcome, the means by which Sidney constructed his self-representation were not uncommon. The ancient model of republican virtue was for him not a "rhetorical flourish" but part of the self, for which he lived and died.

That models are not foreign to the self, not pieces of costume which the actor manipulates at will, is a lesson of both the Cope and the Silver essays. But this is not to go to the other analytic extreme, to the claim that models of behavior, or, to put it another way, particular discourses, actually molded, even constructed, the individual. We are beginning to learn, through close study of the best-documented cases, of the complexity of the relations between language or models and agency.[15] A full appreciation of that complexity is essential to an understanding of almost any aspect of Renaissance selfhood. Again, our post-modern situation puts us in closer touch with the seventeenth century than with the nineteenth. We are prepared to see models as parts of the self, as constitutive of it, in a way that Romantic conceptions of the "true self," independent of social constructions, would scarcely allow. But as the study of particular cases ineluctably demonstrates, the self's relation to its models cannot plausibly be seen as a merely passive one.

The project of consciously fashioning a moral and political agent in seventeenth-century England has rarely been more fully unfolded than in Quentin Skinner's account of Thomas Hobbes's program for William Cavendish. We may be tempted to dismiss the strenuous course Milton lays out in his *Of Education* as simply Miltonic, an idealistic eccentricity. But Hobbes put into practice something that appears likely to have been fully as demanding – with a significant difference. No less devoted than Milton or Algernon Sidney to classical models of thought and style, the young Hobbes seized on Thucydides as exemplar. Hobbes was not merely showing off his Greek and demonstrating his humanist credentials in translating Thucydides from (as he insisted) the best available text; it mattered that his main labor of scholarship was on the most analytical and cold-eyed of classical historians, and one who, as Hobbes noted, "least of all liked the democracy." Milton may have come to an equal distaste for democracy, but Thucydides' dispassionate dissection of the political motives and stratagems of his countrymen was not Milton's primary mode – though it was Hobbes's.

Hobbes may seem to have lived out the injunctions to self-preservation issued by his other mentor, Tacitus; but we should not conclude that the choice of classical models was necessarily predictive of political alignment. J. G. A. Pocock observes in Thomas May the historian a commitment to Thucydides equal to that of Hobbes, and perhaps more passionate.[16] Yet May, who turned to Thucydides as a model for understanding the calamities of a civil war through which the historian himself was living, was a loyal servant of the Long Parliament. Thucydides may have helped to carry both Hobbes and May to thoughtful positions, but certainly not to the same one.

Of course, classical models did not stand alone as guides to writers and readers in the period. We have long known that preachers, on both sides of the political divide, urged their auditors into battle. They sought to bring their congregations and their readers to the point of resolution and political engagement, presenting both the duty of absolute obedience and the duty of resistance as addresses to the conscience.[17] "Conscience" was the great term that, for all but the most purely prudential individuals, spanned as it were the space between the inner life of the individual and the life of action in the public arena. Barbara Donagan demonstrates that in the early 1640s, men heard from some pulpits that their consciences "knew" that the king was "not only not to be resisted, but also to be actively obeyed," regardless of what in particular he commanded, while they also heard from (other) pulpits that "for the defense of religion and the reformation of the church, it was lawful to take up arms against the king" – indeed, that it was a conscientious duty to do so. By which set of duties one felt one's conscience to be bound defined one as a person in that historical crisis. But perhaps, for some at least, only in that crisis. A remarkable finding of Pocock's essay is May's profound sense of the difficulty of understanding, let alone explaining, events of which one has been a witness. May's perplexities of conscience and allegiance in time of civil war were not, he realized, the same as his perplexities as "author," for the fullness of the meaning of the past was lost. It seems likely that he recognized that there had been, for many, the moment of choice that Donagan's casuists tried to argue away; indeed, May came close to a recognition that there had been an existential moment to whose content and meaning even Thucydides could give no guide.

The pulpit, the press, and the classics – as imparted through formal and informal schooling – were great sources of influence on seventeenth-century persons. Yet there was another such locus to which both the pulpit and academia were ambivalent to the point of hostility: the public theater. Yet pulpit-preaching was itself a form of public performance, and this did not escape contemporaries' notice. Stanley Fish teases out the complex relation between the ideal of self-abnegation in George Herbert's poetry and the ideal of "showing holy" in Herbert's advice to fellow clergy in *The Country Parson*. The determination to bring the world to Christian selflessness generated a double paradox. The enactment of holiness and selflessness was envisioned by Herbert as generating an extraordinary power over the lives and selves of others; the loving and selfless scrutiny of the parson over his congregation aspired to something like tyranny. It was, and was known to be, the aspiration of clerical opinion-shapers throughout the period, and it helps explain some of the intensity of anti-clericalism in the 1640s and 1650s. A more visible paradox lay in the way Herbert, the poet of the spirit, offered as advice to his colleagues his own keen awareness of the need to manifest "the holy" in public in concrete, bodily, and well-rehearsed ways.

In a post-Restoration controversy over conformity and conscience, an establishment divine accused non-conformists of treating the pulpit like a "puppet-play" for their use of exactly such devices as George Herbert recommended to the conformists themselves. A non-conforming respondent then threw back the taunt of theatricality at the establishment – "Who so mimical, so theatrical in a pulpit, as some amongst your selves?"[18] An insistence on the importance of public performance, of enacting oneself and one's part, co-existed in this culture with a deep suspicion of hypocrisy. Not surprisingly, when virtue and its representation were so central to public life, the seventeenth century manifested both of these impulses with a remarkable, and unusual, vigor. The world of the stage, and of literature in general, could not be kept separate from the world of the pulpit and politics. As Derek Hirst shows, Marvell's use

of the figure of "Mr. Bayes" to attack the hypocrisy as well as the
religious intolerance of the established church involved a whole complex in which "literary" and "political" considerations cannot (and
should not) be disentangled.

The end of the century brought a solution of a kind to the grand
dilemma of the relation of the self to public life. By then each was
beginning to acquire its own distinctive calculus, in the emerging science
of interest theory and in politeness. But it is ironic that what is perhaps
the most skeptical note was uttered near the beginning of the century.
The greatest figure of the public theater in the English Renaissance was
fully aware of the claims for the transformative power of education, of
the pulpit, and of the theater; *The Tempest* can be seen as interrogating
those claims. The figure of Prospero is at once that of the humanist
schoolmaster, that of the minister who means to stir and afflict the
consciences of the guilty, that of the dramatist who wishes to affect his
audiences through his presentations, and, if Richard Strier is right, that
of the colonial administrator.[19] Here Strier's argument intersects with
Fish's, for the aim of both their central figures, Prospero and Herbert's
Country Parson, is the exercise of power, whether through "virtue" and
learning, or self-abnegation. Strier's reading of *The Tempest* suggests that
Shakespeare, perhaps unlike George Herbert and the pulpit orators of
the early 1640s studied by Donagan, was profoundly uncertain about
the extent to which individuals could wield power transformatively in
any guise. And *The Tempest* can also be seen as mediating the public and
the "private" since, if its skepticism about the transforming capacity of
power extends to the "power" of theater as well, then all those readers
and playgoers from the eighteenth century on who have wanted to see
Prospero as a stand-in for Shakespeare may well have a point after all.

The essays in this volume represent a number of different ways of
approaching their shared concerns. There is, of course, no one preferred or "right" way to read or to write about texts from the past. Some of
the essays in the volume seem plainly the work of their disciplines –
Donagan's essay could perhaps only have been written by a historian,
and Strier's and Fish's perhaps only by literary scholars – whereas other
essays in the volume, those by Hirst and Silver, for instance, have no
obvious disciplinary marks. We feel that this is as it should be. Shared
concerns need not be reflected in set approaches. One of the advantages
of a collection like this is the way in which the essays, pursuing their own
tasks in their own ways, cross-pollinate each other and suggest connections that a more discipline-bound collection might not. No one could

have predicted the confluences between Fish's essay and those of Strier and Hirst, nor known in advance or been able to plan the prominence of Thucydides or of the critique of "romance" politics in this volume. Such connections are themselves truer to the non-discipline-bound realities of the past than any set of merely historical or literary essays are likely to be, however broad their range of reference.

No less instructive than the conclusions are the potentials suggested by the different approaches. For instance, while Fish does not himself extensively contextualize, he discerns a set of structures in his texts that are important data for historical analysis. "Formalism" and "historicism" need not be at odds, though of course they can be and often have been. "Close reading" can be a tool for historians as well as for literary critics, as can awareness of literary allusions and rhetorical modes.[20] Single texts can be profitably studied; multiple texts by single authors can be profitably studied; selected texts by multiple authors can be profitably studied; so can large cross-sections of the discourse of a particular moment. What is important is that scholars attend, sensitively, knowledgeably, and (as far as possible) with their preconceptions suspended, to the multiple ways in which the texts of the past speak to each other and to us; and, as well, that scholars seize and create opportunities, formal or informal, to transcend their disciplinary training by examining shared concerns from their different perspectives, and then communicating with one another. As this volume testifies, some rich and – best of all – surprising convergences occur when such collocations take place.

"I am Power": normal and magical politics
in The Tempest

Richard Strier

Je suis la Puissance.

Prospero, in Aimé Césaire's *Une Tempête*

No play of Shakespeare's is more strongly focused on the matter of service and on the master–servant relationship than is *The Tempest*. Service interested Shakespeare throughout his career, but from the period of *Hamlet* on, the aspect of this topic that most concerned him was the need for servants, subjects, and subordinates of all kinds to resist immoral commands. *King Lear* can be seen as culminating this development, and in the three Romances prior to *The Tempest*, it is taken as axiomatic that "Every good servant does not all commands" (*Cymbeline*, v.i.6). *The Tempest*, however, does not seem to fit into this picture. Its focus seems to be on proper obedience rather than on proper disobedience, and it seems to be much more conservative than the plays that precede it. In earlier work, I opined that the explanation for the conservatism of *The Tempest* "was probably to be found in its colonial context."[1] The chapter that follows tries to sort out these puzzlements. It will show that while the "virtuous disobedience" theme does not entirely disappear from *The Tempest*, the focus of the play with regard to masters and servants is on the extent and possibilities of human power – of power conceived of as pure coercion, as the capacity to force the bodies and, as far as it turns out to be possible, the minds of rational beings. *The Tempest*, in other words, will be seen to be about the practical or existential rather than the moral limits of authority. To this exploration, the "colonial context" will indeed be relevant.

The chapter falls into two parts. The first examines what can be called (by analogy with Thomas Kuhn's "normal science") "normal politics" in the play.[2] This is the politics in which Shakespeare's "axioms" about proper and improper obedience do apply, in which conspiracy and usurpation are familiar, and in which various other topoi

and practices of European politics, Machiavellian and otherwise, operate. The second and larger part of this chapter focuses on features that
are distinctive to *The Tempest*: Prospero's "Art" and, correlated with it,
his two remarkable (and non-European) servants. The dynamics that
operate in this context constitute what I will call "magical politics." My
exploration of this is indebted to Caribbean and African appropriations
of *The Tempest*, the remarkable post-World War II phenomenon of using
The Tempest to explicate actual colonial situations and struggles, an
analytical and literary practice that began in earnest with Dominique O.
Mannoni's *Psychologie de la colonisation* in 1950 and that culminated in
Aimé Césaire's *Une Tempête* in 1969.[3] This chapter goes in the other
direction, using material from the analyses of colonialism derived from
The Tempest as ways of reading *The Tempest*. The post-colonial appropriations are not merely fanciful and anachronistic, yet they have been
acknowledged only fleetingly in criticism on the play and have not been
sustainedly used as a resource. The pro-colonialist afterlife of *The
Tempest* has been taken more seriously by literary critics than has the
anti-colonialist afterlife of it.[4] Mannoni and Césaire will help me explicate the play's "magical" politics. At the very end, the chapter will
return to the "normal" politics of the play and attempt briefly to assess
the relation between its two frameworks. I should state at the outset that
I do not see this chapter as exploring the "political unconscious" of the
play, or as finding meanings in it that the play does not want us to
notice.[5] I understand the meanings that I ascribe to the play as conscious
and intended.[6]

NORMAL POLITICS

The most obvious of the moments in which the "proper disobedience"
theme does get into *The Tempest* is Ariel's reported non-compliance with
Sycorax even though Ariel "was then her servant" (1.ii.271).[7] This non-
compliance, "refusing her grand hests" (line 274), is presented as having
been more an ontological matter, a matter of sensibility or fastidiousness, than a moral one – "thou wast a spirit too delicate / To act her
earthy and abhorr'd commands" (lines 272–3) – but the refusal is clearly
seen as praiseworthy. It is hard not to think of the "earthy and abhorr'd
commands" as sexual – the "abhorr'd"/"ab-whored" pun was readily
available – and the context is smarmily salacious ("for one thing she did
/ They would not take her life" [lines 266–7]). Ariel's refusal of this
"hest" would therefore function to differentiate him, in the dialectic

established in *King Lear*, from the type of servant that Oswald is and that Edgar (as "poor Tom") pretends to have been, one who "serv'd the lust of [his] Mistris heart, and did the acte of darknesse with her."[8] Ariel will not "serve" in this way, but the question remains as to whether there are any other sorts of commands that he will not obey. I have already suggested that the moral dimension of his refusal of Sycorax's grand hests is unclear. Prospero shares Ariel's fastidiousness – "delicate" is one of Prospero's favorite words for Ariel – and Prospero has obtained Ariel's services by freeing him from the punishment to which Sycorax's "unmitigable rage" at Ariel's disobedience confined him. But are there circumstances in which Ariel would disobey Prospero? Are there commands he would disobey that are not physically degrading? We will return to this.

A more straightforward, if less spectacular, example of what we might call the "*Lear–Pericles–Cymbeline*" dialectic on the matter of service occurs in Prospero's narrative of the loss of his dukedom, a key instance of normal European politics. In describing how his wicked brother ousted him, Prospero stresses his brother's skill at personnel management, or, in less anachronistic terms, at working the courtly mechanisms of reward and punishment. Antonio soon got the hang of

> how to grant suits,
> How to deny them, who t' advance, and who
> To trash for over-topping.   (I.ii.79–81)

Antonio truly "perfected" these techniques, and through these familiar and strictly political skills, these management skills (I want to keep the edge of ordinariness), Antonio was able to do something that Prospero finds quite amazing. The language of this speech is extremely interesting; it is verse and we must attend to it as such. Prospero finds what Antonio was able to do so amazing that he needs three different phrases to describe the phenomenon, even though the first phrase seems more than sufficient and the second and third merely synonyms. Playing on the idea of subordinates as "creatures" of their social superiors, Prospero sees Antonio as having "new created / The creatures that were mine" (lines 81–2). The line-break is significant here. For a moment Antonio is like the Christian God, creating out of nothing, rather than the Platonic demiurge creating out of matter. Prospero affirms this description with "I say" ("new created . . . I say") before seeming to back off from it with the diminuendo that ends the line, "or chang'd 'em" (line 82). But he reasserts a strong view at the beginning of the next line with, "Or else new form'd 'em" (line 83). Prospero's "creatures" were mere putty in the hands of this political demiurge, who was able to create, change, and "new form" them. This is an image of political power as truly transformative and god-like. The next lines seem to retreat again, and to present Antonio's power as merely situational ("having both the key / Of officer and office"), but this "key" turns out to be musical and mystical rather than merely practical, for with (or in) this "key" Antonio "set all hearts i' th' state / To what tune pleased his ear" (lines 83b–85a). Antonio established concord; he captured "hearts," not just bodies.

The result of all this was that the entire political class of Milan seems to have obeyed Antonio. He was able to levy a "treacherous army" (line 128) and to find any number of "ministers for th' purpose" of disposing of Prospero and Miranda (line 131). The unexplained love that the "people," presumably plebeian (not, now, the "creatures," presumably courtly) bore Prospero prevented Antonio from having Prospero and Miranda straightforwardly murdered, but no one prevented them from being placed aboard an unrigged, rotten boat and put to sea. The deposed duke and his daughter were aided by a single courtly figure, who, like the virtuously disobedient Camillo in *The Winter's Tale*, "being then appointed / Master of this design" exceeded and countermanded his charge ("Out of his charity") and provided Prospero and his infant with "stuffe and necessaries" and with the books that Prospero prized "above his dukedom" (lines 162–8). It is typical of *The Tempest* that not Gonzalo's moral heroism but his "charity" is stressed, and that the disobedient nature of his action – compare Gloucester's explicitly treasonous "courtesy forbid" in *Lear* – is never made explicit. Gonzalo's act of forbidden charity is completely surreptitious; since it is never discovered by Antonio, it is never labeled as treason. Yet *The Tempest* has a hard time acknowledging even this mild and obviously laudable intervention. At the end of the play, Prospero praises Gonzalo for being "a loyal sir / To him thou follow'st" (v.i.69–70). This is certainly ambiguous, but, in context, it seems to mean loyal to Antonio. Is Prospero being disingenuous here, or does he find it difficult to praise disobedience even when it is virtuous and he himself has been the beneficiary of it?

The theme of virtuous disobedience versus immoral compliance is part, as I have suggested, of "normal politics." In the other major moment of normal European politics in the play, that is, in the other moment of serious treachery – Antonio's subornation of Sebastian to supplant and murder Alonso – Gonzalo is again singled out. Once

Antonio, in a phrase that picks up the theme, "with this obedient steel," succeeds in killing the sleeping king, Antonio assures Sebastian that Alonso's followers will be far from protesting Sebastian's usurpation. In a brilliant image, he says, "They'll take suggestion as a cat laps milk" (ii.i.283). Again the image is of skillfully gaining willing compliance. Shakespeare substitutes the complaisant cat for his normal dog who knows "naught ... but following," but the picture (and the contempt) is the same.9 Gonzalo is marked for death, since he alone is not thus eagerly open to "suggestion."

These themes, as I have said, are very muted in *The Tempest*. There are only a few moments in which the "virtuous disobedience" trope is at work in the dramatized (as opposed to narrated) action. We are perhaps intended to feel a flicker of admiration for Ferdinand's abortive attempt to "resist" Prospero's accusatory power (i.ii.468), and for Miranda's limited disobedience of Prospero (in telling Ferdinand her name [iii.i.36–7]). The most interesting of such moments occur in the Boatswain's dialogue with the aristocrats in the opening tempest and in Ariel's dialogue with Prospero in Act v. In the latter moment, Ariel functions as a good counselor in the full moral sense. Prospero is certainly in a state of high excitement; he has just been in (and is perhaps still in) a towering rage. He has set his dogs on Caliban and company and is exulting that "At this hour / Lies at my mercy all mine enemies" (iv.i.261–2). He has been notably unable to maintain his composure and his role of master of ceremonies at the betrothal of Ferdinand and Miranda. He is at the mercy of his rage. "Some passion works him strongly," says Ferdinand, and Miranda claims (somewhat disingenuously) that "Never till this day / Saw I him touch'd with anger, so distemper'd" (iv.i.143–5). Yet despite Ariel's deep fear of Prospero's anger – which on an earlier occasion prevented Ariel from speaking out ("I thought to have told thee of it; but I fear'd / Lest I might anger thee" [iv.i.168–9]) – Ariel now suggests to Prospero that Prospero ought to "become tender" to his European enemies. Ariel should be seen as following Kent's advice in *King Lear* (borrowed, I think, from the radical theorist, Buchanan) about not "Being oile to fire," not being one of those servants who encourages "every passion / That in the natures of their Lords rebells" (TLN 1148–50).10 Ariel's intervention against the passion that "rebels" in Prospero leads Prospero likewise to side "with my nobler reason 'gainst my fury" (v.i.26). Ariel's intervention is truly an act of virtuous opposition. The fact that it succeeds should not blur its moral and political outlines. He is, at this moment, the virtuously outspoken courtier of Castiglione's fourth Book and of the first scene of *Lear*.[11]

Although the Boatswain of the opening scene can hardly be described in courtly terms, he too can be seen as enacting a form of "virtuous disobedience." The political meaning of his action, however, is quite complex. The Boatswain is peremptory and rude to his social superiors, grandly commanding them to "trouble me not" (1.i.17–18). Yet his rudeness is entirely in the service of attempting to do his job. "You mar our labour" is his complaint (line 13). He understands the nature of the (apparent) situation – both meteorologically and socially. He knows that there is labor to be done and he knows that the aristocrats will not do it. When he says, in exasperation, "Work you then" (line 42), it is an end-game rejoinder, not a serious proposal. His behavior, for all its rudeness, is entirely within a framework of social hierarchy. There is no rebellion here. He orders the aristocrats "to cabin" – the important point is that he does not order them to work. That, apparently, is inconceivable. Shakespeare's presentation here is in sharp contrast to the willingness of aristocrats to labor in a storm that is repeatedly emphasized in the Bermudan shipwreck narrative from which he is deriving some of his details. William Strachey asserted, wonderingly, that "the better sort, even our governor and admiral themselves, not refusing their turn . . . there was not a passenger, gentleman or other . . . but was able to relieve his fellow," and, to hammer the point home, Strachey explicitly noted that this included "such as in all their lifetimes had never done hour's work before."[12] Shakespeare's Boatswain is keenly aware of the limits of political authority in the face of nature – "if you can command these elements to silence, and work the peace of the present, we will not hand a rope more; use your authority" (lines 21–3)[13] – but he questions "authority" only metaphysically, not socio-politically.

MAGICAL POLITICS

The Boatswain's comments on the limits of "normal" – that is, political – authority bring us to the central feature of *The Tempest*, the presence of non-normal authority (and non-normal politics) in the play. As soon as we meet Prospero, we find out that he can "command these elements to silence, and work the peace of the present." The name of this non-normal authority in the play is "Art," which here means magic. Prospero's magic, his special power, is what makes the treatment of "author-

ity" in this play special. It is also, I will argue (following Mannoni) what
makes the focus of the play colonial. What Shakespeare seems to have
intuited and embodied in the figure of Prospero is that, at their cores,
the Renaissance idea of magic and the idea of colonial administration
have the same fantasy content: namely, the idea of omnipotence. Both
figures, the magus and the colonial administrator, are defined by having
special kinds of servants – "spirits" or daemons on the one hand;
"natives" on the other.[14] As Stephen Orgel notes, "what Prospero's
magic chiefly enables him to do is control his servants."[15] As with so
much else in English drama, Christopher Marlowe seems to have
initially given voice to the crucial association between the fantasies.
When Dr. Faustus is first "glutted with [the] conceit" of magical power,
and is stating his resolve "To practise magic and concealed arts" to the
friends (Valdes and Cornelius) who have urged him in this direction,
thoughts of "the new-found world" are strongly present to all of them.
Valdes expresses the core fantasy by coordinating the two kinds of
servants:

> As Indian Moors obey their Spanish lords,
> So shall the spirits of every element
> Be always serviceable to us three.[16]

The rule of the Spanish in the new world is the closest analogue that
Marlowe can think of to the vision of magical omnipotence. Shakespeare remembered this lesson.

The equation between magic and colonial administration helps explain many things in Shakespeare's magian play.[17] Most importantly, it
explains a central fact about which the critics have been remarkably
incurious: why Prospero's "Art" (unlike Faustus's) can only work in a
particular locale. Despite all Prospero's vaunted powers, he can apparently do nothing to bring his enemies to his island ("bountiful Fortune
... hath mine enemies / Brought to this shore" [1.ii.178–80]), and he
cannot, apparently, use his powers directly to get himself home and
re-seize his dukedom. What this means, interpretatively, is that any
attempt to read Prospero "straight" as a magus cannot be right.[18] A
magus could, of course, use his powers anywhere. Seeing magic as
equivalent to colonial administration explains a related point as well. It
explains why, in contemplating his life off the island, Prospero imagines
himself not as "this famous Duke of Milan" (v.i.192), but as a weak and
vulnerable penitent looking toward death. Although there is some
confusion about this in the criticism (to which we shall return), Prospero

does not see his return to Milan as a return to life and work but as an escape from them – he will "retire me to my Milan, where / Every third thought shall be my grave" (v.i.310–11). Life on the island, in other words, is not Prospero's nightmare but his wish-fulfillment dream. This is Mannoni's great insight – the centrality of a certain set of (infantile) psychological satisfactions to the experience of colonial administration.[19] Prospero's life and his "work" are on the island. Sharply as Frantz Fanon and Aimé Césaire criticized Mannoni's views on the mentality of the colonized, they both accepted Mannoni's view of the psychology of the colonial administrator.[20] Fanon admiringly notes "the intensity with which M. Mannoni makes us feel the ill-resolved conflicts that seem to be at the root of the colonial vocation."[21] At the end of *Une Tempête*, Césaire's Prospero chooses to remain on the island.[22]

Mannoni distinguished sharply between the conquistador/explorer, on the one hand, and the colonial governor on the other.[23] Shakespeare could have studied the psychology of the colonial administrator in the many accounts of his countrymen in Ireland and, especially, of the Spanish in the new world.[24] Seeing Prospero as embodying this psychology gets the focus of the colonial dimension of the play on the only place where it can plausibly be: on Prospero's relation to his non-European servants. For, apart from these relations, Prospero is a very odd colonizer. He is not, in fact, by the English definition, a colonizer at all. The *True Declaration of the State of Virginia* (1610) explained that "a Colony is therefore denominated, because they [the settlers there] should be *Coloni*, the tillers of the earth, and stewards of fertilitie."[25] Following the innovation in the practice and theory of colonization that the Spanish made before the beginning of the sixteenth century, the English vision of colonization always included cultivation.[26] Colonies were often called "plantations," as in Bacon ("Of Plantations") and Bradford (*Of Plymouth Plantation*).[27] A "plantation" was a militarily guarded and maintained agricultural settlement.[28] Cultivation, farming, and building were central to the English conception of colonization; they were what made colonization a "civilizing" process.[29] The (attempted) conquest and resettlement of Ireland was the model.[30] Sir John Davies pours scorn on the Irish gentry because (except when they occasionally imitated the English) the Irish never "did build any stone or brick house" and "neither did any of them in all this time plant any gardens or orchards, enclose or improve their lands"; William Crashaw explains that the American savages need (and desire) "civility" for their bodies almost as much as they need (and desire) Christianity for their souls, since "a savage cannot plow, till, plant, nor set."³¹ Prospero looks very odd indeed in this context. He seems to have neither built, planted, nor "set" anything on the island. His "cell" seems to be a cave.³² His Masque of Ceres presents a magnificent vision of fully cultivated and very English (or Dutch) land ("banks with pioned and twilled brims" [IV.i.64]), yet there is no indication that he grows anything, raises anything, or even has a garden on the island.³³

In this context, we can recognize that Shakespeare's emphasis in *The Tempest* is not on what Prospero has done but on the relationships that he has established. We meet him not at the moment of discovery or conquest but at a moment when he has already had a history on the island. The essence of Prospero's situation on the island is not cultivation, except in the mental sense. He is a "governor" rather than a "planter," and "governors" were often thought of as especially (and sometimes only) appropriate for the uncivil and, especially, the non-European. A leader of the defiant local gentry on the Isle of Wight in the 1580s told Sir George Carey, the queen's newly commissioned governor of the island, that "if he would needs be a governor, then he should go into the West Indies among the base people."³⁴ The essence of Prospero's role is rule. As Mannoni suggests, Prospero is in a situation where he is, at least in his own mind, the only true adult.³⁵ As Prospero experiences his situation, he is "among the base people." He has, as he experiences it, no peers, only inferiors: a boyishly androgynous "spirit," a fifteen-year old daughter, and "a salvage and deformed slave."³⁶ Paradise! Not another adult European male (or female) for thousands of miles. In 1774, when George Ogilvie established a plantation on the Santee river in South Carolina, he experienced himself as "like the Tyrant of some Asiatick Isle, the only free Man in an Island of Slaves."³⁷ This is the ideal situation for someone who has, as Mannoni wonderfully puts it, "a grave lack of sociability combined with a pathological urge to dominate."³⁸

And dominate Prospero does. He is concerned, as the Spanish were, not primarily with his claims to land as with his claims to rule, especially to command labor.³⁹ Let us begin with Prospero's relation to Ariel, since it is possible to ignore or downplay the element of domination in this relationship. Prospero first addresses Ariel as "servant" (I.ii.187), and one might think that a distinction is in place here. But Prospero later addresses Ariel as "slave" (at I.ii.270), and Ariel addresses Prospero as "master" (actually, "great master" [I.ii.189]). Roberto Fernández Retamar is correct that, in this regard, "there is no real Ariel–Caliban polarity."[40] Ariel's role in relation to Prospero is to be the embodiment of his magic, the provider of desired results without effort and utterly free of normal constraints: "To answer thy best pleasure, be 't to fly, / To swim, to dive into the fire, to ride / On the curl'd clouds" (I.ii.190–2). In *Totem and Taboo*, Freud saw the essence of magic in the infantile belief in "the omnipotence of thought."[41] Prospero commands Ariel, "Come with a thought," to which Ariel replies, "Thy thoughts I cleave to" (IV.i.164–5). (Significantly, this conception disturbs Frank Kermode, for whom it is part of the evidence that Shakespeare's characterization of Prospero's relation to Ariel is not "theurgically pure.")[42] As far as Prospero is concerned, Ariel exists as pure projection. The affection between Ariel and Prospero needs to be looked at carefully. It is largely part of the service relation. Ariel gives detailed and eloquent accounts of how well he has performed Prospero's bidding ("in the waist, the deck, in ev'ry cabin, / I flam'd amazement" [I.ii.197–8], and Prospero commends him ("Why, that's my spirit!" [line 215b]). Ariel's great slavish question – "Do you love me, master? No?" (IV.i.48) – expresses the nature of the relationship; the context of the question is a profession of total readiness to serve: "Before you can say 'come' and 'go'" (line 44). Prospero loves Ariel as the perfect instrument, and Ariel apparently takes pride in being such.

The merest suggestion that Ariel has an agenda or even a will independent of Prospero's projects produces an extraordinary rage in Prospero (rage – despite Miranda's assertion to the contrary – being one of Prospero's most frequent emotions).[43] Shakespeare dramatizes this early on. In the first conversation between Prospero and Ariel, after Ariel's description of his extraordinary skill and effectiveness at "performing" the tempest and "disposing" the king's ship, Ariel greets Prospero's announcement that "there's more work" (for Ariel) with this response:

> Is there more toil? Since thou dost give me pains,
> Let me remember thee what thou hast promis'd,
> Which is not yet perform'd me.   (I.ii.242–4)

Ariel expects to be an object as well as an agent of "performance." "Performance" is a technical term in contract law, and Ariel reminds Prospero of the "contract" between them. Though addressed and treated as a slave, Ariel seems to have something like the legal status of an indentured servant. In return for perfect reliability – "no lies ... no mistakings" – and a perfect attitude of servility – "without grudge or grumble" – Prospero apparently promised to "bate" Ariel "one full year" (lines 248–50) of their contract (which apparently was for thirteen years, which puts the closing date right at the moment of the play).[44] Prospero is outraged at the idea that he should be reminded of something, that someone else's historical consciousness should be brought to bear on the present moment. He is so outraged at being rather gently reminded ("let me remember thee") that he turns the tables on Ariel and accuses him of forgetting a crucial fact in their relationship. Prospero twice accuses Ariel of forgetting "From what torment I did free thee," and when Ariel twice denies this accusation – very reverently the second time ("I do not, sir") – Prospero bursts out, "Thou liest, malignant thing!" (lines 250–9). This seems a false charge as well as a wildly inappropriate characterization, but Prospero wants his role as savior in the foreground, and he wants, most of all, to make it clear that if his (presumably non-"earthy") commands are not obeyed, his rage will be just as "unmitigable" as Sycorax's (line 276). As a number of critics have noted, despite Prospero's contempt for Sycorax, he threatens, in effect, to become her.[45] It is worth pointing out, however, that there is a significant difference between the actions that are seen as unleashing the particular torture that Prospero borrows from Sycorax. Where she was actually disobeyed, Prospero threatens to bestow the punishment on the mere fact of being questioned:

> If thou more murmur'st, I will rend an oak,
> And peg thee in his knotty entrails, till
> Thou hast howl'd away twelve winters.   (1.ii.294–6)[46]

"Murmuring," it should be noted, was the standard English term for biblical reluctance toward God's commands; biblically alert auditors would have noted this.[47] No wonder Ariel asserts that he will be "correspondent to command" (line 297). And, after Prospero finally does acknowledge that he remembers the contract – all that Ariel asked in the first place – Ariel throws himself into a frenzy of obeisance: "What shall I do? Say what; what shall I do?" (line 300). Prospero finds this attitude totally acceptable.

   The "urge to dominate" is as almost as much a feature in Prospero's relation to Miranda is as it in his relation to Ariel, and it complicates or inflects the issue of love. That a Renaissance prince would spend some "care" on the education of his only child and heir, even if female, and would make great effort to secure her a dynastically advantageous match – these things are not at all surprising. They are part of "normal politics" in the Renaissance, at least as much a matter of prudence and statecraft as of love. That Prospero is to be taken as having had, as he repeatedly says, "care" of Miranda is undoubtedly true (I.ii.16, 174). His represented interactions with her, however, are typically impatient and hierarchical. George Lamming, another analyst of colonialism fascinated by *The Tempest*, emphasizes the weirdness of how long it has taken Prospero to tell Miranda the most basic facts about their history. Lamming notes that "It has taken [Prospero] twelve years to tell the child one or two things which any decent parent of his intelligence would have passed on long ago."[48] We might also note the obvious relishing of power involved in Prospero's repeated postponements of Miranda's enlightenment: "You have often / Begun to tell me what I am, but stopp'd, / Leaving me to a bootless inquisition" (I.i.33–5). Prospero has kept Miranda "innocent" of the most basic features of the behavior and appearance of Europeans so that (as in his response to her "brave new world" remark) he can patronize her "innocence." He has created the conditions that allow him to patronize her. His inability to acknowledge the will of others is operative in his refusal to believe that Miranda is fully and properly attending to his narrative of their shared past – despite the lines just quoted regarding her frequent "inquisition" into the subject and despite the repeated assurances that she offers him, culminating in her final exasperated joke ("Your tale, sir, would cure deafness" [line 106]). As Mannoni says of this interchange, Prospero "tries to treat her as an equal; but he fails."[49] Perhaps most indicative is Prospero's response, even if it is a "mock" one, to Miranda's reasonable plea for gentle treatment of Ferdinand – "What! I say, / My foot my tutor?" (I.ii.468–9).[50] Prospero is always aware of hierarchy and of his "natural" place at the top of it.

This brings us, inevitably, to Caliban. He is first mentioned in Prospero's admonitory "reminding" Ariel of Ariel's story. Although he only grudgingly acknowledges that Caliban has "A human shape" (I.ii.281–4), Prospero is absolutely clear on the social function of "that Caliban, / Whom now I keep in service" (lines 285–6). Caliban seems strictly parallel to Ariel. Shakespeare appears to be introducing us to Prospero's household, and doing so in order of rank: child, upper servant, lower servant (or perhaps, house servant and field servant). As we have already seen, there is no distinction from Ariel implied when Prospero refers to Caliban as "my slave" (line 310). What is distinctive is the specific nature of Caliban's "service." This service is strictly, etymologically, economic – that is, having to do with the *oikos*, the

household. When Miranda expresses a reluctance to interact with
Caliban, Prospero insists, strongly and in explicit detail, on Caliban's
indispensability:

> We cannot miss him: he does make our fire,
> Fetch in our wood, and serves in offices
> That profit us.   (i.ii.363–5)

What exactly these "offices / That profit us" are is left unspecified, but
what is clear is that Caliban's services are indispensable precisely because they are physical. Just as it was inconceivable to Alonso and
company that they might actually help during the storm, it is apparently
inconceivable to Prospero to fetch his own wood or make his own fire (or
catch his own fish or do his own dishes – see ii.ii.180–4). The situation
here strikingly duplicates that of the Virginia settlers, who were much
maligned for their lack of industriousness, and were also, especially as
portrayed in Ralph Lane's report on the first colony in 1584, quite
dependent on help from "the savages" for survival (especially with
regard to "dams . . . for fish").[51] The climate of Prospero's island seems
to be more like that of Virginia than like that of Bermuda, since
Caliban's main task, and the main example of degrading labor in the
play, is the carrying of wood or logs (apparently for heating rather than
for cooking – there is no mention of this – and certainly not for
construction). Prospero intends for Ferdinand to experience his physical
labor as "baseness" (iii.i.12), as, in Harry Berger's words, "degradation."[52] Ferdinand calls it "slavery" (iii.i.62). Prospero's attitude toward
physical labor is clearly the older classical and medieval (and Spanish)
one, rather than the newer Protestant one.[53]

Yet despite the clarity of Caliban's economic role, Prospero's commands to Caliban often seem to be mere exercises in authority. When
Prospero first summons Caliban (with "What, ho! slave!"), Caliban
assumes that what Prospero wants from him is wood-fetching, and
Caliban asserts that "There's wood enough within" (i.ii.316). Prospero
must accept the truth of this, since he asserts that wood-carrying is not
what he wants, but that "there's other business for thee" (line 317). Yet
Prospero ends this initial interaction by commanding, "Fetch us in
fuel" (line 368). So there is no "other business" for Caliban. Prospero
simply wants to exercise power and, as with Ariel, to insist on his
version of history. The history that Shakespeare creates for Prospero
and Caliban is quite complex. Caliban evokes an initial experience of
reciprocity:

> When thou cam'st first,
> Thou strok'st me, and made much of me; wouldst give me
> Water with berries in it; and teach me how
> To name the bigger light, and how the less
> That burn by day and night: and then I lov'd thee,
> And show'd thee all the qualities o' th' isle,
> The fresh springs, brine-pits, barren places and fertile.
>
> (1.ii.334–40)

In this idyllic picture, knowledge, affection, and food are all exchanged and shared. There is no reason to doubt the substantial truth of
this picture. Prospero does not deny it, and the knowledge exchange was
successful: Prospero presumably now knows the "qualities o' th' isle,"
and Caliban did indeed learn the lessons in natural philosophy that
Prospero was teaching him out of Genesis.[54] But obviously something
intervened between this idyll and the present of the play. After Caliban's
speech on their early history, Prospero accuses Caliban of being a "most
lying slave," and one "Whom stripes may move, not kindness" (lines
346–7). These accusations are characteristic of Prospero in their intem-
perateness, their stress on "lying" (compare "Thou liest, malignant
thing" said to Ariel), and their falsity. Both the accusations of Caliban –
that he is a liar and that he is unmoveable by kindness – are plainly false.
Caliban has not told any lies in his narrative, and Prospero did indeed
"move" Caliban through kindness: "Thou strok'st me, and made much
of me ... and then I lov'd thee." Caliban has "lied" in Prospero's mind
in precisely the way that Ariel did – by not including in an account of his
relationship with Prospero information that Prospero considers to be
crucial. For Prospero, not to understand and tell one's story as he
understands it is to lie. Power is quite clearly shown here as including the
capacity to impose upon others one's own version of their history.[55]
   Caliban's narrative has not made reference to the incident Prospero
considers pivotal. Characterizing Caliban as "filth," Prospero fills in
what he sees as the crucial causal link in the break-up of the idyll:

> I have us'd thee,
> ... with humane care; and lodg'd thee,
> In mine own cell, till thou didst seek to violate
> The honour of my child.   (1.ii.347–50)

Caliban is unrepentant about this – again, he does not lie – and
Prospero and Miranda take this episode as revealing the irredeemable,
evil essence of Caliban's "vile race."[56] Yet Prospero's account of

Caliban's sexual transgression is, as Mannoni argues, a justification for rather than a rational explanation of hatred and coercion.[57] Responses other than sadistic enslavement were surely possible. But not for Prospero. What made Caliban's attempt on Miranda unpardonable? One answer to this question may have to do with problems of sexuality and of incest fantasies (a major topic of *Pericles*), but the answer that I want to pursue has to do with Prospero's inability to conceive of another being having desires and an agenda different from his own.[58] Prospero feels betrayed by Caliban, just as Caliban feels betrayed by Prospero. Prospero feels that Caliban – like the Ariel who has murmured and dared to remind Prospero – has been ungrateful. He has betrayed Prospero's trust, and we know that, in Prospero's mind, his trust is an absolute that places an absolute obligation on its object. We know as well that Prospero cannot acknowledge any responsibility for his harsh treatment of Caliban; it is forced on him by Caliban's betrayal of him.[59] In that amazing colonialist document, the *Requerimiento*, the Spanish carefully explain that if their (proper) demands for obedience and reverence are not met, "we shall take away your goods, and shall do you all the mischief and damage that we can, as to vassals who do not obey," and it goes on to explain that all these ills that will be inflicted "are your fault."[60] So Caliban is responsible for Prospero's treatment of him.

But the play takes us further into this matter. We must read the story of Caliban's "betrayal" of Prospero through the story of Antonio's betrayal of Prospero. Why is this "generous" man so constantly being betrayed? Prospero's trust in Antonio was, as he says, "sans bound" (1.ii.97). He put Antonio in a situation of impossible temptation – "casting" the government entirely upon him – and then was utterly startled, shocked, and horrified when Antonio did not play by Prospero's rules and succumbed to the obvious temptation. And Prospero did exactly the same with Caliban. He threw Caliban, an adolescent boy (at least fourteen or fifteen when Prospero appeared on the island), together in his "cell" with his daughter, and was totally startled, shocked, and horrified when Caliban became sexually interested in Miranda once she reached or approached puberty (Prospero's obsessive monitoring of Ferdinand's sexuality can be seen as an attempt to "rewrite" his failure with Caliban). In the cases of both Antonio and Caliban (brother and surrogate son), Prospero's boundless trust "awak'd an evil nature" in the recipient of it (this is said, it should be noted, of Antonio [1.ii.93]). Prospero's "trust" no more acknowledged the personhood of its objects than his impositions of power and narrative do.

The intellectual fantasy embodied in *The Tempest* is of narcissistic withdrawal producing – quite literally – magical power. More clearly than Marlowe, and perhaps as clearly as Bacon, Shakespeare recognized that magic, especially "white" (theurgic) magic, was the Renaissance name for what we would now think of as the Foucauldian conception of "power–knowledge."[61] But Shakespeare is explicit, as Michel Foucault is not, that the ultimate meaning of power is physical coercion (Césaire seems to me to show his typical perspicacity in having his Prospero characterize himself as *"la Puissance"* rather than the more abstract *"Le Pouvoir,"* Foucault's term).[62] After Prospero's "Fetch us in fuel" – the arbitrariness of which we have already noted – Caliban comments:

> I must obey: his Art is of such pow'r,
> It would control my dam's god, Setebos,
> And make a vassal of him. (1.ii.374–6)

Power is the capacity to coerce and enslave, to "control" in the very strong Renaissance sense of that term.[63]

Yet *The Tempest* is also strongly aware of the limits of coercive human power, even in a colonial situation. Through a combination of threats and bribes, Prospero can keep Ariel from "murmuring," but nothing Prospero can do can keep Caliban from cursing. Prospero threatens Caliban with torture – "if thou neglect'st, or dost unwillingly / What I command, I'll rack thee with old cramps" (lines 370–1) – but while Prospero can make Caliban work, he cannot keep him from doing so "unwillingly."[64] In their first exchange, Caliban curses Prospero and Prospero responds to the curses with threats, yet Caliban goes on cursing (1.ii.323–32, 341–2). Neither surveillance nor punishment make a difference. "His spirits hear me, / And yet I needs must curse," says Caliban (11.ii.3–4). Caliban claims that all Prospero's conscripted workers do "unwillingly" what he commands, and that in fact they all "do hate him / As rootedly as I" (111.ii.92–3).[65] "Thought is free," says Stephano (111.ii.121).[66] And so, as Caliban's case makes clear, is the tongue – if one is willing, like Caliban in the play and Henry Paine in Strachey's narrative, to suffer for the use of it (Paine was a rebellious gentleman who specialized in "settled and bitter" anti-authoritarian speech; in the 1611 "Articles, Lawes, and Orders, Divine, Politique, and Martiall for the Colony in Virginea," the second through fifth items concern speech-crimes – impiety, blasphemy, derision, etc.).[67]

The limits of Prospero's power are crucial to the political meaning of the play, both generally and in its local context. Yet the best political critics of the play have either refused to note or refused to give critical weight to these limits. This may be because these critics have assumed that if the play is critical of colonialism, it must be criticizing a presentation of colonial *success*. Brown sees the action of the play as producing a "new solidarity" in the aristocratic class; Hulme is insistent that "in its own terms Prospero's play is undoubtedly a success; it achieves what it wants to achieve."[68] Orgel takes full note of Prospero's failure with Antonio, yet concludes from this that since Antonio remains impenitent, it must be the case that "penitence is not what Prospero's magic is designed to elicit from his brother."[69] What Prospero really wants, says Orgel, is his dukedom back – and this he gets. Greenblatt follows Orgel here. After noting that "the truculence of the villains at the end of the play marks the limit of Prospero's power," Greenblatt withdraws from the point by adding that "at the very moment that the limit is marked, the play suggests that it is relatively inconsequential" – since Prospero gets his dukedom back.[70] Breight takes the "success view" even further and denies that Prospero intends to renounce his power when he returns to Milan.[71]

But just as the play is explicit that Prospero renounces his power, it is explicit that he desires to transform his enemies. He wants to affect their minds, their hearts, their consciences. This (as Greenblatt knows and emphasizes elsewhere in his essay) is one of the great fantasies of power in the period, in and out of the colonial context.[72] Prospero's aim, repeatedly highlighted, is not only to get his dukedom back; he could do that merely by revealing himself. His aim is to produce genuine contrition in his enemies, "heart-sorrow / And a clear life ensuing" (III.iii.81–2) – the precise Protestant definition of penitence.[73] His whole "project" with regard to his enemies consists in their "being penitent" (v.i.28). He succeeds at this in one and only one case, that of Alonso. At the end of Act III, Gonzalo believes that Prospero has succeeded with all his European enemies. Watching the behavior of Alonso, Sebastian, and Antonio after they hear what the thunder says, Gonzalo concludes that:

> their great guilt,
> (Like poison given to work a great time after)
> Now 'gins to bite the spirits.   (III.iii.104–6)

But it turns out that Gonzalo is wrong. Prospero can produce the physical and even the physico-psychological effects of guilt – he can produce hysteria and hallucinations and obscure the group's rational powers (v.i.67–8) – but he cannot affect their "spirits" in the non-physiological sense.[74] He cannot change their moral characters, their hearts in the non-physiological sense. A similar moment occurred earlier when Prospero paralyzed Ferdinand with sword in hand and told him that he (Ferdinand) could not strike because "thy conscience / Is so possess'd with guilt" (i.ii.473–4). Bright argues that Shakespeare is here demystifying the way that power seeks to impose false interpretations on its subjects.[75] Yet Shakespeare may here be pointing not to the emptiness of the fictions of power but to the fullness of their fantasy-content, to the capacities that those in power wish they had.

Like torturers and tyrannical administrators of all sorts, Prospero can "play God," but Reformation Protestants would certainly have held that only the figure who does not have to play God can actually transform the will. Only God can produce "heart-sorrow / And a clear life ensuing." This was the central premise of Luther's "Ninety-five Theses," and of the whole Protestant attack on the penitential system.[76] Fear of punishment may have been "attrition," but it was not contrition (Césaire's Gonzalo points this out).[77] Alonso, as I have noted, is Prospero's one clear success, and it seems to be grief over the (apparent) loss of his son that enables the process to work in him. Sebastian, in Act v, seems to have developed a capacity for wonder (he sees the revelation of Ferdinand and Miranda playing chess as "a most high miracle" [v.i.177]), but relapses into cynicism (at v.i.263–5, "Will money buy 'em?"). Antonio, the major villain of the play – the supplanter of Prospero, suborner of Sebastian, and would-be assassin of Alonso (ii.i.278–9) – remains entirely untransformed. Just as Prospero cannot stop Caliban from cursing, he cannot make Antonio speak. Prospero can "forgive" Antonio, but he cannot change him, even though Antonio is repeatedly characterized as "unnatural" (v.i.74–9). The entire speaking part assigned to Antonio in Act v is a cynical line and a half speculating on Caliban's potential status in Europe as "marketable" (v.i.265–6). Shakespeare's point, I would argue, is not that Prospero doesn't really want to transform Antonio, but that he does really want to and cannot. And this strikes me as deeply consequential.

But perhaps Caliban is transformed. The fantasy of morally uplifting the "uncivil" (whether "natives" or not) is a deep one. Part of the rage of Miranda (and, presumably, Prospero) against Caliban is the fury of outraged humanism. The central premise of humanist pedagogy was that (proper) education was morally transformative.[78] Caliban learned –

but without being morally transformed. In the speech by Miranda attacking Caliban's "vile race," she has to admit that, as she says to Caliban, "thou didst learn" (1.ii.360–2).[79] Yet in Caliban's final speech, Caliban says that he will "be wise hereafter, / And seek for grace" (v.i.295). The question is what to make of this. I do not believe that there is truly a theological dimension here, though Shakespeare obviously wants us to consider this possibility. He is using the language of "grace" in its lowest (socio-political) rather than its highest (theological) register. He wants us, I would argue, to feel the gap between these senses (Leininger would argue that he is trying to cover over this gap).[80] As Berger says, Caliban's words here are "a travesty of what Prospero would like to hear."[81] Where the Reformation deontologized grace in order to exalt it ("grace is not medicine, but favor"), Shakespeare here reduces the deontological to the political.[82] The context is entirely socio-political. Servants are being reassigned to (and recognizing) their "proper" masters: Stephano and Trinculo to Alonso; Caliban to Prospero. Seeing Prospero in full aristocratic garb, with "hat and rapier," in Act v (line 84), Caliban notes "How fine my master is," and immediately fears punishment (lines 262–3). The "wisdom" that Caliban dedicates himself to is merely the ability to recognize the truly powerful and, therefore, the proper object of "worship" ("What a thrice-double ass / Was I, to take this drunkard for a god, / And worship this dull fool" [lines 294–6]). The "grace" that Caliban seeks is merely his true "master's" pardon.[83]

These last remarks bring us to perhaps the most disturbing feature of Shakespeare's portrayal of Caliban. The sexual rapaciousness that is alleged by Prospero and implied by Miranda is never presented to us directly. We hear Prospero's account, but we witness Caliban's desire not for sex but for offspring (for which Orgel suggests a political and dynastic reading).[84] Caliban's hunger for servility, on the other hand, is fully staged. It is a datum. Mannoni used it to illustrate "the dependence-complex in its purest state"; Césaire eliminated it from his play.[85] Caliban's favorite promise to Stephano is to be his foot or boot licker. This occurs three times (II.ii.152; III.ii.22; IV.i.219), and it would, along with Caliban's equally explicit (and related) tendency toward "idolatry," have horrified Shakespeare's largely Protestant audience as much as it does us.[86] Mannoni seems to be right that Caliban feels abandoned by Prospero, and that servility, for Caliban, is a mode of relationship. Where Mannoni is wrong, however, is in asserting that Caliban does not also feel exploited by Prospero, and in asserting that Caliban lacks a conception of freedom. He certainly can imagine freedom from forced physical and menial labor. Prospero can starve – or do his own "dirty work":

> No more dams I'll make for fish;
>   Nor fetch in firing
>   At requiring;
> Nor scrape trenchering, nor wash dish.   (II.ii.180–3)

Yet Caliban does confuse freedom with getting "a new master" (II.ii.185). As Mannoni argues (or ought to argue – he is not fully consistent), the encounter between native slave or servant and European "master" degrades the consciousness of both.[87]

What then do we want to conclude about Shakespeare's attitude in *The Tempest* toward colonial and toward "normal" politics? Certainly the play could have been experienced, in 1611 and throughout James's reign, as reinforcing the emphasis of the Virginia Company and its partisans (many of whom were friends or patrons of Shakespeare) on the need for strong government, for the use of force against native peoples, and for disciplined laborers without Caliban-like "dreames of mountaines of gold, and happy robberies."[88]

And yet the deepest fear of *The Tempest* seems to be not that England's struggling colonial ventures would fail but that they would succeed. It is no accident that the most far-reaching speech in the play celebrates not successful work but peaceful dissolution into nothingness. Shakespeare's emphasis is not on the ease with which Prospero works his "Art" but on the effort that goes into it, the effort that leaves him touchy, impatient, and, in Shakespeare's wonderful word, "vex'd" (IV.i.158). Pierre Bourdieu notes that in situations of direct, unmediated, or, as he happily calls it, "enchanted" domination, before "a system of mechanisms has been constituted capable of objectively ensuring the reproduction of the established order by its own motion," the dominator must work "directly, daily, personally" to produce the conditions of domination, which, Bourdieu adds, "are even then never entirely trustworthy."[89] This perfectly captures the difficulties of Prospero's relations to his island servants (his relations to his European enemies are mediated through Ariel and the "spirits" Ariel commands). As Meredith Skura and John Gillies have pointed out, the question about Virginia at the time of the production of *The Tempest* was clearly, "Is it worth it?"[90] Shakespeare can be seen as giving something close to a negative answer – not as an "aporia" but as a position. "Foison" is the great word in the play for abundance of food. If "foison" could be produced without labor or rule, as in Gonzalo's primitivist vision (II.i.163), "plantation" would not be necessary. But in Prospero's much more "majestic" vision (IV.i.118), "foison" can only be produced by "sunburned sicklemen, of August weary" (IV.i.134). We cannot miss them. Shakespeare does not imagine an aristocracy willingly sharing such labor.

But what of the fantasy of transforming souls? James did not approve of princes who delighted in magicians and occult studies (especially when such concerns distracted princes from their duties), but he reveled in the biblical language of kings "as Gods," who could "make and unmake their subjects."[91] It is surely no accident that the one image of thorough transformation by human means (not a "sea-change") in the play occurs within the realm of Machiavellian rather than of magical politics. The ability to new create and new form "creatures" is attained not by magic but by knowing "how to grant suits, / How to deny them" – by the skillful exercise of "normal" princely prudence. And Prospero's one truly successful political venture is in this realm: he arranges a dynastically advantageous marriage for his daughter.

To sum up the "local" meanings, then, the partisans of the Virginia Company could have seen *The Tempest* as supporting them in the dark days of 1610–11, whereas King James could have seen the play as suggesting that colonial endeavors, for all their glamour, leave one weary and "vex'd." James could have seen the play as advocating a focus on "normal" politics, a policy of concentrating on his own court and on arranging advantageous marriages for his children, especially for his daughter, Elizabeth, who was fifteen in 1611.[92] On the other hand, when we recognize that the play's critique of "magical" politics is profound enough to undermine "normal" politics as well, we have perhaps reached its deepest and non-local meaning.

CHAPTER 2

"Void of storie": the struggle for insincerity in Herbert's prose and poetry

Stanley Fish

"OH THAT I ONCE PAST CHANGING WERE"

In a somewhat neglected poem of George Herbert's entitled "A Dialogue Anthem," two characters, Christian and Death, debate the shape of history, both personal and cosmic. Christian tauntingly asks, "Alas, poore Death, where is thy glorie? / Where is thy famous force, thy ancient sting?" and Death replies in kind, "*Alas poore mortall, void of storie, / Go spell and reade how I have kill'd thy King.*"[1] We are meant to see of course that Death completely misunderstands or misreads the situation: he thinks that because Christ has died, there is no longer any center to Christian's life, nothing in relation to which his actions could have meaning; but Christian knows that meaning, and the continuation of his story, is assured by Christ's death, an act of self-sacrifice that rescues man from the death-sentence (separation from deity) earned by Adam and Eve in Eden. It is only because of Christ's death that man will live.

But live how? The answer to this question reveals a further irony in Death's accusation, "void of storie"; for, correctly understood, it is not an accusation at all, but a precise specification of the requirement that Christ's sacrifice imposes, the requirement that the Christian not have a story of his own, that he be, in that impossible and perhaps inconceivable sense, void of story. The logic is familiar in Christian thought. It is present, for example, when Milton reminds us that the taste of the forbidden tree was "mortal" and brought Death into the world. The point is profound, if tautological: mortality *is* death in the sense that it names a state which is finite, which has an end, a cessation, a conclusion. Once separated from the endless rhythms of eternity, from that "Grateful vicissitude"[2] in which change is "delectable" (*PL*, 5.629) but not needed, man is delivered into a world where change always has reference to the pressures exerted by beginnings and ends. Mortal man always feels time's winged chariot at his back because as a creature whose mode of existence is linear every moment brings an opportunity that will not come again and also brings choices that are at once irrevocable and determining. When Milton says of our first parents that at the moment of the Fall they "knew not eating Death" (*PL*, 9.792), he might as well have said, they knew not eating narrative (story), that wandering and errant course which is theirs once they are no longer incorporate members of a choir who live with and in God and therefore "sing in endless morn of light."³

There is of course another way to put this point, and it is Satan's way when he sneeringly refers to the loyal angels as the "Minstrelsy of Heaven" (*PL*, 6.168) and contrasts their "servility" with the "freedom" (line 169) in whose name he claims to contend. If death is another name for mortality, then freedom is another name for both, for freedom, at least as Satan defines it, is the state of being separate from God, of not being enfolded in the ceaseless repetition of his praise, but, instead, exposed to the world of chance and hazard. In death, then, in mortality, in finitude, Satan finds life, by which he, and Adam and Eve following him, mean an independent story line. By breaking union, by disobeying – or, rather, *in* disobeying – they get to do it their way, and their way, in contradistinction to God's way, is to be finite and to have a beginning, a middle, and an end. It follows then that if fallen man is ever to repair the ruins of his first parents, he must somehow do it *no* way, have no story line, be void of story. We see then another sense in which Death is precisely wrong when he cries, "mortall, void of storie"; to be mortal is to have a story, to have a continuity, to be available to narration; to be void of story is to be enclosed in the story of another ("I live to show his power," "Josephs Coat," line 13), and it is this that Herbert's Christian voice desires, although that desire is itself self-defeating, since to have it is to envision a fulfillment which, if achieved, marks the end and point of a story of which the desirer will then be anything but void.

What to do? Or, rather, how to "do" doing nothing, how to a-void story? The answer to this question often appears in Herbert's poetry in the guise of a complaint. Here, for example, are the first four lines of "Giddinesse":

> Oh, what a thing is man! how farre from power,
> > From setled peace and rest!
> He is some twentie sev'rall men at least
> > Each sev'rall houre.   (lines 1–4)

What Herbert laments here is the absence of continuous being; he bemoans the fact that life brings so many and so violent changes that at the end of an hour he is not the same person he was at its beginning; in effect he has no identity, and is a thing or a no-thing always on the move.

This is the master theme of any number of Herbert's poems. "The Temper (II)" begins by recording the loss of the resolution – of the state of being – achieved at the end of "The Temper (I)": "It cannot be. Where is that mightie joy, / Which just now took up all my heart?" (lines 1–2). The severity of the disjuncture is underlined by the fact that the speaker is not here recalling the moment of loss; he doesn't remember it; he only knows that at this moment he is not what he was a moment ago; and he knows too that what he now feels he may not feel in the moment yet to come. The world of nature, "The grosser world," he complains, "stands to thy word and art" (line 5); that is, once made by you (God) it abides; but the inner (and supposedly superior) world of consciousness, "Thou suddenly does raise and race, / And ev'ry day a new Creatur art" (lines 7–8). It is important to realize that this is not a reference to the Old Man who is made new – transformed – by the grace and sacrifice of Christ; this man is not made new, but newly made; *he* is "rac'd" or erased by a mark that simply writes over him. When Herbert begins "Affliction (II)" by crying "Kill me not ev'ry day," he might as well have pleaded, "make me not ev'ry day": for in relation to a self that would have its own story, killing and making are the same thing, and what they are is killing. In these poems, as Barbara Harman observes, the speaker comes to see himself "not as someone who grows, or fails to grow, 'in a straight line' but rather as someone who dies many deaths and experiences many renewals,"[4] as someone, in other words, who is not a some *one*. The speaker keeps finding himself to be someone else, and this finding, in Harman's words "signals the end of coherence, the end of narrative, the end of *representational* life."[5]

Indeed in almost every one of these poems the moment of unhappiness (and sometimes of despair) is presented as a moment in which a promising story line had been broken off. In "Giddinesse" man is imagined first as fixed on heaven "as of his treasure" (line 5), but then "a thought creeps in" (line 6) – as if a switch on a railroad track had been turned by an unseen agent – and suddenly that same man is fixed on the pleasures heaven will require him to relinquish. In subsequent stanzas he is a soldier, a pacifist, a recluse, a miser, a spendthrift, until finally his mind is characterized as a "whirlwinde" (line 14), as something that continually alters (line 18) with "desires" (line 20) he cannot control and which, like the thought that "creeps in," are not finally his own. In "The Flower," that same variability, without transition and without pattern, leaves the speaker unable at any moment to make continuous sense of his existence: "It cannot be / That I am he / On whom thy tempests fell all night" (lines 40–2). "O that I once past changing were" (line 22), he cries in a line that itself marks a change from the achieved equanimity of the previous stanza, and it is clear that even when the change is from a "shrivel'd heart" (line 8) to one that "buds again" (line 36), from "tempests" (line 42) to "dew" (line 38), it is no less disconcerting than it would be if the direction were malign; for in either direction what the speaker (if he can still be honored by that appellation) is deprived of (a deprivation that leaves him with nothing) is, as the poem precisely says, a "straight line," a directionality that is sustained enough to afford material for a story, for a story of a someone. This speaker, like so many others, is continually discovering that he does not know himself, that there is no himself to know because the stances and attitudes he displays merely follow one another in a succession and do not follow from a set of motives and purposes that would confer on them a coherence.

Of course this is exactly the goal of Christian life, to lose the coherence that makes one's actions a career and gives them a shape independent of the shape imposed on everything by God's will. The variability of which Herbert's speakers so often complain, the sense they have of a story line continually interrupted by forces outside them, the sense of being the vehicle of so many conflicting and temporary voices that they have no voice of their own, is exactly the condition of their salvation. Even as they lament their distance from God, as evidenced by an inability to sustain a sense of his presence ("If what my soul doth feel sometimes, / My soul might ever feel?"), they testify to the annihilation of that distance when they are able to do nothing but helplessly record alterations of mood and understanding so violent and random that they resist intelligibility. "O rack me not to such a vast extent" (line 9), pleads the speaker of "The Temper (I)." The number and extent of the changes he suffers are too great to be accommodated within the canvas of the self which because it cannot contain – manage, order, relate, narrate – them is exploded, disintegrated, dispersed by them; as a result the self is not its own, but another's. "Those distances belong to thee" (line 10) the speaker says in a complaint that should be a celebration of the gain he enjoys in loss.

In some poems that celebration arrives, as it does here in "Temper (I)": "Yet take thy way; for sure thy way is best: / Stretch or contract me, thy poor debter" (lines 21–2); and in "The Flower" the achievement of insight is even more decisively announced:

These are thy wonders, Lord of love,
To make us see we are but flowers that glide:
Which when we once can finde and prove,
Thou hast a garden for us, where to bide.
Who would be more,
Swelling through store,
Forfeit their Paradise by their pride. (lines 43–9)

Or in other words "I see now that what I have been complaining about is nothing more or less than the strategy by which God brings us to the realization that rather than being creatures that grow we are creatures always in transit, never the same, always passing from state to state, never in one place." But if this resolution is satisfying because it renders intelligible something that had previously resisted understanding (the apparently unpatterned succession of extreme mental and spiritual states), that very satisfaction is the vehicle of its own undoing; for in this hard economy, intelligibility undoes the spiritual benefit; gain – especially gain of insight – is loss, since to acquire it is to have written and lived a story: "Once I was perplexed and disoriented by the vicissitudes of my life; now I see how to make sense of them; no longer am I disoriented, once again I am an I, a someone whose struggles are the stuff of a spiritual *bildungsroman* which now displays (and can boast of) a beginning, a middle, and an end."

We can see what is wrong with this by slightly rewriting another of Herbert's poems, "The Holdfast," a short lyric in which the speaker searches for an action, however small, that he can call his own. He determines first to keep the law, but is told that it is beyond his power and that he must trust not in himself, but in God. He then resolves to trust, but this course too is denied him as his interlocutor explains, "Nay, ev'n to trust in him, was also his; / We must confesse that nothing is our own" (lines 6–7). Aha, the speaker says, then I will confess that nothing is my own, only to hear in reply, "But to have nought is ours, not to confesse / That we have nought" (lines 9–10). That is, philosophizing about having nought is not the same thing as having nought, for the very act of philosophizing is a claim to possession and mastery of one's own thoughts. Similarly, if the speaker of "The Flower" claims to have realized that he is transitory, then by the inexorable logic of "The Holdfast" that realization undermines itself because it can only be the product of a consciousness that claims continuity in its ability to sum and pronounce, to be reflective, to speak from a perspective, to have a point of view, to have duration. "But," as

the second voice of "The Holdfast" might say, "To *be* transitory is
ours, Not to *realize* that we are transitory." Harman would have it that
the speaker here "acknowledges the *impossibility* of any full saying, when
he acknowledges that our sentences, like our bodies and like our stories,
are provisional";[6] but of course that acknowledgment is itself a "full
saying" in which provisionality is domesticated and evaded by being
made into a conclusion, an ending, the terminal point of a new (though
ever more sophisticated) narrative.

The very action of having reached a conclusion is the "more" to
which the last three lines of "The Flower" refer: "Who would be more,
/ Swelling through store, / Forfeit their Paradise by their pride" (lines
47–9). Richard Strier wonders about what he calls these "grim final
lines."[7] They are to be explained, I think, as a reaction on the part of
Herbert to the robustness of the lines that precede them, lines in which
he becomes more by seeing through to the other side of his situation
where he finds waiting the pride of successful intellection. "Store"
means "increase" or "addition"; it is a motion exactly opposite to
gliding or diminishing and here it is the motion of adding to one's stock
of insight and therefore to oneself by reaching an extending resolution.
You can't *be* gliding at the moment you become newly able to proclaim
(indeed boast) that you are gliding. Herbert's requirements are always
more severe than the achievements he records, because the basic requirement is that there be no achievement, nothing to report, no story to
tell, not even anything to know.

The point is made at the end of "Gratefulnesse" when the speaker
asks to be given a "thankfull heart" (line 27), but then immediately
qualifies his request in a way that can serve as a comment on all of the
poems we have looked at. I don't want a heart, he says, that is "thankfull when it pleaseth me," but rather "such a heart, whose pulse may be
/ Thy praise." That is to say, he doesn't want a heart that *knows* itself to
be grateful and is therefore, in its knowledge, making a claim. He
wants a heart that is just – without consciousness, without more –
grateful, full of gratitude, its every beat speaking a praise from which it
is indistinguishable. But even to have that want, to be conscious that
your goal is to be without separate consciousness is to be separate from
that goal, is to be too much, to be something in addition, is to swell
through store. Neither Herbert nor his speakers can ever get quite thin
enough, be sufficiently insufficient, sufficiently shallow, sufficiently
without depth, to disappear.

SHOWING HOLY

The one exception to this statement, and therefore Herbert's one success – because it is a non-success – is the title figure of *The Country Parson*. Until recently this pastoral work has always been regarded as a model of sincere piety. In 1908 Joseph Blount Cheshire, then bishop of North Carolina, praised its "simplicity and unaffectedness, its directness of purpose . . . its genuine humility and sympathy . . . its absolute fidelity to truth,"[8] and sixty-three years later W. A. Powell was still sounding the same note: "The simplicity and homeliness of style, the directness of tone . . . and the uses of images which unmistakably present a spiritual truth all combine to depict the simple faith and devout spirit of George Herbert's humble audience."[9] In every discussion of *The Country Parson*, the same words recur, "sincere," "direct," "simple," and "unaffected," and the praise is always for the "integrity" of the title figure, and, by extension, of Herbert whose practice at Bemerton is presumed to be his model.

It is only in the last decade that critics have begun to complicate this pretty picture, usually by bringing *The Country Parson* into the ambit of the courtesy books it is now said to resemble. Cristina Malcolmson quarries both the courtesy manuals and the "character genre" in support of her thesis that "For Herbert, 'character' referred directly to the process of a public self-representation . . . To have a holy 'character' was not to be spiritually minded but to make that spiritual mindedness public."[10] It was for him as for others in these traditions, "a matter of performance."[11] Kristine Wolberg extends this argument and renders it even more pointed: "Herbert's manual in fact instructs the pastor in how to fashion a correct public image. The great bulk of Herbert's advice is not immediately linked to spiritual realities, but to the minister's appearances."[12] And, in what is surely the most nuanced and sophisticated version of this line of analysis, Michael Schoenfeldt finds that *The Country Parson* repeatedly "blur[s] the distinction between social and religious demeanor that it attempts to draw," and he substitutes for the benign and simple figure of an earlier criticism a parson who "imposes upon his congregation a regulation of body and behavior that is continuous with courtly self-control."[13]

I agree with the points made in these analyses but I find them made in ways that leave in place the same familiar oppositions – between surface and depth, artifice and substance, show and reality – that were assumed and honored by those whose view of Herbert and his parson was less critical and more benign. When Malcolmson says that the chief lesson of *The Country Parson* "was not to be spiritually minded but to make that spiritual mindedness public," she assumes that the spiritual-mindedness is securely in place (in its *inner* place) and that the skill required is the translation of that interior condition into a public posture. In her reading, the public performance is anchored in and validated by the parson's private integrity; his life "links internality and appearance, inside and outside, ethical quality and visible behavior."[4] (One has no doubt as to which is the superior and controlling term in each of these phrases.) And in the same vein, Wolberg feels obliged at the end of her essay to detach Herbert from the courtesy tradition in which she has embedded him so that she can reassert his commitment to a higher aim: "[w]hile Herbert, like the secular courtesy author, emphasizes appearances rather than realities, he stands out in his final aims as well as in his confidence that appearances can have a profound mimetic effect upon one's spiritual realities."[5] I would argue, however, that Herbert's emphasis on appearances (and on performance and control) is not so easily domesticated, and that if one reads his little tract in the light of what I have identified as the poet's impossible project – the effort to be thin to the point of vanishing – something quite remarkable, and even disturbing, emerges.

Let me begin with a sentence that conveniently foregrounds the issues that will remain in play throughout *The Country Parson*. "The Countrey Parson, when he is to read divine services, composeth himselfe to all possible reverence; lifting up his heart and hands, and eyes, and using all other gestures which may express a hearty, and unfeyned devotion."[16] What strikes one immediately about this sentence is the tension between its two vocabularies – on the one hand the vocabulary of piety and sincerity – "reverence," "heart," "unfeyned devotion" – and on the other the vocabulary of artifice and theatricality – "composeth," "gestures," and "express." This latter set of words combines to emphasize the extent to which the parson's actions are superficial in the sense that they are "put on" much as one might put on a suit of clothes. The "reverence" is precisely "composed," that is, constructed or confected; the heart is not really lifted up; rather a theatrical gesture stands in for the parson's heart of whose actual posture we know nothing; and as for the "unfeigned devotion," that is the triumph of the composer's art, to express, by means of some outward movement, an inward orientation defined precisely by its scorn of the external. The parson, in short, is skilled in feigning being unfeigned. He is the expert not at being devoted, but at expressing devotion, and in the sentences that follow, the tools of his trade are laid out and anatomized:

This he doth, first, as being truly touched and amazed with the Majesty of God, before whom he then presents himself; yet not as himself alone, but as presenting with himself the whole Congregation... Secondly, as this is the true reason of his inward fear, so he is content to expresse this outwardly to the utmost of his power; that being first affected himself, hee may affect also his people knowing that no Sermon moves them so much to a reverence, which they forget againe, when they come to pray, as a devout behavior in the very act of praying. Accordingly his voyce is humble, his words treatable, and slow; yet not so slow neither, as to let the fervency of the supplicant hang and diy between speaking, but with a grave livelinesse, between fear and zeal, pausing yet pressing, he performes his duty. (*The Country Parson*, p. 231; ch. 6)

As this passage makes clear, not only does he perform his duty; performance *is* his duty, and what he must first perform is the spontaneity of the gestures he so deliberately orders; he must act as if ("as being") he were "truly touched and amazed" and what that action or composition involves is duly detailed, a humble tone, a distinct speech which is slow, but not so slow as to suggest a lack of fervency. All of this is quite accurately and openly characterized as the ability to "expresse ... outwardly." The parson dresses himself in the appropriate gestures and then "presents" himself, that is, makes a presentation or composition of himself. The qualifying, "yet not as himself alone" is exactly to the point. He is never himself alone; he is always in the act of composing himself, that is, of putting together or constructing the role he will then play.

In the next chapter, "The Parson Preaching," that role is called being holy, "the character of his Sermon is Holiness ... A Character that *Hermogenes* never dream'd of, and therefore he could give no precepts thereof" (p. 233; ch. 7). "Character" is the perfect word to capture what is going on here, since it means both distinctive mark or style and inward essence, refers at the same time to a representation and to the thing represented. The parson's sermon is marked (characterized) by holiness, but it is a holiness wholly made up of external marks, of signs. Hermogenes may be unable to present a list of precepts for producing the "holiness effect," but Herbert's parson displays no such inability: "first," he says, choose "texts of Devotion ... moving and ravishing texts"; then, he states that it is by "dipping and seasoning all our words and sentences in our hearts, before they come into our mouths, truly affecting and cordially expressing all that we say ... that the auditors may plainly

perceive that every word is hart-deep" (p. 233; ch. 7). The effect produced is to be one of words coming directly from the heart but it is an
effect that will follow upon a careful rehearsal of the appropriate cries
and gestures. The result will be "truly affecting" in two senses; the
desired effect will have been achieved – the audience will be affected –
and the success will be the product of a true or superior exercise of the
skill of "affecting," of putting on.

The same doubleness of reference is also present in the phrase
"cordially expressing" which again offers a formula for simulating by
outward signs (by expression) the interior ("cordial") reality. The words
may *appear* to be "hart-deep" – the spontaneous and unprompted
exclamation of an unfeigned piety – but in fact they will be taken from a
stock inventory of pious-sounding phrases, an inventory whose contents
the parson begins immediately to list: turn often, he advises, and make
"many Apostrophes to God, as, Oh Lord blesse my people, and teach
them this point; or, Oh my Master, on whose errand I come, let me hold
my peace, and doe thou speak thy selfe." This is how the parson
achieves not heart deepness but its appearance, by piling up layer on
layer of pre-packaged *signs* of sincerity. On this point the prose is precise
and unabashed: "Some such irradiations scatteringly in the sermon
carry great holiness in them." We are then told that holiness is also
"carried" by "frequent wishes of the people's good." Indeed "there is no
greater sign of holiness" than such wishes and therefore one should take
care that they be "woven into Sermons, which will make them appear
exceeding reverend." The last instruction is often to urge "the presence,
and majesty of God, by these, or such like speeches," examples of which
promptly follow. And lest one mistake the point of this amazing sequence, it concludes with the general observation that "such discourses"
– discourses artificially built up in the manner here described – "*shew*
very Holy" (p. 234; ch. 7, my emphasis).

I am aware that the previous paragraph could be read as a severe
criticism of Herbert, indeed as an accusation of hypocrisy. But in fact I
intend no such criticism, and if hypocrisy is the appropriate term for
what I have described, it is so in the root sense of the word – "playing a
character on a stage." Herbert's parson is always play-acting, and
because he is play-acting he is never being himself. In a technical sense
one might say that he practices and counsels a massive insincerity; but in
the context of what Rosemond Tuve long ago identified as Herbert's
lifelong goal of self-immolation,[17] massive insincerity is the mark not of a
failure but of an almost unthinkable achievement (just try it); for if the

parson (and through him Herbert) does in fact manage to be wholly insincere, he realizes, or at least comes close to realizing, the desire to not be himself, to not be more, to not swell through store, to not have a story of his own. That after all is what insincerity is, to not be speaking from the heart, to have a disjunction between one's words and actions and one's innermost thoughts, indeed to have no innermost thoughts, but to be a succession of false appearances, to be all surface, superficial, without depth, thin, to be continually composed, confected, constructed, to feign. What Herbert sees is that, in relation to the mode of life for which the Christian yearns – a reunion with the will of God – sincerity, the claim of saying and doing what *you* mean, is a temptation, is the greatest temptation. And what he also sees and here exemplifies is that the way to defeat the temptation of sincerity is to be always in a posture of affectation, to have the character of having no character by being a number of characters (in the theatrical sense) seriatim, to be a hypocrite, to be always presenting (composing) oneself and therefore never being oneself, to be always other, because you are always dispersed.

It is an incredible project especially in the context of the anti-representationalism that is so prominent in sixteenth- and seventeenth-century thought. In effect, Herbert is reversing the hierarchy of values that is constitutive of Platonic-Stoic-Christian thought as it is found in the works of authors otherwise so diverse as Spenser, Shakespeare, Jonson, Bacon, and Milton. It is as if Jonson were to turn and celebrate (rather than vilify) Inigo Jones for being all show and no substance, for being indeed the "earl of show, for all thy work is show."[18] Jonson ends his vitriolic poem (one of many) by exclaiming that however many surfaces Jones's artistry can paint, however many effects he can create, the one thing he cannot create, either of others or of himself, is an "honest man."[19] An honest man would be a sincere man, a man whose center stood firm against the variable pressures of a protean world, a man whose inner point of reference was the measure of everything he saw and did, a man who took to heart Polonius's famous counsel, "to thine own self be true." He would be what R. A. Lanham (with not a little sarcasm) has named him, Serious Man, and his prototype would be the Socrates of the *Dialogues*, the man who dies rather than betray himself, the "Martyr-of-the-Central-Self ... utterly his own man."[20] Opposed to Serious Man in Lanham's two member taxonomy is Rhetorical Man, *Homo Rhetoricus*, for whom "dramatic motive" – that is, the motive to impersonate, to feign – "forms the groundwork of all 'respectable' motives";[21] that is, of all motives that are supposedly "heart deep."

In the history of Western thought Rhetorical Man has never had a good press while Serious Man has been invulnerable to attack since, as Lanham observes, to quarrel with him would be to quarrel with "a fundamental Western Ideality,"[22] an ideality whose watchwords are integrity and sincerity, values that undergird an essentialism which finds an expression in innumerable places from Sidney's "fool ... look in thy heart and write" to Herbert's own Neoplatonic preference in "Jordan (1)" for a "true" over a "painted chair" (line 5). Of course the dismissal of fine language in favor of the solid things of the world and heart is itself a rhetorical convention (witness in addition to Sidney's Astrophel, Shakespeare's Iago, Coriolanus, and Hotspur, Spenser's Archimago, Skelton's Colin Clout, the speaker of Donne's satires, and even Herbert himself in the third of his extant orations ["*non rhetoricor, Academici*"]),[23] and one could argue, as Lanham does, that Serious Man has always been Rhetorical Man's favorite role. Still, it seems to me that the Herbertian project differs significantly from those others with which it might be compared. The parson is not trying (vainly), as are the protagonists of so many other Renaissance poems and plays, to escape *from* rhetoricity, but to escape *into* rhetoricity, into surface, superficiality, into show; he is not engaged in an (impossible) attempt to be himself in a world of appearances, but in the (perhaps equally impossible) attempt to be nothing more than an appearance, to be nothing more, to be nothing.

Moreover, he sees it as his business to move others in the same (non)direction. To that end he makes surprise visits to his parishioners in the afternoons of weekdays, for then "he shall find his flock most naturally as they are, wallowing in the midst of their affaires: whereas on Sundays it is easie for them to compose themselves to order, which they put on as their holy-day cloathes, and come to Church in frame, but commonly the next day put off both" (p. 247; ch. 14). In a recent edition of the poetry "wallowing" is glossed as "engaged in, without the present negative connotations,"[24] but the editor is betrayed into an historical inaccuracy ("wallow" in its negative connotations is standard usage in the King James bible) by the familiar Platonic prejudice in favor of the natural and the interior. In the editor's reading, the parson is critical of his parishioners for spiritually dressing up on Sundays, for putting on an act; but in fact the parson is critical of his parishioners for not dressing up on the other days, for not putting on an act, for falling back into being themselves – "naturally as they are." The strategy is the reverse of the usual one in which you stagger your visits in order to be sure that your flock is not putting on its best face; here the parson staggers his visits so that his flock will be unable to relax ("wallow") and will always be putting on its best face. He wants his parishioners to "compose themselves to order," to put on holiness, because only a put on – affected, confected – holiness will be free of what he will later in the tract term the "tincture" of the "private" (p. 287; ch. 37). It is in the private mode that they "wallow" and comport themselves "naturally," and not as they would if they knew they were always being watched, performing on stage, "in frame." The church as theater, as show, is not a metaphor the parson avoids; rather he courts it in order to exaggerate the public space in which he wants his parishioners to operate, always afraid lest they be caught not playing a role.

TRACKING GOD'S WAYS

It is at this point that the dark underside of the Herbertian project comes into view. For it would seem that by extending his program of total theatricality – of never being off-stage and "naturally as he is" – to his parishioners, the parson produces a society that is regulated down to the last detail. To the extent that his strategy is successful, no one of his charges ever experiences an unguarded moment, but lives in fear of a visit whose prospect controls behavior even (especially) when it does not occur. The result is an authoritarian regime and one might wonder how so much authority and control can emerge from a project of self-effacement. The answer lies in another one of the parson's self (or anti-self) descriptions: "the Countrey Parson ... is a ... tracker of Gods wayes" (p. 72). That is to say, he walks in the tracks of another and has no way of his own (he copies, exactly in the sense recommended in the last lines of "Jordan [II]"), a posture that seems to breathe humility until one takes in the whole of the sentence as it unfolds: "So the Countrey Parson, who is a diligent observer, and tracker of Gods wayes, sets up as many encouragements to goodnesse as he can ... that he may, if not the best way, yet any way, make his Parish good" (p. 244; ch. 11). Being a tracker of God's ways does not mean that one performs no actions but that one performs actions like God's, which in turn means that, like God, one employs any means that comes to hand ("yet *any* way") in order to effect an end – bringing one's parishioners to goodness – that justifies those means.

A whiff of the unrestrained power this justification authorizes enters the prose with the last clause – "*make* his Parish good" – and the full extent of that power emerges as the parson's activities in relation to his flock are more completely described. The key to everything he does as a tracker of God's ways is that he stands "in Gods stead to his Parish," and therefore, "there is nothing done either wel or ill, whereof he is not the rewarder or punisher" (p. 254; ch. 20). And if one doubts the extent to which this impulse to social control is to be indulged, it is a doubt that does not survive another such description: "The Countrey Parson, where ever he is, keeps Gods watch; that is, there is nothing spoken or done in the Company where he is, but comes under his Test and censure" (p. 252; ch. 18). (At this point, the same editor, again zealous to protect Herbert and his text from what they are obviously saying, glosses "censure" as "[e]valuation, without present negative connotation."[25])

Even this statement falls short of communicating the zeal with which the parson carries out his duties, for it suggests that his parishioners might escape notice when they are not in his company. However, as we learn in a chapter entitled "The Parson's Completeness," he so contrives it that they shall always be in his company by insisting that in his parish all offices of whatever kind shall be performed by him and by him alone: "The Countrey Parson desires to be all to his Parish, and not onely a Pastur, but a Lawyer also, and a Phisician. Therefore hee endures not that any of his Flock should go to Law; but in any controversie, that they should resort to him as their Judge" (p. 259; ch. 23). Even so, one might think that there would be times when his flock has need neither of judge nor lawyer, nor physician, nor pastor, and is therefore (quite literally) out of his sight, but it is at these times that the parson betakes himself to a hill from whose vantage point, we are told, he is able to survey his flock and "discover" its vices (p. 264; ch. 26). It is his particular skill to spy not the obvious vices of "Adultery, Murder, Hatred," etc. but those of a "dark, and creeping disposition," whose "natures are most stealing, and beginnings uncertaine" and whose detection requires the kind of vigilant "canvasing" (pp. 264–5; ch. 26) the parson so assiduously practices.

This particular aspect of the parson's performance is recounted in a chapter entitled "The Parson's Eye," and given the titles of surrounding and related chapters – "The Parson as Father," "The Parson in Sentinel," "The Parson in God's Stead," "The Parson Punishing," "The Parson's Surveys" – Herbert's idealized pastor begins to look like the engineer and operator of a system of surveillance that answers perfectly to the account of Bentham's Panopticon in Foucault's *Discipline and Punish*.

All that is needed, then, is to place a supervisor in a central tower... By the effect of backlighting, one can observe from the tower, standing out precisely against the light, the small captive shadows in the cells of the periphery. They are like so many cages, so many small theatres, in which each actor is ... constantly visible. The panoptic mechanism arranges spatial unities that make it possible to see constantly and to recognize immediately... Full lighting and the eye of the supervisor capture better than darkness... Visibility is a trap.[26]

As Foucault points out, one justification of the Panopticon and other "Enlightenment" disciplinary spaces is that the power they exert is not the power of a single person (such as a sovereign) but of the impersonal face of society, and therefore it could be said that disciplinary techniques were not carried out in the name of anyone in particular.[27] It is exactly in these terms that Herbert defends his parson against the charge that in zealously discovering the faults of offenders in his parish he violates the biblical injunction to be charitable:

But this is easily answered: As the executioner is not uncharitable, that takes away the life of the condemned, except besides his office, he add a tincture of private malice in the joy, and haste of acting his part; so neither is he that defames him, whom the Law would have defamed, except he also do it out of rancur. (p. 287; ch. 37)

Here in a concise form is both a rehearsal of Herbert's theory of (non)personality and an analysis of the way in which that theory negotiates the passage from a dispersal of power and the loss of story to a reconcentration of power in a story that is at once seamless and totalitarian. Like the executioner, the parson is never himself, is never anything "besides his office"; he is always acting his part and thereby making no claim to have a story of his own; but this very condition of being void of story – of having no continuous being, no personal desires, no inner orientation, no tincture of the private – frees him to act as an agent of a larger story – the story of a bureaucracy or of a God – and thus to acquire a prepared-in-advance justification for anything he does. The result is a narrative that unites absolute contingency and absolute design. The design belongs to the parson, but it is experienced as contingency by his charges who live with no certainty except the certainty that their own designs can be interrupted and unlinked at any moment. Because they never know when he is going to show up, they are unable to give themselves to the purposes of their "own affairs" and instead must await the eruption into those affairs of a purpose whose springs remain hidden. By providing his charges with the experience of continual anxiety, the parson fulfills one of his chief obligations, which is "to reduce [the members of his flock] to see Gods hand in all things, and to beleeve, that things are not set in such an inevitable order, but that God often changeth it according as he sees fit, either for reward or punishment" (p. 270; ch. 30).

This is an extraordinarily complex statement which repays analysis no less than a line in one of Herbert's poems. The order *is* in fact inevitable; it is the order of God's will, but it is shown in the frustration of other orders – the natural, the logical, the cultural – on which man is tempted to depend. In short, God disrupts the plots in which man attempts to insert himself and insists that he see himself as an unwilling actor in a plot that is forever escaping his understanding. God prevents man from making sense of his existence, except by the reference to the extra-rational category of "God's hand" (or what he "sees fit"), a category one invokes in feeble response to a universe of pure chance. If chance and randomness are the only thing you can count on, it becomes difficult, if not impossible, to wrest meaning and intelligibility from your experience. By removing predictability, God and his parson prevent their charges from making coherent sense of their lives and ready them to rely for sense on the will of their masters.

The result is a narrative of cosmic jealousy ("Thou shalt have no other gods before me") abetted by absolute power and it is a narrative that Herbert rehearses with an almost unholy glee: "God delights to have men feel, and acknowledge, and reverence, his power, and therefore he often overturnes things, when they are thought past danger; that is his time of interposing" (p. 272; ch. 30). That is, it is God's practice and delight to look for those times when men have deluded themselves into thinking that events have now acquired an intelligible shape, and then he intervenes in an act which replaces shape and pattern with contingency:

As when a Merchant hath a ship come home after many a storme, which it hath escaped, he destroys it sometimes in the very Haven; or if the goods be housed, a fire hath broken forth, and suddenly consumed them ... So that if a farmer should depend upon God all the yeer, and being ready to put hand to sickle, shall then secure himself, and think all cock-sure; then God sends such weather, as lays the corn, and destroys it: or if he depend on God further, even till he imbarn his corn, and then think all sure; God sends a fire and consumeth all he hath. (pp. 270–1; ch. 30)

And God does these things not because he loves disorder and discontinuity for their own sake, but for the sake of their effect on those who might be tempted to a prideful self-confidence: "Now this he doth, that men should perpetuate, and not break off their acts of dependence, how faire soever the opportunities present themselves ... [one] ought not to break off, but to continue his dependance on God ... and indeed, to depend, and fear continually" (p. 271; ch. 30).

This description of God's intention and practice is, as we have seen, also a description of the parson's intention and practice; this, then, is what it means to be a tracker of God's ways and be "in his stead." The difference of course is that God's surveillance is not something for which he has to work; it comes along with his omnipresence, with his all-seeing eye. The parson on the contrary enjoys no such supernatural power and he must contrive to simulate God's easy surveillance with a complex system of social, political, and juridical mechanisms in which the area of contingency is progressively reduced until every moment and every action bears the mark of a controlling design; the citizens who live in this system must "depend and fear continually," that is, they must never be allowed to feel that anything they do is unrelated to the pressure of a master plot of which they are not the authors. Rather than being void of story, this world is replete, indeed overflowing, with story, a story of dependence and manipulation that everyone is forced to enact.

OLD AND NEW PIETIES

A reading of *The Country Parson* so at odds with the traditional accounts of the tract raises more than a few questions. Why have so many missed the darkness and terror of Herbert's vision, and why *is* the vision so dark and terrible? How does one account for it? To the first question I would respond by pointing to the history of Herbert criticism, a history inaugurated by Izaak Walton's hagiographical life, and a history that to this very day cannot free itself from hagiography. To the second question – how does one account for the Herbert I have described? – there are a range of possible answers, no one of which is wholly satisfying. One might begin by linking the parson's efforts to monitor, and by monitoring, eliminate the inner life of his parishioners, to Herbert's response to Andrew Melville's attack on rites and ceremonies. Repeatedly mocking the puritan proclivity for undressing or "living without clothes," Herbert warns that a soul, "bare of sacred rites," has been rendered "bare to conquest / By Satan."[28] Nothing could be further from his religious temper than Milton's declaration (in answer to the question, "What, no decency in Gods worship?") that "the very act of prayer and thanksgiving with those free and unimpos'd expressions which from a sincere heart unbidden come into the outward gesture, is the greatest decency that can be imagined."[29] In Herbert's theology it is the "outward gesture" that makes good what a heart, naturally and totally foul, cannot, by itself, perform. Where Milton wishes to encourage spontaneity, Herbert wishes to extinguish it.

Still, this does not explain the parson's program of surveillance, his imposition of a control so total that he is jealous of any to whom his parishioners might turn for aid or counsel. Once again, however, there are historical materials that would seem to provide an explanatory context. In a culture obsessed by the mysterious workings of an all powerful and omnipresent deity, it is hardly surprising that men would think of God as someone by whom they are being continually disciplined. This is the argument, persuasively made, by Debora Shuger under the rubric of "absolutist theology." What she says of Donne could apply equally well to Herbert: "His preaching, and his king are all analogously related, all participants in absolutist structures of domination and submission."[30] Jonathan Dollimore makes the same point with the help of a passage from William Perkins's "A Discourse of Conscience":

The master of a prison is knowne by this to have care over his prisoners ... and so Gods care to man is manifested in this, that when he created man and placed him in the world, he gave him conscience to be his keeper, to follow him alwaies at his heeles, and to dogge him ... and to prie into his actions, and to beare witnesse of them all.[31]

The emphasis on conscience and an inner discipline is of course puritan, but one could turn to Thomas More's *Dialogue of Comfort Against Tribulation* for quotations that would externalize the discipline in ways Herbert's parson would recognize and approve.

God our chiefe gayler, as himselfe is inuisible, so vseth he in his punishments inuisible instrumentes, and therfore not of like fashion as the tother gaylers doo, but yet of like effect, and as paynfull in feeling as those. For he leyeth one of hys prisoners with an hote feuer, as euill at his ease in a warm bedde, as the tother gayler layeth his on the cold ground: he wringeth them by the browes with a meygreme: he collereth them by the neck with a quinsye [sore throat]: he bolteth them by the armes with a paulsy ... he manacleth their handes with the gowt ... he wringeth them by the legges with the crampe in their shinnes: he byndeth them to the bedde borde with the crycke in the backe, and layeth one there alonge, and as vnhable to ryse, as though he laye by fast the feete in the stockes.[32]

Statements like this one support Schoenfeldt's assertion that in Renaissance Europe there is a close connection between divine power and torture. He cites Luther's confident declaration that when princes punish, "It is not man, but God, who hangs, tortures, beheads, strangles."[33] In comparison to this, the discipline of the God of Herbert's parson, working as he does largely on grain and ships, seems almost tame.

Another possible explanation for the severity of the parson's regime is more theoretical and less historical. Jonathan Goldberg turns for illumination to Freud's linking of the notion of conscience with the pathology of paranoia: "Patients ... complain that all their thoughts are known and their actions watched and over looked."[34] This, as Goldberg points out, is exactly the complaint of so many Herbert speakers, who always imagine themselves "in the position of subjection"; and as "the *object* of scrutiny."[35] Following Goldberg's lead, we could argue that the paranoid fantasy of perpetual surveillance is an inevitable consequence of Herbert's strong monotheism, and that since one response to that fantasy is to identify with the surveillant, the program of the country parson is merely a logical extension of that response. Here the moral would be precisely that of Herbert's poem "The Reprisall": if you can't beat him (and you certainly can't), join him; that is, join your will or your wing to his – and thereby gain for yourself – no longer *your* self alone – the power that is properly his; turn submission and lowliness into the exercise of power. This is precisely what is done in innumerable sermons composed by preachers on every conceivable side of every conceivable debate in which every conceivable action is justified by its having been performed at God's behest and in his name. Or one could, as many historicists have now begun to do, invoke those manuals of courtesy that instruct in precisely this art, in the myriad ways by which gestures of humility and deference can be the means of seizing and maintaining power. It would then be a simple matter to argue (as Schoenfeldt does) that as a practiced courtier and court rhetorician Herbert would have quite naturally conceived of his relationship with God in terms analogous if not equivalent to his relationship with James I. Again Shuger provides a gloss: "The theological corollary of royal absolutism is radical monotheism, the total concentration of power into a single figure."[36]

With so many explanatory paths in prospect, it would seem that the answer to my question – how are we to account for the dark and sinister aspect of Herbert's work? – is that it is overdetermined; we should have expected nothing else. It is, however, an answer I want to resist because

by giving it we run the danger of making the Herbertian experience
disappear into its possible sources and analogues. Instead, I would agree
with Schoenfeldt when he insists that "Herbert's poems ... chillingly ...
imagin[e] God as wielding various implements developed by western
culture specifically for the imposition of pain."[37] It is the chill I want to
emphasize, for even in an age that refuses the pieties of literary high
humanism, the piety that has always characterized Herbert studies
continues, albeit in a different form. At the beginning of this century we
were still reading, or so we thought, a Herbert of simple, almost childlike
piety. In the revisionist period that began with the studies of Rosemond
Tuve and Joseph Summers, the piety was shown to be anything but
simple, but piety nevertheless. And even in the most up-to-date discourses of the very newest Historicists, we are told of a Herbert who
"attempts to break through the surfaces of social experience to a nearly
immediate communication from heart to heart," and who produces "a
'plain,' fully transparent speech which makes impossible all artificial-
ity."[38] The critic who writes these words acknowledges the theatricality
of the parson's performance, but avers nevertheless that it is a performance whose aim is "to exclude the theatrical by basing what is fabricated, the public image, on what is essential, the holiness within."[39] A
statement like this testifies to the desire (apparently irresistible) of so
many professional readers to transform their favorite poets into exemplars of an inner integrity they also share. But this will not do for the
Herbert I have been describing, who sees that the way to holiness is not
to break through surfaces, but to multiply surfaces, indeed to become a
surface; not in order to have holiness within, but to have nothing within,
not to purify "inner states of mind and feeling,"[40] but to achieve the
absence of inner states and feeling.

"Achieve" of course is the wrong word; the requirement, as I noted at
the beginning of this chapter, is more severe: to not achieve, to not be
conscious of an achievement which would thereby – by consciousness of
it – be forfeit. That is why the most remarkable thing about *The Country
Parson* is its total lack of interest in the interiors of either its title figure or
his parishioners. In the poetry, the weather of the inner life is a continual
obsession, and as an obsession – with the status of the self, of a being that
would have duration – it constitutes a temptation. In *The Country Parson*
that temptation seems to have been mastered, and Herbert is able, in
the person of his parson, to give himself over completely to the externals
of saving ceremonies, to vestments that wear him. There are poems like
that too, notably "Aaron," a poem about dressing up, about putting on

the armor of God, and thereby becoming dead to the self, "Christ is my only head / ... / ... striking me ev'n dead" (lines 16–18); not bringing new life to me, but extinguishing me. As the armor goes on – and it just goes on; we don't see him putting it on; we don't see him do anything – each piece "replaces," rather than revivifying or refurbishing, what it covers, until, in the manner of the transformation so brilliantly presented in the film *Robocop*, there is something entirely new, an animated suit of clothing where there was once a person. Of course once liberated from personhood this animated automaton can then proceed (again like the hero of *Robocop* but with even less vestigial memory) to do absolutely terrible things in the name of a higher power.

What remains startling (if not wholly original) in Herbert's work and thought is this relationship between the drive toward self-abnegation and the appropriation by the radically diminished self of everything that self-abnegation would supposedly have relinquished. In "Josephs Coat," Herbert cites triumphantly, "I live to show his power" (line 13) and in that single half line he displays the ambiguity that lends such a strength – such terrible beauty – to his work. He lives in order to be an illustration of God's power as it acts on him, to be a canvas for God's pencil, a showpiece of his irresistibility; and he also (or is it therefore?) lives in order to *show* that power to others by exercising it on their persons even as it has been exercised on his. If this is piety it is difficult to say whether the appropriate response to it is admiration or fear, both of which are demanded by the God whose ways Herbert tracks.

CHAPTER 3

Sir Kenelm Digby's rewritings of his life

Jackson I. Cope

What follows is a meditation upon aspects of the seventeenth century composed upon the observation of one man, the extravagant courtier Sir Kenelm Digby. He is a man who was accorded attention by his contemporaries extraordinarily disproportionate to the romantic bit roles to which history has reduced him in later accounts: something of a *miles gloriosus* and cuckold, yet a buccaneer in both love and war. English Roman Catholic son of a father executed for his part in the Gunpowder Plot, Digby was a supernumerary attendant to his uncle's negotiations for Charles I's marriage to the Spanish Infanta; became famous (or infamous) for his frustration of the Venetian fleet at Scanderoon; published a self-glorifying account of a duel for Charles's honor in France; was a charter member of the Royal Society; was a cherished and much-praised patron to Ben Jonson; and, finally, was the suitor, husband, and widower of Venetia née Stanley, perhaps the most gossiped about and most celebrated courtesan of the salad years of Charles's reign during the twenties until her death in 1633. It is this complex love relationship that has been the focus of later attention to Digby; sixty years ago a talented amateur chronicled it in a charming little book,[1] and thirty years ago the Italian scholar Vittorio Gabrieli made public a series of manuscripts which were, in large part, Digby's own accounts of his marriage to Venetia and her loss to death.[2]

It is to this relationship that I want to return attention yet again, because Digby's accounts of it would seem to exemplify with naively dramatic boldness the psychic interaction between *eros* and *thanatos* that we identify in its full mature articulation with Sade, and which Philippe Ariès, in his magisterial history of Western attitudes toward death, has found nascent in the baroque, with manifestations in painting, poetry, and the theater of cruelty, not least among the English Jacobeans who were Digby's contemporaries. Ariès argues that in the seventeenth century the artists' "tendency to place love in the midst of death ... takes place in the realm of the unconscious and unadmitted rather than in that of the inadmissible . . . But their contemporaries suspected neither the perversity nor the sexual basis of their taste for horror . . . Neverthe-less, the reader and spectator must have been profoundly aroused in spite of themselves, on an unconscious level; this can be felt in a vertiginous quality that we sense today in baroque art and literature." Ariès's sense of confusion at this point of lamination between historical data and psychological interpretation on a grand scale becomes evident when a few pages later he opines that "in the first half of the seventeenth century, the baroque era, a whole undiscovered world of emotions and fantasies began to stir. But the undercurrents that were created barely reached the surface of things; contemporaries did not even notice them."[3]

It will be my argument that Digby's baroque treatment of love and death in his own "loose fantasies" was quite conscious, and self-con-sciously aimed at his contemporary audience through a calculated manipulation of genres. Ariès, whose achievement in making us aware of death in new ways is humbling and admirable in many respects, joins many cultural historians and New Historicists in an underlying psycho-logical progressivism. While demonstrating on the level of annals a series of successive paradigms focusing attitudes toward death which he considers anything but a triumphant progress, having arrived at our own modern effort to obscure its presence with the language and tools of the hospital and clinician, there is yet observable in Ariès's attitude toward baroque attitudes the assumption of a progressive uncovering of the unconscious. It is an unconscious hubris about the moderns' insight into the oversights of the predecessors whose documents, available but in half light in their own time, awaited the psychological recoding of ours. "I began with the desire to speak with the dead": this statement stands at the opening of a set of theoretical, historiographic essays collected in a recent anthology.[4] In spite of disclaimers, a large number of such recent essays into cultural history, less magisterial than Ariès's, impose a modern idiom upon these dialogues with the dead. Digby, too, wanted to converse with the ancients. The conversation, though, was a probing of conscious intentions: what were the *rhetorical* modes of ma-nipulation that Tacitus employed? What did the Tacitean "dark style" reveal, in its abrupt truncations, about the anticipated audience? What structural aspects of the Isocratean panegyric were apt for adaptation by Digby in an era of rapidly shifting political forces? The questions raised by rhetoric, questions of choice couched in genres and style, are answerable by intentions not undercurrents. Historians who focus upon the unconscious gestures, the unrecognized pressures of the past may conceal more than they uncover. The case of Digby is a caveat suggesting that we may have a good deal of unlearning to do in preparation for conversations with the seventeenth-century dead.

The nineteenth-century antiquarian who first printed a version of Digby's erotic romance of the Hellenic variety popularized by Sidney's *Arcadia* created a radical misunderstanding when he labeled it as "private memoirs"; it was anything but that. If not printed, the *Loose Fantasies* was written and revised over a period of years to be circulated among those in Digby's court-centered group as a romance displaying the author's narrative and stylistic skills, with the added attraction of a frequently titillating allegory of coded names, as well as an embellished autobiography cum *apologia* for his much remarked marriage. It was just such distribution to just this court circle, gathering at the table of Richard Weston, Under-Treasurer of the Exchequer, and like Digby, a friend and patron to the poet, that Ben Jonson anticipated for his epigram "To my Muse, The Lady Digby, on her Husband, Sir Kenelm Digby":

> What reputation to my lines, and me,
> When he shall read them at the Treasurer's board?
> The knowing *Weston*, and that learned Lord
> Allows them? Then, what copies shall be had,
> What transcripts begged?

We are just now coming to realize that scribal and print publication moved in tandem throughout the seventeenth century in England; that, indeed, if we are to accurately evaluate the function and impact of these texts, the identification of publication with printing is one of those things we must unlearn.[5] The Jonson–Digby relations present an exemplary opportunity to "seek through a process of recontextualization to understand the ways in which scribal publication served to define communities of the like-minded."[6] Since Venetia, Lady Digby died in 1633, it is clear that Jonson's later poems were circulating among the members of such a community for several years before Jonson's death in 1637, as well as before the printed publication of *Under-Wood* in 1640 under the aegis of Digby, to whom, as the laureate's literary executor, "severall of the writings and workes of Benjamin Johnson ... were some tyme before his decease presented ... to dispose thereof at his will and pleasure."[7] The last and longest original piece published in *Under-Wood*, presumably by

Digby's arrangement, was "Eupheme, or, the Fair Fame Left to Prosperity of that truly-noble Lady, the Lady Venetia Digby, late Wife of Sir Kenelm Digby, Knight." And this elegy echoes so faithfully the themes of saintly charity and apotheosis elaborated in Digby's letter-book "In Praise of Venetia" that one must conclude that the latter had passed through Jonson's hands during the parallel development of both men's tributes.

I will here enter an only apparent digression, in noting that the poems of Robert Southwell, the English Catholic martyr who introduced the structures of religious meditational manuals into English poetry, were not printed until immediately following his execution in 1595. Southwell himself refers to a collection of poems which he prepared for circulation, and which were variously copied and given diverse devotional arrangements in numerous manuscripts of which some still exist; Southwell's modern editors have had recourse to these over the "printed books where the original intention of the Catholic missionary priest is overlaid by the commercial caution of the London printing houses."[8] Digby, too, was, one temporary and politic "conversion" aside, a Roman Catholic son of a Roman Catholic martyr. Indeed, in the *Loose Fantasies* he quotes the first line of the poem that opens and gives title to *St. Peter's Complaint*, Southwell's first printed collection; the allusion, underlined (and with the marginal note ["South."]) is applied to Venetia's own conversion to a life of penitential piety. This looks very much like a coded pointer for Catholic readers, entered after Digby's reconversion in 1635, especially inasmuch as the meditation would become formal principle for his letters "In Praise of Venetia." But this is to get ahead of the story.

In the years following his reconversion, Digby, too, assumed the mission of conversion, and was twice successful. Once it was with Lady Frances Purbeck, who had left her mad husband, been cited for adultery, and had fled to Paris and Rome, where she met Digby. He provided her with spiritual advice that survived for circulation in at least two morocco-bound manuscripts, both dated "Paris, 13. Jan: 1636."[9] It was only two to three years after this date that the guide toward conversion was printed in Paris as *A Conference with a Lady about Choice of Religion*. The other conversion guided by Digby, following close upon that of Lady Purbeck, was that of his cousin George Digby. During 1638 and 1639 they had an exchange of letters that focused the differences between Roman and Anglican theology in the doctrine of infallibility, and the letters' "immediate interest caused them to be widely read, and subsequently published."[10] They were not, however, printed until 1651.

These were not the only Digbean works to circulate in manuscript among a "community of like-minded," but they are sufficiently exemplary to provide a context for publication of the *Loose Fantasies* and "In Praise of Venetia." I couple the earlier romance and the widower's retrospective not only because they both narrate the love relationship, but because the later work dictated the narrative reformation of the earlier one. The meditational form that Southwell introduced would reshape the Hellenic romance into a history of providential salvation.

Venetia, Lady Digby was wept over in verse not only by Ben Jonson, but by Aurelian Townsend, Owen Felltham, Randolph Rutter, her relative William Habington, and Digby himself. Van Dyke painted her in life and death; accompanied by pious "inscriptions in copper gilt" affixed around it, her effigy topped a noble tomb in Christ Church before the Great Fire. But there had been another Venetia Stanley; before penitence the Magdalen had lived in sin. The antiquarian Aubrey off-handedly coupled her with Elizabeth Broughton, whose "price was very dear – a second Thais. Richard earle of Dorset, kept her (whether before or after Venetia, I know not, but I guess before)." Venetia had been nurtured on a country estate, "but as private as that place was, it seems her beautie could not lye hid. The young eagles had espied her, and she was sanguine and tractable," Aubrey reports elsewhere, and he continues: "I have now forgott who first brought her to towne, but ... she was so commonly courted and that by grandees, that 'twas written over her lodging one night ... PRAY COME NOT NEER, BUT DAME VENETIA STANLEY LODGETH HERE." Whoever brought her into society, "Venetia Stanley was (first) a miss to Sir Edmund Wyld; who had her picture," but "The earle of Dorset ... was her greatest gallant, who was extremely enamoured of her, and had one if not more children by her."[11] In a public fit of pique the Venetian ambassador called her a whore, and the Earl of Clarendon counted as a handicap under which Digby labored "his own marriage with a lady, though of an extraordinary beauty, of as extraordinary a fame."[12] Digby's sensitivity is revealed in an extravagant boast that he must have made on more than one occasion; Aubrey twice reports that Sir Kenelm "would say" that "a handsome lusty man that was discreet might make a vertuose wife out of a brothell-house."[13] It was just this extravagance that Digby elaborated into the romantic narrative of *Loose Fantasies*.

Of all the young eagles in Oxfordshire, Digby was the first to spy out the beautiful Venetia, and it is with this early stage that his prose romance begins the history of their relationship, under the fictive names of Theagenes and Stelliana. In spite of a conventional disclaimer at the end, that this is a public performance, and far from Edward Nicholas's presentation of it as "private memoirs," is evident from the early declaration that it is to be written "in a plain style, and without endearing [*sic*] any thing to the advantage of either of them beyond the reality of truth," because such partiality would be recognized by "those that knew how near friends they are unto me."[14]

Briefly, brought by fortune to neighboring country estates, Theagenes and Stelliana conceived a mutual love as small children ("and whereas other children of like age did delight in fond plays and light toys, these two would spend the day in looking upon each other's face" [*Loose Fantasies*, p. 12]). Their relatives fall out, and Theagenes's mother sends him to begin his studies, while Stelliana's father sends her to the court of Morea (read "London") where "all men of eminency" gather for the marriage of the princess. Here (in confirmation of Aubrey's report), Stelliana begins to draw too-early attention. Her nurse abets the courtier Ursatius in his seduction and kidnapping attempts upon the young beauty. What the narrator withholds as a literal account, he reveals in allegory when Stelliana escapes the hands of Ursatius only at the cost of being laid prostrate and bloodily wounded in the forest of error by a "wolf's merciless teeth," from which Mardontius rescues her. She heals from her wounds to body and reputation in the house ("styled the school of temperance and goodness" [p. 30]) of Artesia; here she learns that Theagenes has refused a pre-arranged marriage, and meets him once more. Before the young courtier departs for a long tour of continental courts to deflect his mother's marital ambitions, what had been a soul-mating enters a more physical phase: "the last of [his vows] he breathed into her mouth ... whilst their souls, ascended to the very extremities of their tongues, beggan a mystical discourse ... his hands ... in their dumb language expressing what it was that he desired" (p. 38). The lovers' restraint triumphs here, but the maturing Theagenes soon is thrust among the perils of the Athenian (read "French") court; he almost becomes victim to the unnatural heat of the Queen (Marie de' Medici), but escapes by the ruse of pretending to have been killed in a revolutionary skirmish. Unhappily, this false tale crosses the Channel and reaches the grief-stricken ears of Stelliana. After mourning her lost love, she gradually succumbs to Mardontius, and is betrothed until he displays himself as a fickle deceiver and is righteously spurned. Theagenes has himself been having adventures of blade and boudoir, driven to despair by news of Stelliana's engagement. When one of his dueling triumphs is recounted in Morea, Stelliana becomes remorseful at having compromised herself in the wake of his reported death. Theagenes returns, forces Mardontius to restore a symbolic token and, with it, Stelliana's reputation. She, in turn, pledges her fortune to advance his political ambitions. Mutual confidence recovered, they marry although, "moved by sundry weighty respects" (his mother and uncle disapprove of Stelliana's past), Theagenes keeps the marriage secret through the birth of a son and on through the seafaring adventures that culminate in a great victory at Alexandretta (Scanderoon) and his arrival at Milos. These are the barebones events of the simple secular romance that Digby began, along with the journal of his buccaneering voyage through the Mediterranean, while becalmed for a few days on the island of Milos in August 1628. He had "set down in writing [his] wandering fantasies ... in loose sheets of borrowed paper ... so that ... it might serve for an index to reduce the rest into my remembrance" (p. 173).

Over the next several years, Digby states that this initial index brought him "many times [to] retire my looser thoughts within their own centre, and with serious meditation fix them upon this subject" (p. 3). The extant fair copy manuscript (possibly transcribed by Digby himself, who "wrote a delicate hand, both fast-hand and Roman," Aubrey reports)[15] contains numerous revisions, and incorporates knowledge of Venetia's death five years after the first draft. The privateering voyage through the Mediterranean which occasioned the writing of the romance is itself explained within the text as an action that motivated such disapproval at court "that it was necessary for him to employ himself in some generous action that might give testimony to the world how his affections had nothing impaired the nobleness of his mind" (*Loose Fantasies*, p. 161). Quite the reverse. Venetia was as beautiful as her reputation was ugly; Digby was a young and ambitious courtier; naturally, it was "much against his mother's, etc., consent, that he maried that celebrated beautie and courtezane," as Aubrey again reports.[16] The "etc." included Digby's older cousin, John Digby, first Earl of Bristol, whose romance counterpart Aristobolus chides Theagenes and draws forth the lengthy "philosophic" defense of his marriage in *Loose Fantasies* (pp. 139–57). This is the rationale and certification for the publication through manuscript circulation of the romance. Aristobolus accuses Theagenes of having fallen into a "servile affection" that draws "if not contempt, at least a mean esteem, especially when it is conferred upon one that hath been known ... to have been formerly engaged unto another, and hath lived altogether at liberty under her own conduct in the world" (p. 140). Theagenes, in response, constructs a simple but audaciously personal *scala paradisiaca*. Man's greatest attribute is will; the will's highest desire is to draw near God, who cannot be approached but through his creatures. All who know her know that Venetia is the paragon of female beauty, and "the love of a virtuous soul, swelling in a fair and perfect body, is the noblest and worthiest action that a man is master of; it exerciseth in due manner that superior talent that God and nature hath given him; and by choosing a perfecter object than himself to love, it exalteth and refineth those seeds of goodness that are in him ... and to that idea that he hath framed to himself, he raiseth himself up" (pp. 131–2). But how can this soiled courtesan serve as Digby's English Beatrice? First, if Digby's philosophic ground-plan has inextricably associated body and spirit, chastity, as an act of omission, mere "frozen virtue," has little value. But women "are capable of worse corruptions" than immature sexual surrender ("there are innumerable vices incident to them"): "if a noble affection, and their being deceived with sacrilegious vows, do win them to antedate their favors ... they are pardonable" (p. 145). In a version of Digby's reported habit of repeating that a discreet man could "make a vertuous wife out of a brothel-house," Theagenes asserts that "A wise man should not confine himself to what may be said of the past actions of his wife ... But in choosing her, he ought to see that she be nobly descended, beautiful to please him, well formed to bear children, of a good wit, sweet disposition, endowed with good parts, and loves him; then it will be his fault if he make her not a good wife" (pp. 146–7). Stelliana, in fact, will be a better wife for her earlier unhappy experience: "if indiscreet unstayd youth, or rather childhood, have at any time cast a mist over her judgment, and so caused some innocent error in any of her actions, the goodness of her nature hath converted it into this benefit, that she is fully warned and armed never to incur the like." Theagenes concludes his defense of marriage to his modern Magdalen with the invocative citation of Southwell: "but weak conjectures can be made of what one doth before the intellectual part is grown to his full strength; for they were once brittle mould that are now saints" (pp. 148–50).

Saintly Venetia Stanley became; Ben Jonson's eulogy *Eupheme* concludes its litany of her pious deeds with the fantasy of her final vision of Christ's ascent: "In this sweet *Extasie*, she was rapt hence. / Who reads, will pardon my Intelligence, / ... To publish her a *Saint*. My *Muse* is gone" (lines 225–8). A saint but, in her reformation, all too saintly, perhaps, for the adventurous and curious courtier. The religiosity that the old poet could unstintingly admire in the muse who was his patron's wife, the young husband found excessive – an attitude that seeps out through the letters formally "In Praise of Venetia." The great romance led to a separation of souls that Digby seems intent upon bridging in the posthumous accounts. He was a restless adulterer and compulsive confessor: "Even when she suspected or knew I had scattered else where what was onely her due, and that upon her taking unkindnesse att me for it I grew sadde and sorrowfull . . . she would blame her selfe and aske pardone for what she had caused in me . . . I neuer stayed her asking; but such a strainge and impatient loue I had that the wrong I did her burned in me till I had told her of it."[17] The result seems to have been less healthy for her than for him: "the extremity of [her sorrow for receiuing so sharpe affliction] would worke strange effectes and alterations upon her bodie" ("In Praise of Venetia," 9, 13). Digby thought it a face, though, "not extremely winning att the first sight" (9, 129), and in the cheeks of which, at the best of times, "one might happily haue wished a little addition [of colour] to what ordinarily was in them" (9, 130). One learns from an early letter written before Venetia's death that these cheeks had been scarred by smallpox ("Ça et la il y a quelques marques et vestiges d'autre fois un mal discourtois quand il attaque les visages des belles dames" [10, 104]); the posthumous word-portraits make no allusion to this cosmetic disaster. Untutored ("she was beholding to nature for all she had; art had no share" [10, 84]), she was limited in song, as in conversation: "She had a very sweete and pleasing voice, and of a great compasse until the bearing of children did something restrain that" (9, 131), and "One that had knowne her but in her familiar coruersation would scarce haue belieued she had had so strong partes of the braine" (10, 84). But the mind, like the voice, must have deteriorated greatly, since at the autopsy "when they came to open the head, they found the braine much putrifyed and corrupted: all the cerebellum was rotten" (9, 134). Venetia, if fat, nonetheless had become a difficult spiritual anorexic: "She fasted many meales besides those she did by obligation; and those she did by her owne election she would seeke to steale from the knowledge of me and of her family." Before her morning grooming, Venetia became accustomed "to pray and meditate two howres in her oratory" without fire or gown even in winter; "in the afternoones she seldome missed two or three hours of her prayres"; for "particular deuotions of that time she euer assigned a whole hour before she went into bed; and there meditated until sleepe stole upon her" (9, 132). What from one perspective was saintly behavior in a thirty-year-old lady of the court ("she often mortifyed her selfe with disciplining and wearing a shirt of haire"), from another could seem dangerous obsession. While she was alive in those last months, Digby clearly sensed that she was growing unbalanced: "Seeing her rirednesse (for often she would not stirre in a fortnight, three weekes or a month) I was faine many times to use importunity to gett her abroade" (9, 128). Privately, he said, "I have oftentimes considered ... what issue and periode this her course of holinesse might haue; and I haue feared for my owne sake that she was to farre aduanced in her journey towardes heauen" (9, 133).

It was Venetia herself who nurtured this notion in the mind of Digby – and of others. "Any time above this yeare [she] hath expected and talked of dying suddainly," Digby tells his aunt, repeating what he had told their children more specifically: "she did in a manner foresee and prophecy her owne death; for of late times she would be speaking of it, and would affirme constantly that she belieued the houre of it was not farre ... my wife euer had a presaging apprehension of a soddaine death, and would often say to my selfe and many of her frendes that she expected such a one" (9, 133). A strange locution, that of referring to their mother as "my wife" in a memorial portrait for the children, but it appears by attraction, by being drawn into the recollection of Venetia's talk to friends. All of the portraits of Venetia that I have pieced together here consist in fragments buried in the hagiographic floor of repetitious adoration that is the collection of documents Digby labeled "In Praise of Venetia." But isolated, they offer a quite different perception of the marriage and its end from that intended for his public by Digby, and both perpetuated and misunderstood by his modern biographers.

Digby, a busy administrator at court where he was a Gentleman of the Privy Chamber, and an experienced advisory officer for the navy, was also busy as a self-proclaimed philanderer, doubtless both cause and consequence of the prayers and hair shirt that came between him and the reformed courtesan with whom he had had such a romantic, if notorious, beginning. And those who knew them took her predictions of imminent sudden death in a somewhat different light from a premature call to God's side. Sir John Finch knew Digby in Paris where he lived "After the death of his Lady V.S. whom the King caused to be opened upon suspition of some poyson his enemies had suggested to have been given."[18] This is all we know of the origin of the autopsy, but Aubrey confirms the rumors abroad: "She dyed in her bed suddenly. Some suspected that she was poysoned ... spiteful woemen would say 'twas a viper-husband who was jealous of her that she would steale a leape."[19] A

well-connected husband, both famous and notorious at court for his
boasted sexual prowess, for "chemical" experiments with the painter
Van Dyke, who made a posthumous portrait of Venetia on her death-
bed (delaying the eventual autopsy), a man carrying all the baggage of
suspicion surrounding Roman Catholics in England; an equally notorious wife who had gone from loose mistress of several courtiers to a
physically deteriorating religious hysteric warning of her imminent
death. These were the elements that gave credence to the rumors of
murder sufficient to motivate the autopsy upon Venetia's body. And this
is the historical context in which one must read the letters "In Praise of
Venetia" to realize that they represent neither the modern romance
depicted so convincingly by Bligh, nor the unconscious sexual depths
discovered by Ariès in the baroque psyche's coupling of *eros* with *thanatos*.
Rather, they are Digby's public rhetoric of self-defense, couched in the
form of the religious meditation, against dangerous suspicions.

One should notice that in describing his retreat during which the
letter-book was written, Aubrey emphasized Digby's motives in terms
consonant with the display (the "signs") of mourning rather than unrestrained grief: "After her death, to avoyd envy and scandall, he retired
in to Gresham Colledge at London, where he diverted himselfe with his
chymistry, and the professors' good conversation. He wore there a long
mourning cloake, a high crowned hatt, his beard unshorne, look't like a
hermite, as signes of sorrowe."[20]

And self-conscious display, the enhancement of private feelings in
public exhibition with the stylistic resources of the practiced rhetorician,
was a principal generic effect of the meditation. John Wallace said of
Traherne that "he used the meditation much as Cowley employed the
ode, to arouse powerful feelings in an age which was becoming increasingly distrustful of enthusiasm."[21] This may remind us that "scribal"
publication for engaging with an audience both circumscribed and
prescribed was the vehicle Traherne chose for his meditations in poetry,
as it had been for that first English Catholic poetry of meditation, the
collections by Robert Southwell. Digby's letters are no more extem-
poraneous private ejaculations than such carefully wrought poetic performances; no distracted scribbler wrote such Donnesque prose (it is not
infrequently encountered throughout the letters) as this carefully bal-
anced alliterative and assonantal sentence: "My soul can resist sorrow
and make me submitt my will to the will of God, and be appay[s]ed with
whatsoeuer he pleaseth to do; but God knoweth other motions raigne in
my sense and will tyrannize there whiles my flesh hath sense" ("In Praise

of Venetia," 9, 122). Such calculated rhetoric belies the *pro forma* disclaimer in the same letter, where Digby says: "You may not expect here studied, or indeed orderly, expressions of what I desire to deliuer you . . . my sorrowes are to fresh and to deeply imprinted in my heart to lett me dresse my wordes with any ornamente" (9, 121). It is a pose of spontantous sincerity doubly appropriate to the courtier as author and to the author of spiritual meditations.

"Meditation" is a term Digby uses in describing Venetia's religious discipline ("her life for seuerall yeares of late hath bin but a continuall meditation of death" [10, 88]), and is repeated like a leitmotif throughout the letter-book, even in relatively impersonal communications. Only days after the event, Digby writes to an unidentified Mr. Gell that "All I have now to doe is by continuall reflection on my deare wifes death to meditate upon my owne." A few days later yet, in a letter of business arrangements with Secretary of State Sir John Coke, Digby refers to his "sorrowfull meditations."[22]

Let us briefly recall what this term encompassed as a psychological structure prescribed in the popular Catholic guides written by St. François de Sales, Luis de la Puente, and St. Ignatius Loyola, those authors most widely consulted in Digby's England. The meditation is a self-examination, "spoken as one friend speaketh unto another, when he talketh with him of some weighty affaire." It first rouses the memory by concentration upon a scene, that "composition of place" which imaginatively locates one at the site of spiritually intense moments; this is succeeded by the understanding's analysis of the significances to be derived from such a contemplation; and, finally, the will is employed in the colloquy proper to attain that end of spiritual growth, that redirection of the affections that is the object of the exercise.[23]

Digby was focusing his image as a reformed man reevaluating his life and afterlife in a retirement motivated by his loss. One can see this motive in a letter to his brother written on June 19 that follows the meditational structure paradigmatically (and incidentally informs one that Digby, unlike the perfervid Venetia, carefully regulated his spiritual calendar): "as I sate this morning meditating deeply on my blessed wifes death (which I use to do in particular manner every Wednesday), her old servant brought in a picture and sett it downe before me." It is the Van Dyke deathbed portrait; but so strong is his concentration that he relives the moment he discovered her dead, through "an effect of the imagination that, being deeply and wholy busied upon one object, did (after it had raised itself to such heate) represent it thus lively to me."[24] The

recollections turn upon the ease with which she passed almost imper-
ceptibly from life to death, while he survives "upon this wretched earth
drowned in teares and sorrow," his only companion Venetia's portrait
which "att night when I goe into my chamber I sett ... close by ... and
by the faint light of a candle, me thinkes I see her dead indeed; for that
maketh painted colors looke more pale and ghastly then they doe by
daylight."[25] The icon, like its subject, has metamorphosed from life to
death. But the redirection of Digby's will through these meditations is
quite unexpected, unless one has realized the public self-exoneration
toward which Digby has adapted the meditational genre. His friends
urge him to divert his attention from this obsessive concentration upon
loss. But that very obsession is a vehicle toward his salvation; the
reformed Magdalen's death has reformed the penitent philanderer: "Is
it not a strange thing that griefe should bring to passe what love and
beauty could not? When my wife was alive, I could be contented
sometimes to steal a houres delight with other women ... But now she is
dead, methinkes the goodnesse and beauty of all her sexe is gone with
her."[26] This brief letter is characteristic of the meditational form into
which Digby's almost daily correspondence falls, as he writes those
letters, most addressed to his brother, that constitute the collection "In
Praise of Venetia."

The most interesting is that of May 24, which seems a prime document to exemplify Ariès's thesis of a subconscious *frisson* in the baroque
merger of love and death, until one supplies the personal contexts of
Digby's published performance. And, in this most striking instance, one
must remember not only the author's self-defense against the talk of
adultery and murder, but his experimental interest in the body and his
philosophic interest in justifying the notion of corporeal resurrection in
the face of the scientist's focus upon decay, interests in 1644 embodied in
*Two Treatises, in the one of which, the Nature of Bodies; in the other, the Nature of
Mans Soul, is Looked into.*

The event the memory revives in this meditation is, as usual, Venetia's
death; the scene imagined is the house of death. "My thoughtes haue ...
tumbled euery corner of her graue. This day three weekes, late att night,
she was buried; and by this time God knoweth what alteration that faire
bodie hath sustained." God knows, but Digby conjectures: "by this time
peraduenture her louely face ... is farre gone towardes being turned to
earth, and is couered ouer with slime and wormes. Her eye ... is now
farre unlike what it vsed to be. Her fine-shaped bodie and full thighes that
were so tender ... haue now their dainty flesh consumed, and haue the

bones and sinewes naked and deformed ... and her heart that was the seate of goodnesse, truth and vertue, hath now nothing in it but peraduenture some presumptuous worme feeding in the middle of it" ("In Praise of Venetia," 9, 455). If this description suggests the self-torment of a perverse sensual obsession, one should recall a meditation in which Digby warned against another obsession, that with "learning and sciences": "peraduenture he that is fascinated with these is worse then who is immersed in sensuall voluptuousnesse, by how much these affect the minde the more immediately and with a greater peruersity" (10, 96). And recalling this, one realizes that Digby's corpse-side fantasy is presented in bad faith: Venetia had been anatomized before burial, and perhaps before her husband's eyes. Digby recounts the details: "she lay dead as she was aliue, like an Angell. The last day her bodie began somewhat to swell vp, which the Chirurgions said they wondered she did not more and sooner, being so fatt as afterwardes vpon opening she appeared to be, and lying in so warme a roome" (9, 133). "When she was opened, her heart was founde perfect and sounde ... In her gall was found a great stone bigger then a pigeons egge ... All her other partes were admirably strong and sound ... But when they came to open the head, they found the braine much putrifyed and corrupted: all the cerebellum was rotten, and retained not the forme of braine but was meer pus and corrupted matter." The scientist has replaced the lover, and presents the findings of the autopsy as evidence that clears away the suspicions that he had poisoned Venetia: "the decay they found there was not the work of short time, but had bin some yeares in growing to this passe" (9, 134). It is the scientist who will proceed to elaborate the significance of Venetia's corporeal decay, whether fictive or factual.

The long middle section of the meditation develops a version of the topos we most readily identify with Spenser's argument for "eterne in mutabilitie." As Digby phrases it, "Nature aymeth at perfection in euery thing ... So that all the variations of nature are but a most orderly progression to perfection; and by euery change we gett a betterment, then change must cease" (9, 456). The truth of this is evidenced from Paracelsian "chymicall operations" or "the spagyrike art" of distillation. The operations prove empirically the familiar argument that form is ultimately inseparable from matter. In making an "Elixir (which in more familiar expression may be called a resurrection and perfection)," the chemist brings it to "putrefaction," makes it "the most corrupt and foetide masse that it is possible to be." This is the process in which the soul seems to lose the body to the ravages Digby has envisioned; but thus purified of dross, the soul will be reunited with the corporeal vehicle in its quintessential, perfected form. This same double metamorphosis will occur in a chemist's "little glasse and a furnace, working vpon any substance whatsoeuer," and in the history of the earth, whose parts were opened to "a generall decay and putrefaction" by the flood, only to be prepared for the perfecting final conflagration (9, 457). It is a grand cosmic expansion from Digby's having "tumbled euery corner of her graue" to his observation of the earth's millennial renewal. As is usual with Digby, the impassioned conclusion that he draws is unexpected. "This earth ... when it is thus renewed, will be a fitt habitation for the bodies that rise againe out of it, and are purifyed with it." But in the meantime, why must we think the souls impatient for a pure and permanent corporeal reunion are "in the outermost conuexe superficies of the world"? They are with God, but God is everywhere, and thus, our heaven is everywhere. Venetia's soul, then, may be Digby's muse: "why may she not now be close att my hand, and desirous (if it were lawfull for her) to informe my understanding and guide my pen in writing of these things"? (9, 458). Meditating as a scientist upon the beloved's death, Digby becomes the inspired prophet of the afterlife. What had seemed a personal obsession with loss evolves into an inspired philosophic optimism; and it is the philosopher who speaks what are perhaps the most personally revealing words in Digby's collection of meditations: "Mine is a kind of rationall madness" (9, 458).

Meditation upon the loss of Venetia's body to the presumptuous worm has brought Digby to realize that her hovering soul has exalted him to a voice prophetic of human reunion in a purified state when apparent decay has metamorphosed into permanent transcendent perfection. But this is but another version of what the younger Digby had argued in defense of his marriage to Venetia. In the *Loose Fantasies* we learned that a man's "love of a virtuous soul, swelling in a fair and perfect body ... exalteth and refineth those seeds of goodness that are in him ... and to that idea that he hath framed ... he raiseth himself up." Substituting "form" for "idea," the philosophic rationale for this claim is provided in the later meditation: "it is not in the power of any agent to destroy the forme" of any creature, "but that it will still retaine a seede or rather a sparke of fire that hath power to assimilate other fitt matter into its owne nature, and to make an other substance like the former, but much more noble and perfect" ("In Praise of Venetia," 9, 455). In death as in life, his own Saint Mary Magdalen spiritually resurrects the wandering sinner.

Digby's life continued through thirty turbulent years after Venetia's death, though. A Catholic and a royalist, he was on the continent through much of the Civil War; served the queen mother in various capacities, was an agent in Rome, was briefly imprisoned in England, and became intimate enough with Cromwell to raise another set of rumors. Throughout these years, Digby kept up his scientific and philosophic studies, publishing widely if not well upon them. In this context the *Loose Fantasies* took on a new significance and structure: the "looser thoughts" Digby would not "with serious meditation" fix upon "the perfect friendship and noble love of two generous persons, that seemed to be born in this age by ordinance of heaven to teach the world anew what it hath long forgotten" (*Loose Fantasies*, pp. 4–5). In retrospect, the narrative that rationalized a scandalous marriage will be rewritten as a providential personal history that metamorphoses the romantic protagonists into the spiritual model for a new age. Providence not only brought forth this model when it was most needed ("such an example . . . Infinite Wisdom, that disposeth all things, deferred until his season, wherein affections are so depraved that they had need of the liveliest pattern" [p. 6]), but intervened at every internal turn of the history. Separated after their childhood companionship had begun, "if their fates had not been written above in eternal characters, even then their affections had been by a long winter of absence nipped and destroyed" (p. 13). During this separation, Stelliana reasons that "it is ordained by heaven that I must harbour no other flame within my breast, since this long absence . . . has not been able to smother this" (p. 20). Providence provides its mysterious aid in paradoxical ways: "Oh how unsearchable is the Providence of heaven!" the author cries out when Mardontius arrives to save Stelliana from the wolf (p. 929); when this same Mardontius becomes infatuated, however, he becomes a pawn in God's paradox: "the just heaven, whose judgements are inscrutable . . . useth oftentimes to effect the greatest actions by the most unlikely means, so it made her consent to marry Mardontius to be the first cause of dissolving it" (pp. 67–7). And now "the fortunes of Theagenes did mingle themselves with . . . the actions of great princes, and but that they were guided by a secret working of Divine Providence, did run in such a way as none could have expected" (p. 69). A Christian stoic quite as active as Hamlet, Theagenes neither seeks nor rejects service to the king or country: "I conceive the surest way to leave the disposing of one's course of life to the Divine Providence, and for the rest, to bear an even mind and a quiet soul" (p. 98); he knows "how weak all the wisest propositions of men are, and that God reserveth to himself the right of disposing all things" (p. 139).

Expanded, revised, and rewritten in light of Venetia's death, *Loose Fantasies* nonetheless incorporates none of the sexual adventures that prompt so much remorse in the meditative letters, none of the social and physical limitations of Venetia, nor her obsessive religious rituals which we learn from the letters only partly "in Praise of Venetia." Both are allegedly autobiographical works, but each molded within the clear confines of a literary genre. After his wife's death, the courtly widower revised his *roman à clef* into the history of a chosen man's providentially guided career, repatterning a Catholic courtier's life into a counterpart to the popular puritan spiritual autobiographies.

The principal impetus for each of Digby's literary projections of his affairs was provision of a public antidote to negative reactions that his relations with Venetia Stanley roused at both the beginning and end of their marriage. He adapted religious literary genres as political documents promulgating a public fiction among a relevant court circle for private ends.

I began by suggesting that Digby's case offers a caveat not only against Ariès's anachronistic misreading of the baroque psyche, but against a wide range of the conversation with the dead that passes as cultural history. If this chapter seems to have probed into obscure psychological motives as ruthlessly as the revisionists whose historical success I question, it does so not to discover the unconscious springs of his action, but Digby's full consciousness of the possibilities for psychological manipulation of the public rhetoric of genres. One might offer as a last conjecture that the original genius of the early modern writer was not for originality of forms, but for their misappropriation.

CHAPTER 4

Thomas Hobbes and the Renaissance studia humanitatis

Quentin Skinner

John Wallace was one of the first scholars to provide a convincing account of the intellectual context within which Hobbes worked out his civil philosophy. His was a pioneering attempt to demonstrate that, as he puts it in *Destiny his Choice*, Hobbes can be "brought into relation with contemporary political thought instead of standing outside it."[1] There are at least two routes, however, by which writers can be brought into an instructive – and perhaps explanatory – relationship with their immediate intellectual surroundings. One is by identifying the precise range of debates to which they contributed, treating their texts in effect as responses to the controversies in which they were involved. This is the approach followed by John Wallace in *Destiny his Choice*, in which he shows how far Hobbes's theory of political obligation was occasioned by, and in turn helped to advance, the arguments about "engagement" after the execution of Charles I in 1649.[2] But it is possible to take a different though complementary route, focusing on the intellectual resources available to a given writer and seeking to assess how far he or she may have been molded and affected by them. This is the approach I shall adopt in what follows, in which I too shall be principally concerned with the figure of Thomas Hobbes. My aim will thus be to add a footnote to John Wallace's pathfinding scholarship not merely on Hobbes's political theory but on the discipline of contextual reading itself.

We are frequently assured that, as one of Hobbes's best recent commentators puts it, Hobbes's philosophical ideas were "formed" by the scientific revolution spanning the seventeenth century.[3] I shall argue that this orthodoxy rests to a misleading extent on emphasizing the period in which Hobbes began to put into print his ideas on the natural and moral sciences, beginning with his first major treatise, *De Cive*, in 1642. If we focus instead on the period before *De Cive* was published, a strongly contrasting picture begins to emerge. Hobbes is revealed not as a product of the scientific culture to which he later contributed so extensively, but rather as a student and exponent of the predominantly literary culture of Renaissance humanism.

A number of commentators have already pointed out that Hobbes's intellectual development may be said to have passed through a "humanist period" before he turned to the sciences, natural and moral, in the course of the 1630s.[4] Little attempt has been made, however, to explore the extent to which his earlier studies may be said to conform to the Renaissance ideal of the *studia humanitatis*, and thus to the distinctively "humanist" range of genres and disciplines.[5] And no attempt at all has been made to examine how far the works he published prior to *De Cive* embody an authentically humanist understanding of how philosophical texts should be organized and presented to maximize their argumentative force. These are the gaps I hope to fill in the current literature, although I can only hope to do so in a preliminary way.[6]

According to Renaissance pedagogical theory, the first and basic element in the five-fold syllabus of the *studia humanitatis*[7] was grammar, the study of the classical languages.[8] John Aubrey's biography makes clear that Hobbes acquired an exceptional mastery of these linguistic skills at an early age. After four years of "petty" training between the ages of four and eight, he was sent to a school run by a young man called Robert Latimer, whom Aubrey describes as "a good Graecian."[9] Aubrey tells us that Latimer "delighted in his scholar, T. H.'s company, and used to instruct him, and two or three ingeniose youths more, in the evening till nine a clock."[10] The young Hobbes "so well profited in his learning," Aubrey goes on, "that at fourteen yeares of age, he went away a good schoole-scholar to Magdalen-hall, in Oxford."[11] As proof of the high level of proficiency in Greek and Latin that Hobbes had by then attained, Aubrey adds in admiring tones that "it is not to be forgotten, that before he went to the University, he had turned Euripidis Medea out of Greeke into Latin iambiques, which he presented to his master."[12]

These literary interests must have been seriously interrupted by the scholastic curriculum Hobbes was obliged to follow at Oxford, a curriculum he recalls in his verse *Vita* with unmixed contempt.[13] But he seems to have had the idea of returning to his humanistic studies as soon as he left Oxford in 1608.[14] He immediately joined the household of William Cavendish, later the first Earl of Devonshire. Hobbes was employed as tutor to Cavendish's son, the future second earl, who also bore the name William Cavendish.[15] Hobbes and his charge began by removing to the University of Cambridge, where the young Cavendish was awarded the degree of Master of Arts in July 1608, while Hobbes was incorporated as a member of St. John's College.[16] The choice of college is interesting in view of the fact that St. John's had been a leading center of humanistic learning ever since Roger Ascham and Sir John Cheke had begun teaching there in the early 1530s.[17] However, this particular educational scheme appears not to have worked out. We learn from the account-book kept by Cavendish *père* that Hobbes was paid twenty shillings in November 1608 for hiring a coach to take the young Cavendish back to his father's estates in Derbyshire after what appears to have been only a single term of residence in the university.[18] So far as studying at Cambridge was concerned, that was that.

After this failed experiment, Hobbes at first abandoned his studies more or less completely. "During the year that followed, I spent almost the whole of my time with my master in the city, as a result of which I forgot most of the Latin and Greek I had ever known."[19] After returning from a trip to France and Italy with the young Cavendish in 1615, however, Hobbes seems to have settled down once more to a regular and scholarly mode of life.[20] He informs us that "my master provided me with leisure throughout the ensuing years, and supplied me in addition with books of all kinds for my studies."[21] As he makes clear in his autobiographies, moreover, his reading largely centered on the five canonical disciplines of the Renaissance *studia humanitatis*: grammar, rhetoric, poetry, history, and moral philosophy.

Hobbes tells us in his prose *Vita* that he began by setting himself a course of study specifically designed to recover and extend his mastery of the classical languages. "As soon as I got back to England, I started carefully to read over the works of a number of poets and historians, together with the commentaries written on them by the most celebrated grammarians."[22] He adds that "my aim was not to learn how to write floridly, but rather to learn how to write in an authentically Latin style, and at the same time how to find out which particular words possessed the meaning best suited to my thoughts."[23] He must have begun to recover his knowledge of Greek at the same period, Lucian being one of the authors on whom he seems to have concentrated. Lucian is praised in the Appendix to the Latin *Leviathan* as an excellent writer of Greek,[24] and Hobbes exhibits a knowledge of his writings in several different works. He is mentioned in the *Critique* of Thomas White's *De Mundo*[25] as well as in *Lux Mathematica*[26] and the *Historia Ecclesiastica*,[27] while in *Leviathan* he is cited (although without acknowledgment) at several points: the story in chapter VIII about the learned madness of the people of Abdera is taken from Lucian's account of how to write history,[28] while the description of human law in chapter XXI is presented as a commentary on Lucian's version of the fable of Hercules.[29]

No doubt as part of this process of reeducating himself in the classics, Hobbes appears to have renewed acquaintance with the ancient theorists of rhetoric at the same time, and thus with the second element in the *studia humanitatis*. He must have made a close study of Aristotle's *Art of Rhetoric* at this juncture or in the early 1630s, given that a paraphrase he made of the text was in print by 1637.[30] He must also have read, or more probably reread, the major treatises on Roman rhetorical theory in the course of the 1620s. Existing studies of Hobbes's intellectual development have tended to leave the impression that his detailed knowledge of ancient eloquence may have been confined to Aristotle's *Rhetoric*.[31] But in the introduction to his translation of Thucydides, which he published in 1629, Hobbes makes it clear that he was no less familiar with a number of leading works of Roman rhetorical thought. He not only refers familiarly to Cicero's *Orator*, *De Optimo Oratore*, and *De Oratore*, but also quotes from each of these texts.[32] Finally, it seems likely that it was during the same period that he immersed himself in Quintilian's *Institutio Oratoria*, a treatise to which he makes explicit reference in several of his later works.[33]

There is plentiful evidence that Hobbes was also much preoccupied in the 1620s with the third element in the Renaissance *studia humanitatis*, the study of classical poetry. He informs us in his verse *Vita* that he read a great deal of ancient poetry and drama at this period, specifically mentioning Horace, Virgil, and Homer among the poets, together with Euripides, Sophocles, Plautus, and Aristophanes among the dramatists.[34] Aubrey confirms that, although Hobbes in later life possessed relatively few books, his visitors could always expect to find copies of Homer and Virgil on his table.[35] Both poets are invoked on numerous occasions in Hobbes's later works, and there are direct quotations from Virgil's *Aeneid* in the *Critique* of White's *De Mundo*, in *Leviathan*, and (although unacknowledged) in *De Corpore*.[36] Hobbes's verse *Vita* adds that this was a time when he read many other ancient poets.[37] One of these must have been Statius, to whom he alludes in chapter 12 of *Leviathan*.[38] Another must have been Martial, one of whose epigrams is quoted in *De Cive*.[39] Another must have been Lucan, whose *Pharsalia* he cites in his essay on heroic poetry and praises for having achieved "the height of Fancie."[40] Yet another must have been Ovid, whom Hobbes might have been expected to include in the list of his favorite ancient writers, especially as he modeled his verse *Vita* on the autobiography included by Ovid in his *Tristia*.[41] But of all the ancient poets Horace was unquestionably Hobbes's favorite, with references to the *Epistles* in particular being sprinkled through several of his later works.[42]

It is evident from Hobbes's autobiographies that he also devoted himself after his return to England in 1615 to the fourth of the five elements in the *studia humanitatis*, the study of history. He informs us that "in my early years I was drawn by my natural bent to the historians no less than to the poets,"[43] and he explains that this made him turn "to our own historians as well as to those of Greece and Rome."[44] He does not tell us which English historians he read, but he emphasizes that, among the Greeks, "it was Thucydides who pleased me above all the rest."[45] Aubrey reveals that, among the historians of Rome, Hobbes chiefly admired Caesar, and particularly his *Commentarii*.[46] He adds that Hobbes never abandoned these early interests, and that in later life it was not uncommon to find him reading "some probable historie."[47]

Hobbes must in addition have made a close study of several other classical historians at this time. This is evident from *The Elements of Law* and *De Cive*, both of which reveal a detailed knowledge of Sallust's *Bellum Catilinae*;[48] it is also evident from *Leviathan*, in which Hobbes not only refers to Plutarch's life of Brutus[49] but also puts the life of Solon to elegant though unacknowledged use.[50] The same point emerges still more clearly from Hobbes's translation of Thucydides. One of the distinctive features of Hobbes's edition was his attempt to locate all the place-names mentioned in Thucydides' text. Hobbes entered the names on a map of ancient Greece which he drew himself, and which he arranged to have engraved and inserted into his book.[51] He explains in his opening address that he was able to discover the location of all the towns and villages "by travel in Strabo, Pausanias, Herodotus, and some other good authors."[52] His index confirms that he made extensive use of all these authorities, and also read a number of other historians with the same purpose in mind. One was Appian, whose account of the Roman civil wars he mentions at several points.[53] A second was Polybius, whose *Histories* he refers to with some frequency.[54] But the most important was Livy, whose authority he invokes on dozens of occasions, drawing his information from at least ten different books of the history.[55]

During the long period of reading that followed his return to England in 1615, Hobbes also seems to have taken a special interest in the fifth and culminating element in the traditional *studia humanitatis*, the study of moral and civil philosophy. His reading must at least have encompassed Lipsius' *De Doctrina Civili*, which he quotes in the Introduction to his translation of Thucydides,[56] as well as Bacon's *Essays*, several of which he helped to translate into Latin.[57] He must have known More's *Utopia* and Bodin's *Six livres de la République*, both of which he mentions in *The Elements of Law*, the latter in tones of considerable respect.[58] We learn in addition from one of his letters to the Earl of Newcastle that he began reading John Selden's *Mare Clausum* as soon as it was published in 1635,[59] and from references in *The Elements of Law* that by 1640 he had mastered a number of classical texts in moral and civil philosophy including Aristotle's *Politics* and the works of Cicero and Seneca.[60]

It is in some ways even more striking that Hobbes's pupil William Cavendish should have taken such a professional interest in the moral sciences at the same time. Cavendish made his debut as a writer on moral philosophy in 1611, when his *Discourse Against Flatterie* was published by the London firm of Walter Burre. Although the *Discourse* appeared anonymously, it was known to the booksellers as Cavendish's work,[61] and was dedicated to his wife's father, Lord Bruce of Kinloss.[62] There seems no reason to doubt – as some scholars have done[63] – that Cavendish was the principal author of the *Discourse*.[64] But if it is true that the work was commissioned by his formidable father-in-law, it would hardly have been surprising if Cavendish had called upon his tutor to help him make a satisfactory job of it.

After returning from his travels with Hobbes in 1615, Cavendish continued to read and write on similar themes. The first outcome was a set of ten short pieces[65] to which he gave the Baconian title of "Essayes" and which he presented to his father in the form of a manuscript volume inscribed from "Your Lordships mos [*sic*] observant and dutifull sonne W. Cavendisshe."[66] Hobbes must have been acting as Cavendish's secretary at this time, for the volume is actually in Hobbes's hand,[67] although it includes corrections by Cavendish in addition to the signature claiming the volume as his own work.[68] Again there seems no reason to assume that Hobbes rather than Cavendish must have been the real author,[69] especially as some of the essays contain opinions diametrically opposed to those later expressed by Hobbes on the same subjects.[70] As in the case of the *Discourse*, however, it is hard to believe that Cavendish would not have discussed the contents of the volume with his former tutor, particularly as the opening essays are all devoted to issues so close to Hobbes's heart: "Arrogance," "Ambition," "Affectation," "Detraction," and "Selfe-will."[71]

Cavendish's final contribution to moral philosophy took the form of a volume of essays entitled *Horae Subsecivae* or "Leisure Hours." This collection was first published anonymously by Edward Blount in 1620,[72] although when the firm of Legatt and Crooke registered the same work for republication in 1637 they described it as "Lord Cavendishes *Essaies*."[73] The first half of the *Horae* contains twelve short pieces entitled "Observations," and consists of a slightly extended version of the manuscript volume already presented by Cavendish to his father.[74] The second half is given over to four longer "Discourses," the titles of which are "Upon the Beginning of Tacitus," "Of Rome," "Against Flattery," and "Of Lawes."[75] Of these the third is a revised and abbreviated version of the *Discourse Against Flatterie* originally published by Cavendish in 1611. But it has now been contended that the other three[76] were almost unquestionably written by Hobbes[77] – a dramatic suggestion that would push back by over twenty years the date at which he first embarked on the publication of his civil philosophy.

So far I have concentrated on Hobbes's humanistic studies during the period of his service to the second Earl of Devonshire. This period came to an unexpected end in 1628 when the earl suddenly died and was succeeded by his ten-year-old son, yet another William Cavendish.[78] These developments at first caused Hobbes to lose his position in the Devonshire household, but he regained it in 1631 when the second earl's widow invited him to return as tutor to her young son.[79] There then ensued what Hobbes describes in his verse *Vita* as "seven painstaking years"[80] in the course of which he served as tutor and traveling companion to the son of his former pupil, continuing in these roles until the third earl attained his majority in 1638.

Hobbes's verse *Vita* includes a revealing account of the syllabus he drew up in his renewed tutorial capacity. He mentions that he taught the young William Cavendish some logic, arithmetic, and geography,[81] and it is evident from other sources that he also gave him some instruction in geometry.[82] As the *Vita* makes clear, however, he took his principal duty to be that of inculcating the main elements of the Renaissance *studia humanitatis*. He accordingly started his pupil off with Latin grammar, his aim being to instil "an understanding of the meaning of the speech used by the Romans, and of how to join Latin words together in the proper way."[83] Some evidence of Hobbes's method of

teaching this basic skill can be seen in one of William Cavendish's
surviving exercise-books at Chatsworth. From this it appears that
Hobbes dictated in Latin, subsequently going over his pupil's version
and pointing out his mistakes. One of the texts on which they worked
together in this way was Aristotle's *Art of Rhetoric*. Cavendish's exercise-
book contains a Latin paraphrase of Aristotle's text, with numerous
marks to suggest that it may have been dictated to him in short sections,
and with a large number of corrections and additions in Hobbes's
hand.[84]

After this, Hobbes's verse *Vita* explains, they moved on to the second
element in the *studia humanitatis*, the study of rhetoric. Hobbes's account
implies that he was following a recognized scheme of instruction at this
juncture, rather than teaching what he might ideally have wished to
impart, since his description of the *ars rhetorica* is far from neutral in tone.
What he taught the young earl, he declares, was "how Orators write,
and by means of what art Rhetoricians are accustomed to deceive the
uninitiated."[85] As we have seen, Hobbes's method of imparting this
additional skill took the form of combining it with the teaching of
grammar, concentrating on a number of texts – such as Aristotle's
Rhetoric – capable of serving both pedagogical purposes at once. This
had been the normal method of instruction in the grammar schools of
Hobbes's youth, in which the rules of composition had generally been
taught from a study of the best authors together with handbooks of
rhetorical style.

There is considerable evidence that Hobbes paid no less attention in
his teaching to the other three elements in the traditional *studia
humanitatis*. He mentions in his verse *Vita* that he taught the young
Cavendish "what a Poet does,"[86] and it is clear that he also introduced
him to some ancient history and moral philosophy. The main evidence
about the young Cavendish's historical studies is contained in another of
his surviving exercise-books, in which a large number of biographical
sketches and famous incidents from Greek and Roman history are
translated and copied out.[87] A hundred and twenty of these brief
extracts survive, reflecting various stages in the development of Cavendish's handwriting, and it is striking that a majority of them concern the
early history of republican Rome. A number discuss the military leaders
from the era of the Punic Wars: there are extracts on Publius Claudius,
Lucius Paullus, Quintus Metellus, and Marcus Regulus in addition to a
series of ten extracts on the Scipio family. A still larger number celebrate
the heroes of the early republic:[88] there are extracts on Lucius Brutus,

the liberator of the Roman people from their kings; on the severity of Camillus and Postumius as censors; on Gaius Flaminius and Tiberius Gracchus as leaders of the plebs; on the elder Cato, who carried into extreme old age "a youthfull courage in defending the Common-wealth";[89] and on the military greatness of Publius Rutilius and Fabius Flaccus, the first of whom "begot in the legions a more subtle way of avoiding and of giving strokes," while the second discovered the value of using nimble velites against cavalry.[90]

The humanist handbooks of the English Renaissance had invariably emphasized that an education in the *studia humanitatis* should culminate in the study of moral philosophy. As Sir Thomas Elyot had explained in *The Book Named the Governor*, "by the time that the child do come to seventeen years of age, to the intent that his courage be bridled with reason, it were needful to read unto him some work of philosophy; specially that part that may inform him unto virtuous manners, which part of philosophy is called moral." By way of embarking on this final stage of the syllabus, Elyot goes on, "there would be read to him, for an introduction, the first two books of the work of Aristotle called *Ethicae*, wherein is contained the definitions and proper significations of every virtue."[91]

Hobbes appears to have followed these humanist precepts to the letter. As a way of introducing the third earl to the rudiments of moral philosophy, he seems to have commissioned the production of a Greek and Latin manuscript, found among his papers, which is headed *Aristotelis Parva Moralia, sive de Ethicis virtutibus*.[92] Hobbes's choice of author is perhaps surprising, given that he later denounced Aristotle to Aubrey as "the worst teacher that ever was,"[93] but the explanation is perhaps that he again saw himself as following an approved pattern of instruction rather than his own inclinations at this point. Certainly the contents of the *Parva Moralia* are largely Aristotelian in character. The title is not of course the name of any authentic work by Aristotle, but was doubtless intended to recall the best-known of the post-Aristotelian epitomes, the *Magna Moralia*, which continued to be printed as a text of Aristotle's in Renaissance editions of his works. The *Parva Moralia* manuscript is mainly devoted to considering the specific virtues discussed by Aristotle in Books III to VI of the *Nicomachean Ethics,* together with a number of the apparent virtues discussed in Books II and VII. The Latin terms conventionally used to translate Aristotle's vocabulary are used throughout, the individual chapters being entitled *De Prudentia, De Temperantia, De Modestia et Magnanimitate, De Fortitudine, De Iustitia Particulari, De Liberalitate et*

Magnificentia, De Comitate et Urbanitate, De Mansuetudine, and *De Veritate &*
*Veracitate.*94 To these are added, again in Aristotelian vein, the virtues
"improperly so-called," the first being *De Verecundia* and the rest *De*
Indignatione, De Continentia, De Tolerantia, and *De Heroica Virtute.*95 The
manuscript contains a large number of marginal references to the
sources of its arguments, all of which correspond to the chapters in
which Aristotle had discussed the same issues in the *Nicomachean Ethics.*
While Aristotle's arguments are supplemented as well as truncated and
rearranged, the manuscript undoubtedly offers a basically Aristotelian
account of "the definitions and proper significations of every virtue" in
exactly the manner recommended by Elyot in *The Book Named the*
Governor.

It would seem, however, that Hobbes may have principally taught the
young Cavendish the elements of moral philosophy in the more homely
manner also recommended by the humanist writers of advice-books on
good conduct. His method appears, that is, to have been to turn to the
moralists and historians of antiquity as sources of sententious maxims
and instructive anecdotes. The exercise-book in which his pupil translated and paraphrased the Roman historians includes a great deal of
material of this kind. From Pomponius Rufus, for example, Cavendish
recounts the story of Cornelia, the mother of the Gracchi, who was
shown some precious jewels and ornaments by a guest. She waited for
her children to come home from school, "and these, saith shee, are my
ornaments." The moral is said to be that "Certainly hee hath all things,
who desireth nothing."96 From Book II of Cicero's *De Oratore* Cavendish
similarly takes the story of Simonides, who was called away from a
banquet just before the roof collapsed and killed everyone else present.
The moral in this case is even more high-flown. "What is more rich than
this happinesse, Which neither the Sea nor the Land raging was able to
destroy."97

As well as repeating these edifying tales – and a great many others in
similar vein – Cavendish was clearly encouraged to treat the historical
figures about whom he read as exemplars of particular virtues and vices.
Hobbes appears to have accepted the conventional view that the lives of
the philosophers provide the most instructive examples. The life of
Solon reminds us about the importance of industriousness.98 Diogenes'
conduct toward Alexander the Great illustrates the value of independence and continence.99 Socrates' willingness to study a musical instrument in old age suggests that it is never too late to learn.100 Carneades,
who wonderfully addicted himself to learning for ninety years, exemp-

lifies the value of a life committed to the pursuit of wisdom.[101] And so on. It seems, in short, that Hobbes's method of instruction was based on the typically humanist assumption that history and moral philosophy can be taught together, since history serves as the light of truth[102] and thus as philosophy teaching by examples.

Throughout his three decades of service as tutor and secretary to the Devonshire family, Hobbes was continually occupied in studying and teaching the *studia humanitatis*. But of even greater significance is the fact that his own writings from this period are overwhelmingly humanist in character. If we turn to consider the works he published prior to the appearance of *De Cive* in 1642, we not only find that he contributed to all five of the recognized humanist disciplines; we also find that his published works are wholly confined to these distinctively humanist genres.

The most obvious way of demonstrating a mastery of the primary element in the *studia humanitatis*, the *ars grammatica*, was by making translations of classical texts. This in turn helps to explain why the art of translation attained such an unparalleled degree of prestige and prominence in the Renaissance. If we reflect on Hobbes's scholarly activity in the 1620s, it becomes clear that he was much influenced by this humanist scale of values. He initially worked as a translator of English into Latin, a skill he exercised at some stage in the early 1620s as secretary to Francis Bacon.[103] It is not clear how this secondment from the Devonshire household arose, but it must have occurred at some time between Bacon's dismissal from the Lord Chancellorship in May 1621 and his death in 1626. One of Bacon's projects during these years was to rewrite his earlier vernacular works in Latin. He published an extended version of *The Advancement of Learning* as *De Dignitate et Augmentis Scientiarum* in 1623, and at the same time began to translate some of his *Essays* into Latin. For this latter undertaking he needed some help, and according to Aubrey it was Hobbes who supplied it. Aubrey not only records that "The Lord Chancellour Bacon loved to converse" with Hobbes, but that Hobbes "assisted his lordship in translating severall of his Essayes into Latin, one, I well remember, is that *Of the Greatnes of Cities*."[104]

Hobbes made a much more important contribution to the study of the classical languages when he published his translation of Thucydides' history as *Eight Bookes of the Peloponnesian Warre* in 1629.[105] Hobbes concedes in his opening address that Thucydides' text has already been rendered into English, and that he has seen a copy of this earlier version, which Thomas Nicolls had issued in 1550.[106] But Hobbes objects that

Nicolls's rendering is not merely full of inaccuracies, but offends against a more fundamental tenet of humanism by failing to use the best available text. Nicolls had been content to work from a French translation (published by Claude de Seyssel in 1527) which in turn derived from Lorenzo Valla's Latin edition of the 1450s.[107] By contrast, Hobbes stresses, he has worked directly from Thucydides' original Greek, using the newly corrected edition of Aemilius Portus[108] and supplementing Portus' text with an up-to-date scholarly apparatus, "not neglecting any version, comment, or other help I could come by."[109] The outcome, Hobbes proudly announces, is a version as free as possible from errors, for "I can discover none, and hope they be not many."[110]

Soon afterwards Hobbes made an important contribution to the second discipline in the *studia humanitatis* when his paraphrase of Aristotle's *Art of Rhetoric* was published. Hobbes had first encountered the editor of the *Rhetoric*, Dr. Theodore Goulston, as a fellow member of the Virginia Company in the early 1620s.[111] But it appears to have been as part of his duties as tutor to the third Earl of Devonshire in the early 1630s that Hobbes made a close study of Goulston's Greek text.[112] As we have seen, he began by translating sections of it into Latin, dictating them to his pupil as a series of comprehension exercises.[113] His Latin version was then turned into English and anonymously published as *A Briefe of the Art of Rhetorique* in 1637.[114] This was the first English translation of Aristotle's *Rhetoric* to be printed, and Hobbes's achievement in truncating, reshaping, and supplementing the text[115] was recognized at the time not merely as an exercise in grammar but as a contribution to the study of rhetoric as well.

During his first period of service to the Devonshires Hobbes also made an ambitious contribution to the third element in the *studia humanitatis*, the study and imitation of classical verse. He presented to the second earl, around the year 1627, a poem of some 500 Latin hexameters entitled *De Mirabilibus Pecci, Carmen*,[116] a description of the "wonders" of the Peak district in Derbyshire which Hobbes published a few years later.[117] The most striking feature of his poem is its continual use of themes and motifs derived from classical epic verse. This admittedly gives rise to a tone of bathos in several passages, but from the perspective of my present argument the important fact is that the aspiration is such a typically humanist one. The poem centers on the Homeric idea of a memorable journey, describing a trip from the Earl of Devonshire's seat at Chatsworth to the neighboring town of Buxton and its surrounding countryside. Recounting seven wonderful episodes – the ancient magic number – Hobbes permits himself copious use of the classical trope to the effect that he cannot hope to do justice to his extraordinary experiences. He nevertheless attempts to describe them, and in doing so repeatedly ornaments his verses with Virgilian echoes and references. The groves of Chatsworth are cooler than Virgil's beeches;[118] the fountains in its gardens are finer than the sacred font of Callirhoe;[119] the descent into the vaporous depths of Elden Hole is similar to Aeneas' visit to the underworld;[120] the robber's cave visited at the end of the journey is reminiscent of the Gorgon's lair.[121]

Throughout the early part of his career, Hobbes also took an active interest in the fourth of the humanistic disciplines, the writing of history. We find him displaying considerable historical erudition in his edition of Thucydides, particularly in the footnotes and marginal glosses he appended to the text. There are learned references to the patterns of alliances at the outbreak of the Peloponnesian war, the nature of Greek religious observances, the methods of waging the war itself, and so forth.[122] As his introductory essays make clear, moreover, Hobbes decided to make more widely available this masterpiece of ancient historiography for reasons of a preeminently humanist kind. One reason he gives is his wish to show that Thucydides discharged "the principal and proper work of history" more effectively than anyone else, that of seeking "to instruct and enable men, by the knowledge of actions past, to bear themselves prudently in the present and providently towards the future."[123] A further reason is that we can hope to learn something of importance from the fact that Thucydides "least of all liked the democracy."[124] He shows us that any community dependent on large assemblies for its processes of decision-making will be liable to suffer dangerously from "the emulation and contention of the demagogues for reputation and glory of wit." With their continual "crossing of each other's counsels," they will be sure to undermine any concern for the public good and eventually bring about the dissolution of the commonwealth.[125]

Of even greater importance as a contribution to the study of history is Hobbes's *Discourse upon the Beginning of Tacitus* from the *Horae Subsecivae* of 1620. Following the typically humanist method of quoting key passages from a classical text and commenting on them, Hobbes devotes a large part of his *Discourse* to narrating the rise of the Emperor Augustus to power and his successful conversion of Rome from a republic into a principality.[126] Hobbes first invokes Tacitus' authority to explain "the means *Augustus* used in acquiring and confirming to himselfe the supreme and Monarchical authoritie."[127] He then adds an extensive account, again in the form of glosses on Tacitus' text, of how Augustus thereafter managed to perpetuate his imperial authority "and derive it to posterity."[128]

Reflecting on this narrative, Hobbes adds in typically humanist vein that a number of general lessons can be drawn from it, especially in view of the fact that Augustus followed "the best order that can be, to assure a new soveraignty."[129] The situation in which Augustus found himself was that of a usurper seeking to impose the "restraint and pressure of Monarchicall rule" upon a people only recently "weaned from liberty."[130] He thus found himself facing the very predicament which, as Machiavelli had notoriously argued in *Il Principe*, is above all fraught with danger for a new prince.[131] This makes it particularly instructive, Hobbes suggests, to observe what courses of action Augustus followed: how he never engaged in policies that "a new Prince ought to avoid," how he concentrated with exemplary skill on the lines of conduct "best for a new prince."[132] Watching Augustus in action, in short, we can hope to learn from "a master in the Art of government."[133]

The early part of Hobbes's career culminated in the production of two major treatises of civil philosophy, traditionally the fifth and final element in the *studia humanitatis*. Hobbes explains in the Preface to his *De Cive*[134] that "a few years before the civil war broke out, my country started to seethe with questions about the right of Sovereignty and the obligations of citizens to obedience," in consequence of which he felt it a matter of urgency to put his thoughts on these matters into publishable form.[135] He began by circulating *The Elements of Law, Naturall and Politique*,[136] which he completed in May 1640,[137] and shortly afterwards published *De Cive*, which first appeared at Paris in April 1642.[138] As we have seen, however, it is now known that he had already published a work of civil philosophy over twenty years earlier. This was his *Discourse of Lawes*, which he had contributed anonymously to the *Horae Subsecivae* in 1620. While Hobbes makes no attempt in this earlier work to present his arguments in the form of scientific proofs, he already announces a number of conclusions that he later claimed in *De Cive* to have demonstrated. He already tells us that "common reason" is at once "ingrafted in our natures" and is at the same time "a *Law*, directing what we are to doe, forbidding the contrary."[139] He further assures us that reason prescribes complete obedience, since we "are rather bound to obey, then dispute; *Lawes* being, as it were, the Princes we ought to serve, the Captaines we are to follow."[140] Finally, he confirms this central contention by arguing that any attempt to live together in the absence of law would bring such confusion "that the differences of Right & wrong, Just and unlawfull, could never be distinguished."[141]

I began by suggesting that, if we are to lend some precision to the suggestion that Hobbes's early intellectual allegiances were predominantly humanist in character, two main questions need to be addressed. The first is whether his early studies conform to the Renaissance ideal of what it means to contribute to the humanistic disciplines. We have now seen that this can be answered in a resounding affirmative. But there remains the second and arguably more significant question: whether Hobbes's early writings are presented and "disposed" in an authentically humanist style.

Before considering this question, we need to recall the leading assumptions about the organization of literary texts that the humanists of the English Renaissance had inherited from their classical authorities and put into currency by this time. The most important was that all public utterances must conform to one or other of three rhetorical genres. That this contention became so widely accepted was undoubtedly due in large part to the fact that, as Quintilian had noted, almost every ancient rhetorician had repeated the list of *genera* originally put forward by Aristotle in his *Art of Rhetoric*.[142] Aristotle had laid it down that – in the words of the translation attributed to Hobbes – "there are three kinds of *Orations; Demonstrative, Judicial, Deliberative*."[143] The pseudo-Ciceronian *Rhetorica ad Herennium* had opened by repeating Aristotle's categories,[144] while Quintilian had later taken over the same classification, commending Aristotle at the same time "for establishing this tripartite division of oratory into the judicial, the deliberative and the demonstrative."[145]

The ancient rhetoricians had almost invariably begun by discussing the *genus demonstrativum*. Aristotle declares (in the translation attributed to Hobbes) that the proper office of such epideictic orations is "*Praysing* and *Dispraysing*," while their proper end is to point out what is "*Honourable*, or *Dishonourable*."[146] He stresses that things as well as persons can be commended or condemned, and lists among the things most worthy of praise "Monuments" and, more generally, "things that excell."[147] When offering such laudations, we should bear in mind that "to praise the Worke from the Vertue of the Worker, is a circular Proofe," and instead concentrate on "declaring the magnitude" of the work concerned.[148] Among Roman rhetoricians, Quintilian particularly takes up this analysis, agreeing that our praises can properly encompass animals, inanimate objects, cities, public works, and "every other kind of thing."[149] If we are praising a city, we should remember that "antiquity brings with it a great deal of authority";[150] if we are praising specific buildings or public works, we must emphasize "not merely their honourable character but also their beauty and usefulness."[151]

This inclusive understanding of the *genus demonstrativum* was enthusiastically revived by the rhetorical theorists of the Renaissance, many of whom exhibit a special interest in re-establishing the genus of panegyric both in prose and verse.[152] One resulting development was the emergence of a sub-genre specifically devoted to praising the *magnalia* or signs of greatness in cities. The most celebrated example is Leonardo Bruni's *Laudatio Florentinae urbis* of 1403–4,[153] but a number of earlier examples survive, several dating from before the dawn of the Italian Renaissance. These include the anonymous poem in praise of the city of Lodi, *De Laude Civitatis Laudae*, which was probably written as early as the 1250s,[154] and Bonvesin della Riva's panegyric on Milan, *De Magnalibus Mediolani*, which was completed in 1288.[155] Quintilian's further suggestion that almost anything can in principle be praised was also much developed in the Renaissance. Richard Rainolde, for example, in his *Foundacion of Rhetorike* of 1563 – a widely used textbook in the Elizabethan grammar schools[156] – assures us that "All thynges that maie be seen, with the iye of man, touched, or with any other sence apprehended" can equally well be commended or condemned: "as Manne. Fisshe. Foule. Beaste. Orchardes. Stones. Trees. Plantes. Pettals. Citees. Floodes. Castles. Toures. Gardeins. Stones. Artes. Sciences."[157]

The second form of utterance to which the classical rhetoricians had addressed themselves was the *genus deliberativum*. Aristotle had laid it down in the *Rhetoric* (in the translation attributed to Hobbes) that the office of such speeches is "*Exhortation* and *Dehortation*," and that their proper end is "to proove a thing *Profitable*, or *Unprofitable*."[158] He goes on to explain that "an Orator in *exhorting* always propoundeth *Felicity*, or some part of *Felicity* to be attained by the actions he exhorteth unto," to which he adds that "by *Felicity*, is meant commonly, *Prosperity with vertue, or a continuall content of the life with surety*."

The implication that an orator who deliberates must in effect be counseling was subsequently taken up by the leading Roman writers on the rhetorical arts.[159] They also accept that, as the *Ad Herennium* puts it, the purpose of offering such counsel will normally be *suasio et dissuasio*, to persuade or dissuade someone from acting in some particular way.[160] The only point at which they express any doubts about Aristotle's analysis is in considering his claim that the goal of deliberative oratory is to indicate which of various possible actions should be treated as especially advantageous or profitable. As Cicero explains in the *De Inventione*, "whereas Aristotle is content to regard *utilitas* as the aim of deliberative oratory, it seems to me that our aim should be *honestas et utilitas*, honesty allied with advantage."[161]

The last form of utterance discussed by the classical and Renaissance rhetoricians was the *genus iudiciale*. Once again they generally take their definitions from Aristotle's *Rhetoric*, in which the office of judicial oratory is described (in the version attributed to Hobbes) as that of *"Accusation and Defence"* and its goal as that of discovering in some particular instance what is *"Just, or Unjust."*[162] It follows that "the thing to be prooved is, that *Injury* has beene done."[163] Among the Roman writers, Cicero provides the fullest restatement of these categories. He agrees that the *genus* takes the form of accusation and defense;[164] he agrees that "the question at issue is always what is equitable";[165] and he speaks at length of the need to establish whether some injury has in fact been suffered in order to ensure that equity and justice are upheld.

If we now return with the above considerations in mind to Hobbes's early writings, we find that they fall into two strongly contrasting categories. By the time he came to draft *The Elements of Law* and *De Cive*, he was in full revolt against the literary culture of Renaissance humanism. Both these texts explicitly repudiate the ideals of rhetorical organization in favor of what Hobbes takes to be the canons of science. But if we turn instead to the works he allowed to appear in print before the publication of *De Cive*, we find him confining himself entirely to the accepted rhetorical genres.

Among these early writings are two contributions to the *genus demonstrativum* so conventional as to count as little more than rhetorical exercises. One is the Latin poem of 1627, *De Mirabilibus Pecci, Carmen*. Hobbes takes especially seriously Aristotle's injunction that, if we are praising monuments or other such works, we must concentrate on their sheer magnitude. The first "wonder" Hobbes describes is Chatsworth, which he commends for its fame and size.[166] The second is the Peak itself, which he praises for its grandeur and frightening appearance.[167] The third is Mam Tor, the "maimed rock," which he admires for its mighty scale.[168] And so on. The poem concludes, admittedly with something of an anticlimax, with a *Laudatio* addressed to the robber's cave near Buxton, which is described as well worth visiting.[169]

Hobbes had earlier written an even more conventional exercise in the *genus demonstrativum* in the form of his *Discourse on Rome* of 1620. The *Discourse* is an instance of one of the most popular forms of *Laudatio* revived in the Renaissance, that in which a city is praised for its signs of greatness. It is true that Hobbes's account is in part a *Vituperatio* as well, since he ends by pointing to the corrupting implications of the fact that the city is nowadays "wholly subject to the Pope, which hee holds as a temporal prince."[170] Hobbes criticizes the leaders of the church in exactly the manner prescribed by ancient theories of rhetoric, stressing their absence of *honestas* and their consequent failure to follow a virtuous way of life. He particularly concentrates on the extent to which their conduct is founded on the worst of all the vices, the sin of pride. Fascinatingly, in view of his long polemic against Cardinal Bellarmine in *Leviathan*, he specifically exempts Bellarmine from this charge, stressing that he is chiefly noted for his learning and retiring mode of life (pp. 400, 402). If, however, we consider the Pope and the rest of the Cardinals "it is strange to see their pride" (p. 400). They "violently desire honour, and superfluity in wealth" (p. 404). They are "proud, seditious and covetous" (p. 406). They have nothing to teach us apart from "ambitious thoughts, and unsatisfied desires after the wealth and glory of this world" (p. 404). We can safely conclude that "the sumptuousnesse of the *Pope*, and the pride of his government, is one token of the falsity of their doctrine" (p. 403).

Apart from this concluding *Vituperatio*, Hobbes's *Discourse* consists entirely of what he himself describes as a "Laudatory" to Rome (p. 353). As we have seen, Aristotle had argued that monuments are particularly susceptible of being effectively praised. Hobbes duly informs us that he will concentrate on the city's "*Ethnicke* Antiquities," "Christian Monuments," "moderne Buildings, Gardens, Fountaines, &c" as well as on its "Colledges, Churches, and Religious Houses" (pp. 229–30). Aristotle had gone on to propose that, in praising monuments, we should focus on their sheer magnitude, to which Quintilian had added that we should seek to commend their antiquity and if possible their beauty and usefulness. Hobbes duly begins (p. 325) by observing that Rome remains unchallenged for antiquity as well as greatness, and subsequently illustrates his claim by emphasizing the great age and size of the amphitheater, the "wonderfull great compasse" of Diocletian's baths, the "great length" of St. Peter's, and so on (pp. 344, 346, 364). He speaks too

(p. 353) of "the singular use and profit that may be gathered" from an understanding of these antiquities, and continually draws attention to their beauty and elegance. Rome's many statues are choice and lifelike; her triumphal arches are of great height and exquisitely engraved; her ancient temples are singular and rare; St. Peter's is remarkable and magnificent (pp. 341, 344, 345, 357, 368). Finally, Aristotle had added that we should speak of "things that excel," thereby couching our praises in the form of superlatives. Hobbes duly assures us that Rome's "Statues and other Antiquities" have "exceeded all that went before" (pp. 356–7); that her ancient temples have ever afterwards "beene esteemed the best" (p. 357); and that the Cathedral of St. Peter's not only possesses "the most goodly *Facciata*, or forefront of the world," but has now been ornamented "by the most famous Painter and Statuist in the world, *Michael Angelo*" (pp. 364–5). The entire city is, in short, "in every kinde Superlative" (p. 358).

Hobbes's early publications also include two contributions to the *genus deliberativum* in which he offers advice – again in exactly the manner prescribed by the classical theorists of eloquence – about how political leaders should conduct themselves if they wish to obtain honor and advantage. This furnishes the theme of his *Discourse upon the Beginning of Tacitus*, in which he draws from the political career of Augustus a number of general lessons about how new princes should act to "assure a new soveraignty" and to provide the people with "the sweetnesse of ease, and repose" (p. 260). Hobbes's other contribution to this *genus* is his *Discourse of Lawes*, which follows the prescriptions of the classical rhetoricians even more closely. As we have seen, Aristotle and his followers had argued that, when counseling someone to act in some particular way, we should try to persuade them that the line of conduct we are proposing will at once prove virtuous and profitable, and will bring them not merely surety but continual contentment of life. Seeking to persuade us in the *Discourse of Lawes* that it will always be better to obey, Hobbes attempts to establish his point in exactly this way. He begins by arguing that the rule of law brings "a double benefit," since it guarantees "the generall good, & government of the *State*" and at the same time "the quiet, and peaceable life of every one in particular" (p. 506). He goes on to describe laws as "the peoples bulwarks, and defences, to keep them in safety, and peace," to which he adds that the equal administration of justice "is the true knot that binds us to unity and peace" (pp. 506, 508). A constant willingness to obey the law brings honor to kingdoms and safety to kings, while enriching and securing their subjects (pp. 514–15). The laws can thus be described as "the true *Physicians* and preservers of our peaceable life, & civill conversation," and as the means of "sowing peace, plenty, wealth, strength, and all manner of prosperity amongst men" (pp. 520–1).

Hobbes's early writings culminate in a notable contribution to the *genus iudiciale*, widely regarded as the most important of the rhetorical genres. His essay *Of the Life and History of Thucydides*, which he published in 1629 as the Introduction to his translation of the history, takes the form of a full-scale classical oration in defense of Thucydides' achievement. As we have seen, the ancient rhetoricians had argued that the aim of writing in this *genus* should be to establish that some injury has been done, thereby enabling a verdict to be reached in line with the requirements of equity and justice. Hobbes duly assures us that a grave injury to Thucydides' reputation has been perpetrated by a number of envious detractors, especially Dionysius of Halicarnassus, who "hath taken so much pains, and applied so much of his faculty in rhetoric, to the extenuating of the worth" of Thucydides' masterpiece (*Of the Life and History of Thucydides*, p. 19). Developing the case for the defense, Hobbes follows with almost mechanical precision the rules for the correct "disposition" of a forensic speech as laid down by the classical theorists of eloquence.[171] As a result, he assures us at the outset, he is able to vindicate the cause of justice by reestablishing that, in spite of Dionysius' unrelenting attack, Thucydides must be accounted the greatest of all the historians not merely for the presentation but for the contents of his thought.[172]

Hobbes's early rhetorical writings stand in marked contrast with the self-consciously scientific approach adopted in *De Cive*, in which he proceeds by framing definitions and pursuing their implications in a purportedly demonstrative style. The suddenness and completeness of this change of front have not perhaps been sufficiently recognized. Hobbes provides us with one of the most dramatic instances of a major philosopher in the midst of whose intellectual career we encounter a genuine *rupture*, followed by a virtual reversal of his previous literary and intellectual allegiances.

CHAPTER 5

Casuistry and allegiance in the English Civil War

Barbara Donagan

"I am resolved by Gods grace to keep my conscience."[1]

Many years after the English Civil War Captain John Hodgson reflected on the examination of conscience he had then undertaken: "When I put my hand to the Lord's work, in 1642, I did it not rashly, but had many an hour and night to seek God, to know my way."[2] In 1645 Sir William Campion had written in similar terms to an old friend and present enemy, "I did not rashly or unadvisedly put my life upon this service, for it was daily in my prayers for 2 or 3 months together to God to direct me in a right way, and besides I had conference with diverse able and honest men for advice who confirmed me in my judgment."[3]

Hodgson was a long-serving soldier of parliament, and we are familiar with prayer and conference as the means by which godly men resolved hard questions, but Campion was a respected royalist who was to die in 1648 in the fruitless defense of Colchester. Both men, however, presented the decision to take action as a decision of conscience reached only after serious reflection. The Civil War, as John Wallace pointed out, "presented itself . . . as the most colossal case of conscience" of most Englishmen's lives, and forced them to seek "to discern what God's part demanded."[4] Hodgson's "serious thoughts" led him to join those who, foreseeing evil, "prepare[d] such instruments as they possibly could to defend themselves" against the king.[5] Campion's reflections drove him the other way, though he was no less certain of the dictates of conscience: "I had rather die a beggar, than wittingly to violate my conscience towards my God, and king."[6] Recent studies of the outbreak of war have made much of religious passion or constitutional conviction, of *force majeure* or local connection, in shaping allegiances. They have given less attention to the moral and intellectual plight of those who were forced to choose. Nor have they noted the prevalence in 1642 of casuistical argument and its implications.

This chapter is not concerned with why English men and women preferred one side or the other in 1642, with the matters that, as Richard Baxter put it, "did . . . byass me to the Parliaments side" – or, in other cases, to the king's.[7] It is, rather, concerned with how they legitimated taking action in support of preference. Even for the undeviatingly royalist Campion, "meer duty of allegiance" had not of itself been enough to bestow legitimacy on his course.[8] There were two parts to what, in John Morrill's words, "made civil war happen."[9] Between preference and action lay a step that historians too often ignore when they address the "choices" leading to war. However great the passions aroused by religious or political differences, war was not the only possible outcome. Contemporaries were well aware of alternatives, from submission to passive disobedience to emigration. When Morrill writes, "It was the force of religion that drove minorities to fight, and forced majorities to make reluctant choices," he denies primacy to constitutional issues; he also conflates two processes.[10] Historians commonly distinguish between long-term causes and immediate occasions of war, but they have paid little attention to the intervening step between cause or occasion and action, namely the validation of formal recourse to arms as a proper response to the situation. Even the godly regicide Colonel Hutchinson applied himself to an extensive course of reading before concluding that there was a "cleare . . . ground of the warre" which was not religion but parliament's "civill right" and defense of "just English liberties." And still he was slow to act.[11] As we shall see, what justified the choice and action of such men was belief concerning the nature of secular power, as authorized by God.

The great "popular" propagandists of legitimization were clergy who shared and elaborated the views of secular thinkers like Henry Parker and Edward Hyde.[12] They brought to the issues of war or peace, resistance or non-resistance, the skills and authority of pastoral casuistry to which their readers and hearers were already accustomed. The power and ubiquity of casuistry in seventeenth-century England – as in the rest of the Christian world, Protestant and Catholic alike – as the means to resolve what are often loosely and mistakenly referred to as dilemmas but are more properly described as hard questions or difficult cases, are by now well known.[13] In 1642 clergy, as preachers and authors, heightened their attention to the public arena, using methods familiar from their labors to satisfy troubled consciences in the private sphere. The literature of casuistry was profuse, pervasive, and influential.[14] It found its way into the libraries of the literate and anxious, but it was a genre in which the relation between spoken and written word remained close, for the substance of private conference and public sermon alike appeared on the printed page. It was no accident that Hodgson based his decision to take arms on "things that I read and heard."[5]

When casuists approached the hard questions of 1642 they faced two issues: justification of war, and justification of civil war. The first need not detain us long. The catalogue of reasons that rendered war just and therefore legitimate was long, well known, and adaptable. Nations are seldom at a loss to prove their cause just and their war defensible. And once justified, national wars rarely present a problem of choice. Critics may oppose government policies, objecting to the selection of a particular enemy or to the way a war is conducted, and for this they may face public censure. Yet they are not confronted by the question of where their loyalty properly lies unless they are tempted actively to aid and comfort the foreign foe. Even pacifism rarely presented a problem until the introduction of universal conscription, which spurred development of the legal concept of conscientious objection to a nationally imposed obligation.

Civil wars, however, are problematic, some more so than others. Where, as in the United States, there was geographic division – an admittedly simplified formulation that ignores such issues as border states and ideological commitment across regional lines – the allegiance of most Americans was a function of where they lived. In wars of religion, as in France, confession largely decided choice of side – although that formulation too is simplistic, ignoring for example class and faction. The English Civil War fits neither category. Geographically, contrary to old stereotypes of a royalist north and west and a parliamentarian south and east, partisanship and indeed war itself ranged untidily across the whole country. Confessionally, the picture was even more confused. While there were Laudians and Arminians at one extreme and sectaries and hedge preachers at the other, between them was a mass of clergy and laity with a shared doctrinal and institutional past; many had been critical of the Caroline church and had common agenda for its reform. Yet some of those critics became committed royalists, while others were equally devoted parliamentarians.

The criteria by which such people chose sides and then chose to act in support of that choice (and we must always remember how many, lay and clerical alike, stayed as neutral as they could for as long as they could), cannot be forced into any simple pattern. For some, choices were little more than continuance of long-held positions, for others they entailed apparent repudiation of part of their past. What follows is an examination of the ways in which some mainstream royalist and parliamentarian clergy, who were formed by common education and experience and shared many opinions and modes of expression in the prewar decades, differed when they came to justify taking arms. They intended their arguments first to persuade men it was their duty to move from passive to active support, from preference to action, and then to sustain them in that choice, and they sought to establish the legitimacy of their own actions as participants and those of their hearers and readers. They endeavored above all to justify a *civil* war and thereby to stiffen men engaged "against ourselves our brothers," to urge to success in battle, and to account for failure.[16] What they said on that issue may help us to understand the hierarchies of conscience and loyalty by which men chose to act in the Civil War.

It may be objected that to focus on the clergy is to give disproportionate weight to the opinions of men with a predictable bias toward religious argument. But while as clergy, and because clergy, they were vocal and authoritative public spokesmen, their message on this issue proves oddly secular, their arguments derived crucially from political theory. Although the ultimate legitimator of any constitution remained God, we are confronted by the irony of clergy publicly and vocally addressing fundamental constitutional issues in what much current historiography has decided was a war of religion.[17] Their opinions were not of course always accepted as oracular; rather, these clergy had much in common, in visibility and claims to authority, with secular pundits of a later age. They mediated between the high theorists of politics and religion and the public that heard their sermons or read their polemic, a public that ranged from the educated to the unlettered. Their subject was the casuistry of participation in civil war – we are not here concerned with what they had to say about the conduct of war once entered into. Their contributions to this topic made up only a part of the vast output of sermons and controversy of the 1640s, but the casuistical approach they took was widespread, and spoke to a near-universal assumption that conscience was central to this war. It spoke, too, to another assumption: that the conscientious must follow their conscience, they must act. Politics was about duties, not rights.[18]

In this study of choice and justification, it may be helpful to begin with the manner in which the case was presented and with its moral context, although neither the power of the word nor the strength of reformist passion was sufficient explanation for taking up arms for parliament; nor was either the exclusive property of parliament's preachers.

The first point is literary and theatrical. The difference between royalist and parliamentarian style of sermon and polemic is less, in most cases, than those who focus on the great high Anglicans of the past like Lancelot Andrewes or the new, rationalizing figures of what would become the Restoration church would suggest. Clerical training produced a recognizable form and style across party lines. In view of similarities of education, of social networks, and often of reformist programs, we should not expect to find radical differences before the war or radical change after it began. Royalist sermons exhibit the same careful, logical structure as parliamentarian, they dismember and gloss texts in the same way, their language is similar and, like their parliamentarian counterparts, their preachers consciously adopted "high" and "low" styles to suit the educational sophistication of their audiences. In 1646 a royalist preacher assumed that there was a moderate, mainline sermon tradition when he dismissed innovative Arminian techniques as a minority aberration, nothing but "the ridiculous, over-acted postures and gestures of some few busie, fanaticall men, whose Popery lay in making discreet men laugh, to see them so artificially devout, and so affectedly ceremonious."[19] He was equally dismissive of those parliamentarian ministers who were like "furies, rather than Preachers ... Men who speaking to the people in a whirle-winde, and breathing nothing but pitcht-fields, and sieges, and slaughters of their Brethren, do profess no Sermon to be a Sermon, which rends not the rocks and Mountains before it; forgetting that God rather dwells in still soft voyces."[20] Parliament's clergy may indeed have been more addicted to the bible's language of violence and warfare than royalist, but the difference was one of degree. It was a royalist sermon that was admiringly described in 1646 as "such a piece as never had ... paralell [*sic*] for an invective."[21] Old opponents of the Laudian church did not change their linguistic habits when they became royalists: Edward Symmons and Stephen Marshall visibly remained polemicists from the same stable after they ceased to be allies, despite Symmons's claim that Marshall's public and private manner of argument, as well as its matter, changed radically when war came. The claim was part of an exchange in which he impugned Marshall's sanity.[22]

Parliamentarian sermons were nevertheless generally held to be better and more rousing than royalist, as royalist ministers themselves admitted and regretted.[23] In view of puritan emphasis on preaching and the attention devoted to cultivating effective pulpit technique, it is not surprising that, as the products of this training manned parliamentarian pulpits, they maintained a higher overall level of histrionic performance. Indeed, puritans recognized the dangers of becoming "too Histrionian-like" and of bringing "the Stage into the Pulpit."[24] Unfortunately style of delivery is rarely recoverable from the printed page. The pulpit melodrama of Stephen Marshall, "the Geneva bull," was not unique, and occasionally we can gain an impression of the distinctive delivery of such "gifted" preachers. A jaundiced account by a scholarly royalist identified the "light, fluent, running, passionate zealous style, which should make [the preacher] ... seeme religiously distracted, or beside himselfe," in a sermon that had "flowne from him in ... an *Ex-tempore* loose career of devout emptinesse and nothings" while "the sands of his glasse have ... fleeted for two tedious houres."[25] But dramatic "awakening" delivery only rarely echoes on the printed page.[26] That printed page does suggest, however, that many royalist ministers transferred puritan habits of controversy to the royalist cause. A revolution of style and manner does not necessarily accompany a shift of political position. The literature of war and religious controversy as practiced in the earlier seventeenth century was strident; it is not surprising that its manner was perpetuated by both sides.

If zeal and style do not serve as criteria to distinguish between royalist and parliamentarian, neither do moral recommendations. A wide-ranging sermon of late 1642 reminds us of common ground between parties. Preached to an audience of soldiers, it addressed such familiar topics as God's judgment on an erring land, the need for moral reformation among those who claimed to serve God's cause, and the importance of a religion of the heart. Mere outward shows were condemned: without true piety "men ... vainly hope to please God with externall formalities" which "make the Church a Stage whereon to act our parts and play our pageants." Men "dallied" with God when they did not employ "requisite industry" to root out sin. What was needed was faith, repentance, and study of the scripture, not the hypocrisy of "personating of devotion in the Psalmes, the Letanies, the Collects." Many professed religion, but few were sincerely faithful. And there followed a diatribe against a traditional calendar of sins:

How few of the gallants of our time doe or will understand, that it is not lawful for them to be ... expensive and costly in apparell? ...

Would it not be strange newes to a great many, that not onely *adultery* and *fornication*, but even *uncleanenesse* and *lasciviousnesse*; not onely *idolatry*, and *witch-craft*, but *hatred, variance, emulations, wrath*, and *contentions*; not onely *murthers*, but *envying*; not *drunkennesse* only, but *revelling*, are things prohibited to Christians, and such as, if we forsake them not, we cannot inherit the Kingdome of Heaven?

Sin incurred God's judgments on earth, while the delusion that repentance sufficed for salvation "hath sent thousands of soules to hell in a golden dreame of Heaven." Instead there must be "effectuall conversion and reformation of life." But like all Protestant moralists, the author recognized the risks inherent in preaching moral reformation: this was not "to preach workes as the Papists doe," but, following Christ and the apostles, "to preach the necessity of them, which no good Protestant, no good Christian ever denied." All of this seems familiar as the puritan program. Yet the preacher of this strenuous sermon was the admired royalist William Chillingworth.[27]

Looking about them, both parliamentarian and royalist clergy saw a desperate need to reform their countrymen. The moderate royalist Henry Ferne, later Bishop of Chester, and the unrelenting parliamentarian Edmund Staunton alike saw suffering as the consequence of the nation's sins. Lusts at home were the causes of their miseries, Staunton declared in 1644, as he railed against sins from lying and swearing to "pride in Apparell, naked breasts," and beauty spots, all of which made it necessary to pacify God. In 1643 Ferne warned the king's army against "swearing, cursing, blasphemy," against "Oathes and Curses" that had infected the civilian population as well as the army and that were "the way to hasten judgement." "[D]runkennesse, rioting, whordome, and the like uncleannesse," "unlawfull pleasures of Excesse and Riot, of chambering and wantonnesse," joined blasphemy and sins (such as "bloodshed [and] oppression") in which public policy and private conduct mingled, to "hasten judgement" and to make his royalists "loosers in the spirituall warfair, and . . . cut . . . off from Gods protection and blessing." Ferne would have had no quarrel with a parliamentarian like William Meeke who in 1646 warned against pride and the "bravery" and "ornaments" of women's dress, and deplored the "most horrid oathes and curses" now heard on all sides. Nor would he have disagreed with Meeke's conclusion: "We cannot expect . . . to be free from Gods judgements, or plagues, as long as we continue in our sinnes."[28] Spiritual warfare against sin, anti-popery, a scriptural and inward religion not dependent on formalities, a providential world in which God's judgments were there for the interpreting, and vivid reformist rhetoric were scarcely the marks of puritanism alone. The sins ministers saw around them, like the language in which they deplored them, were not party-specific.[29]

Many of the clerical partisans whose sermons survive were not seriously at odds doctrinally: they retained a Calvinist core, unpersuaded by Arminian revisionism. Nor was conversion to Arminianism, such as that of Samuel Hoard, the rector of Moreton in Essex, who managed to retain his living until his death in 1658, either a prerequisite for royalism or necessarily a portent of it.[30] Neither do attitudes to moral reformation or doctrine offer a sufficient explanation for the decision actively to support one side or the other. In fact, when they committed themselves most clergy and laity did not need to abandon one set of opinions to adopt another. Rather they were comfortably able to take their moral and doctrinal baggage with them to join others with similar baggage.

There were limits to bipartisanship, however, and an Oxford sermon of 1644 serves as a sharp reminder of these. Its author was the young gadfly John Berkenhead, the man behind the royalist newsletter *Mercurius Aulicus*. Delivered at Christ Church in the king's presence in November 1644, its aggressive and confident tone suited a time of relative royalist good fortune.[31] Uncompromisingly royalist and untroubled by doubts, ambivalences, or any lurking puritan sympathies, it presented a constitutional case for active royalism, validated as ever by religion and morality and, as was normal in the controversies of the 1640s, by denunciations of the irreligion, immorality, and unconstitutionality of the enemy. Berkenhead's text was Romans 13.5, his theme "the Necessity of Christian Subjection": "we must performe passive obedience and absolute subjection, suffering without resistance, being subject without rebellion, even if [superiors] should command the most unjust superstitious, idolatrous, prophane, or irreligious things which can be imagined; yet I say we must not rebell, unless we will renounce Christianity."[32] Subjection was required by conscience; it did not depend on the threat of force. Monarchy was God's chosen form of government, and the king was parent to his people. As obedience in family, church, and state were inseparable, failure in one sphere entailed disaster in the others; interruption of the hierarchy that articulated state, family, and church led to chaos. When there was "not one Supreme, but the multitude tooke power into their own hands," when men sought to alter government and "introduce a new deformed device of their own ambitious invention," the consequences were not only political dissension but robbery, rape, murder, and extortion.[33] The obligation to obey, even without the persuasion of "Armes and Armies, Racks and Gibbets," was imposed by "right Reason ... naturall equity ... morall civility ... [and] Christian Religion and conscience."[34] Yet for all his intransigent royalism Berkenhead was not eager to countenance popery, and he conceded that there was a limit to obedience: "we must ... do ... all their commands which are not directly against God."[35] The royalist, as so often, could recognize the initial premise of the parliamentarian's doubts. But what was against God and what was required of the uncertain Christian lay too often in the eye of the beholder. For obvious reasons, Berkenhead did not linger over this awkward issue, but it is evidence of shared ground that he felt the need to raise it.

Berkenhead's apologia was both intensely polemical and narrowly focused on political theory. When the moderate Chillingworth left moral reformation and "c[a]me a little nearer to the businesse of our times, ... [to] this bloudy Tragedy," his simple message proved remarkably close to Berkenhead's. Resistance to the sovereign power could not be justified. It was the subject's duty to defend the king, but his enemies "sh[ot] Musquets and Ordinance at ... his Sacred Person." Did they know, demanded Chillingworth "the generall rule without exception or limitation left by the Holy Ghost for our direction in all such cases, *Who can lift up his hand against the Lords Anoynted, and be innocent?* Or doe they consider his Command in the *Proverbs of Solomon, My sonne feare God and the King, and meddle not with them that desire change?*"[36] Thus, like Berkenhead, he argued for obedience and maintenance of the status quo, and stressed as well the sacredness of the kingly office and the horror of physically harming a king who was both human and sacred person. Together, provocative polemicist and irenic advocate of reason in faith urged the essential royalist justification for fighting fellow Englishmen on the king's behalf. The king was both sacral entity and embodiment of the state; to neither could resistance be justified.

Before pursuing some of the finer points of royalist theory we should consider the parliamentarian case. If royalists found no problem in asserting an absolute duty to obey, parliamentarians hesitated before asserting a right to resist. Their case was perforce more complex. Theories of resistance had a long history, but they did not come naturally or easily to English Protestant parliamentarians accustomed to seeing the royal supremacy as a bastion against Rome.[37] Yet although public commitment to non-resistance had been virtually universal this should not be confused with ignorance of resistance theory, while as we have seen even arguments for obedience normally stopped short of actions patently contrary to God's will. This last flexible criterion was further modified by distinction between "venial" matters, in which obedience might be reluctant or uncomfortable but was in the overall Protestant and national interest, and others on which no person of conscience could compromise. The latter proved in practice to be few.[38] To reform-minded clergy, theories of resistance had a dangerously popish ring.[39] A set of Yorkshire sermons from the troubled spring and summer of 1642 reveals the reluctance even of "godly" ministers to seek a human rather than a providential resolution to the dangers, of which the king seemed by now to form part, confronting the country.[40]

Royalists assigned the doubtful honor of being the first to "Preach Treason" to Calybute Downing who, in September 1640, affirmed in a sermon at the London Artillery Garden *"that for defence of Religion and Reformation of the Church, it was lawfull to take up armes against the King."* What had previously been whispered was now publicly endorsed by the Smectymnuans, that dangerous group of clergy of whom Stephen Marshall was one.[41] Yet neither Downing nor Marshall had a long history as advocate of resistance. Downing's *Discourse of the state ecclesiasticall of this Kingdome, in relation to the Civill* of 1632 had indeed emphasized the role of religion and clergy in the commonwealth, but it did so with the assertion that "good manners cause obedience and Religion naturally begets good manners"; and it declared furthermore that "our King [is] a most absolute Monarch."[42] Marshall, when later charged with reversal of previous unexceptionable views, "confessed" that Downing's sermon of 1640 had led him to reexamine his position. His colleague Edward Symmons likened Marshall's consequent *"Apostacy"* to "the fall of a great *Oake*," although Marshall struggled to assert a fundamental consistency:

Before the beginning of these unhappy differences, I had both learned, and taught to this purpose. First, that it is agreeable to Gods will, that in all Countreys ... Magistracie be set up, with a sufficiencie of power and authority to rule for the publike good ... Secondly, that among the divers kinds of lawfull governments, *Monarchy, Aristocracy,* and *Democracy,* no one of them is so appointed of God, as to exclude the other from being a lawfull government. Thirdly, that the bounds and limits of the Magistrates lawfull power of commanding and the subjects necessary obeying, must be found, and taken out of the severall lawes, Customs, and Constitutions of those severall States, and Commonwealths.[43]

In this apologia Marshall's position is both strikingly secular and subversive. On the one hand, he weakened the sacral conception of the king when he denied that monarchy is God's only chosen form of government.[44] On the other, while acknowledging that God sanctions authority in the state, whatever form it takes, he allowed for purely secular criteria by which resistance to that authority might be justified. The magistrate derives his authority from law, custom, and constitution; when he exceeds the power granted to him by these secular institutions its exercise ceases to be legitimate. Resistance in this formulation has constitutional, not religious, grounds. Marshall thus continued to assert both the legitimacy of a central power in the state and the duty to obey it, but added the possibility of release from that duty by magistrates' constitutional dereliction. This formulation was to prove infinitely adaptable. Obedience was "necessary" – but only for so long as the magistrate ruled for the public good and in accordance with the powers that were properly his.

Conditional obedience might in practice mean no more than passive disobedience. But when ministers who came down on the side of parliament were confronted by the need to justify actually bearing arms against the king they found the means to do it. The upshot in all cases was to release the subject from his obligation to obey. The king was a tyrant; the power of parliament outweighed that of the king; public safety overrode other considerations; the person and the power of the king must be distinguished; parliament's actions were purely defensive; and so on.

As tyrants go Charles I cut a poor figure.[45] Nevertheless parliamentary apologists took the facts of the case to be self-evident; then, granted that the king had tyrannically commanded action against God's law, the question was what the response should be. As Marshall declared, "there is power sufficient *legally* placed in the Parliament to *prevent* Tyrannie."[46] Yet even admitting that parliament had such power, could it justify using it, for was it not God's ordinance that rulers should be obeyed? But if a tyrant's orders were against God, to argue that he could not be resisted because one must not resist God's ordinance to obey rulers was to say that tyranny was God's ordinance. And that, the presbyterian Francis Cheynell concluded triumphantly, was blasphemy.[47] Subjects might also be freed from their duty to obey even if princes' abuse of power was not personally and actively tyrannical and ungodly. As Marshall's account suggested, princes could delegitimize themselves by omission as well as commission. Subjects' duty to obey was matched by the king's duty to protect them and to defend the faith. It was a reciprocal contract – "everie Schoole-boy hath learned so much of State matters." But King Charles had notably failed to keep his side of the bargain; he had not protected subjects against "the Irish vermine," nor the faith against Rome, and when finally a remedial parliament was called he had tried to kill it for his own ends.[48] It was "the supreame Law of all Nations," said Marshall, "that *Publique safety is the highest and deepest Law*, and that it is requisite that *every State have a power in time of danger to preserve it selfe from ruine*."[49] This argument of public safety when the prince failed in his duty, which owed much to the influence of Henry Parker, lent itself to dangerous extension. If it was lawful to defend the commonwealth and true religion (and the bible showed this to be "a matter of equity"), then the proposition could be established that "[a] lawfull cause makes the action lawfull and warrantable," and the end justified the means.[50]

These arguments relating to public safety reveal two other important elements in the parliamentary case: their claims first, that their actions were defensive, and second, that the proper protective agent on behalf of the people was parliament. The claim to be fighting a defensive war was made by both sides, as they sought to bring the cause – either cause – under the rubric of just war. Royalists declared that the king had been driven to exercise his power defensively by the "insolencies" of a "vulgar rabble" unrestrained by parliament, and by the threat of violence to his person.[51] For parliamentarians, the claim sanitized taking arms against "the Lords Anoynted," a term conceded even by strenuous and unwavering opponents of the king like the earl of Warwick who could still, in November 1642, remind his army of their "deare Anointed King."[52] So Marshall established at considerable length that it was both lawful and necessary for parliament "to take up these defensive Armes." His grounds included the Army Plot, the threat from Ireland, the king's meddling with the membership of parliament's guard, the case of the five members, the attempt to seize the magazine at Hull, obstruction over settling the militia in safe hands, and the raising of an army in the north – a list that is notably secular rather than religious. They amounted, he said, to "pregnant preparations both at home and beyond the Seas: And the civill Lawyers say that pregnant preparations are the beginning of a War."[53] Royalists might deny that the king was initiator of the war, but parliamentary apologists insisted that there was "an Army intended against them."[54] Far from willfully taking arms against the Lord's anointed, they had been driven to defend themselves.

It was parliament, not individuals, that had been thus driven to self-defense. This was in no way an argument sanctioning the individual rebel or inspired assassin. It was, furthermore, a secular argument, in which constitutional law became part of a casuistical justification of resistance. Parliament's place in the constitution, and its embodiment of wisdom, power, truth, and the people, refuted any claim that the king could act unilaterally. It was representative of England: "[W]ho can deny that the Common-wealth of *England* is assembled in this Parliament?" asked Francis Cheynell, as he and other parliamentarian preachers went on to present their accounts of the constitution. So powerful were the provisions of English law that Jeremiah Burroughes saw the right to take up arms in defense of religion as a peculiarly English "Civil Right" which did not need the support of international or abstract theory. Law had become the defender of the Englishman's religion.[55]

The king could alienate powers to the people, but he could not recall them. The "priviledges, grants, liberties" of people and parliament, although "not originall, yet they are irrevocable."[56] The fundamental constitution was thus hardly immutable, but all legitimate change ran in one direction. It was unlikely to reverse itself if, as Marshall claimed, parliament "judgeth all, and itself is judged of none." The king's charters, writs, and proclamations could be nullified and repealed by this "highest Court from whence there is no appeale." To say that "the Parliament judged so" was to clinch an argument. As the royalist Edward Symmons sharply pointed out, Marshall had replaced an infallible popish church with an infallible parliament.[57]

Neither parliament's powers nor the legitimacy of resistance were in doubt for these apologists of parliament and its armies. Yet one awkwardness remained: the king himself. Like most of their countrymen, they continued to think in terms of a monarchical constitution; they were neither republicans nor supporters of some alternative candidate for the throne. How then to deal with the problem of the king, justifying resistance to him while maintaining a plausible fiction of loyalty, of assenting that in his person he was the Lord's anointed? Lip service to the old "jog-trot" constitution of king, lords, and commons took years to fade in parliamentary rhetoric, but it required some agility to render it plausible. One device, attractive to laymen and clerics alike, is well known, that of attributing blame to evil counselors rather than to the king personally. Warwick's "deare Anointed King" was surrounded by bloody and inhuman papists and blasphemous, tyrannical, destructive cavaliers. The king had been "seduced by wicked councell," said Marshall, and his "ill counsellors" had a design to overthrow the laws, enslave subjects' liberties, and alter religion.[58] Cheynell elaborated. The original quarrel was not between parliament and the king at all, but between parliament and delinquents and, particularly, the queen. The king was a puppet in her hands, and now there was a plot to pass the crown to her, or rather to "her idoll *the Crucifixe.*" Conspiracies are heady, and Cheynell played the theme to the hilt: "[P]lot on my Masters," he exhorted, as he acquitted the king of responsibility for at least the initial stages of aggression against parliament.[59]

The fiction grew increasingly difficult to sustain the more visibly the royalist cause became the king's war. He was perceived as an intransigent obstacle to peace even before he was accounted "that man of blood Charles Stuart." A speech by Burroughes at the Guildhall in October 1643 showed the retreat from the comfortable device of distancing the king from his party. To proposals for an accommodation he replied, "You have to deal not onely with his Majesty, but with a Popish party that are about him." He then introduced a new and more dangerous factor. How was the security of an agreement to be ensured? Rights that citizens wrested from the monarch were never safe, for kings neither forgave nor forgot.[60] Appeal to history – incoherent though it might be, as in Burroughes's case – thus became a counterweight to the powerful claim of divine anointment. Indeed, an Essex minister declared at the beginning of the war that it was "a common thought . . . *that William the Conqueror was an usurper; and so were all his successors, and therefore it was fit, that this King would be called to answer for William the Conquerors sin of usurpation.*"[61] The argument for transferred and retroactive guilt remains familiar.

Evil counselors, historical proof of the untrustworthiness of kings, the illegitimacy of a hereditary usurper, all undercut acceptance of the king's authority as divinely ordained. A more sophisticated argument distinguished the power of the king from his person or title.[62] It did not challenge the king's legitimate place on the throne, and it could assert loyalty to his person, even while claiming that his power had been illegitimately used and should be curbed. "[W]ee did never so much as once question his Majesties title, whether it be limited or no?" claimed Cheynell. Nevertheless "[i]t is confessed that his power, and therefore much more the exercise of his power, is limited by the Priviledges of the

Parliament, the Immunities of the Subject, and the King's own oath."[63] No force or violence was offered against the person of the king, insisted Robert Derham, in a passage that revealed the need to rebut the "great Objection" that to levy war against him was "an Act in itselfe impious" and contrary to divine law. "[W]e conceive his person onely free from the Sword," he said, but it was an error to see person and power as co-extensive. The king's person and the "power raised by him illegally" must not be "together confounded." It is hardly surprising that, as Derham admitted, this distinction remained "somewhat darke and Enigmaticall to the ignorant."[64] Furthermore, it proved difficult to eradicate a sacral conception of kingship. In 1643 parliament could still issue a pass for a child to go to Oxford to be touched for the king's evil; after the Battle of Naseby the story circulated that a parliamentary soldier had cried, "Its the King, *touch him not!*" at which the attacker "stayed his hand."[65]

Royalist apologists had an easier task, in part because they counted on familiarity with a body of approved, established ideas, namely royal supremacy and the duty of obedience. Parliamentarians, while claiming to conserve the ancient constitution, were forced anxiously and aggressively to justify change: they had either to adapt accepted and bipartisan theories to new purposes, or to give standing to opinions formerly held to be dangerous. The royalist position, by contrast, was ideologically defensive, although this did not lessen the forcefulness of its polemics. Royalists too supported their case empirically, asserting that Charles was a good king, in the hope of rendering irrelevant arguments that a tyrant or bad king could be removed, but this had its dangers, for it opened the way to claims that in other circumstances resistance might be justified.[66]

Royalist and parliamentarian clergy used common vocabulary and ideas to reach different conclusions. When George Wilde preached to the king's House of Commons at St. Mary's in Oxford he, like his counterparts on the other side, lamented the evils that war brought; he too linked suffering and divine judgment, telling his hearers "[Y]ou have drunke deep of the dregs of Gods wrath." No less sure than his opponents that a just cause rendered a war just, he was equally confident that God would decide appropriately between the parties. Wilde's "Text," however, diverged from his parliamentarian colleagues': "[F]irst set a good King upon his knees to pray for the Peace of *Ierusalem*: and then set him upon his legges agen ... to fight for that Peace."

Although his rhetoric of justified war shared concepts, vocabulary, imagery, and biblical reference with parliamentarians, there was no problem of choice for Wilde: cause and king were so self-evidently good and just that his apologia could hearten his Oxford audience without recourse to hard questions.[67]

Other royalist apologists felt driven to confront the doubters, and presented cases that ranged from the moderate and nominally concili-atory to the absolutist and unrepentantly confrontational. The king himself had set a tone of moderation in early declarations to his soldiers couched in terms that differed little from those employed by his oppo-nents. In September 1642 he promised "to maintain the just Priviledges and Freedome of Parliament, and to govern by the known Laws of the Land . . . and particularly to observe inviolably the Laws consented to by Mee this Parliament." There was here no threat to parliament or law and hence no justification for recourse to arms. In October he reiterated his determination "to maintain the Law, and Liberty of the Subject, with the just Priviledges of Parliament."[68] The theme was echoed by moderate clergy like Henry Ferne, royalist chaplain and former protégé of the Calvinist Bishop Morton. He proclaimed his own "affection" for parlia-ments and agreed that the king did not have power to make law alone or to act arbitrarily. His royalists were not mere loyal automata but thinking constitutionalists. He hoped, like them, that parliaments would flourish in due power and freedom: "I presume that many of the Thousands which follow his Majesty, have engaged themselves in the Cause, not only out of meer duty of Allegiance, but also out of a sense of that very desire, they are confident it is in Him, to the continuance of Parliaments."[69] Ferne admitted that the two houses of parliament "are in a sort Coordi-nate" with the king, but co-ordination did not mean parity, for they were not in "fellowship" with him in "the Supremacy it selfe." Nevertheless the tone of these statements about relations between crown and parlia-ment was on the whole restrained. Such royalists insisted that they believed in parliament, while their king forswore any right to aggressive war and declared his actions purely defensive.[70] Even arguments for a prince's right to choose his own advisers, apparently inflammatory in the light of Strafford's fate, became less provocative when given – as Wilde did in 1643 – a Machiavellian and utilitarian twist: favorites, he said, are useful for they "may receive the shafts of Envy upon Themselves, which otherwise would light upon the sacred Person of the King."[71]

Such views seem moderate and conciliatory. Yet a distinctive royalist stance is evident in Wilde's insistence on the sacredness of the king's person and on the proper shows of "Respect and Reverence" due to the "Lords Anoynted." Those who rejected the etiquette of respect and reverence "Pillage[d] him of his Divinity. Princes are *Gods*, to teach us, not to Play with that holy flame which an awfull distance Warms, but burns upon too neer & bold Approaches."[72] If kings were gods and divine there could be, as Ferne observed, "no warrant for the Armes now taken up by Subjects."[73] It was in development from this line of thought that royalist views became adamant, non-negotiable, and sometimes extreme.

Griffith Williams, Bishop of Ossory, in the comprehensive title to his *Vindiciae Regum* of 1643, summed up the position of royalists like Berkenhead and Chillingworth. Confronted by "the Grand Rebellion," he turned to scripture, church fathers, martyrs, and the best modern writers to prove "that it is no wayes lawfull for any private man, or any sort or degree of men ... for any cause, compelling to Idolatry, exercising Cruelty, practizing Tyranny, or any other pretext, how fair and specious soever it seems to be, to Rebell, take Armes, and resist the authority of their lawfull King."[74] This epitomizes royal claims to a monopoly of legitimacy. The defensive royalist argument that Charles was a good king so justifications for resistance were irrelevant, became itself irrelevant. As Williams reiterated, "no *cause*, and ... no *pretext*" made it "lawfull for any Subject to *rebell* against his soveraigne governour." The last phrase signaled an extension of the claim beyond King Charles and beyond monarchy, and we should note how far Williams was prepared to go. Despite the apparent justifications of equity, love, and religion, Moses and St. Peter had, he claimed, "*transgressed* the commandement of God": "to strike any one without lawfull authoritie, ought not to be done ... for what *cause* or *religion* soever it be; especially to make insurrection against his King, contrary to all *divine* authoritie."[75]

This simple and absolute position was elaborated by Ferne in a series of careful distinctions intended to persuade his opponents. "Ordained powers," for example, could issue commands that were either legal or willful; the power and its agent could be conceptually separated; and obedience, which could be active or passive, was sharply distinguished from resistance. The important thing in applying theory, Ferne made clear, was not to know what was required, but what was forbidden. Active obedience was to be granted to "ordained powers" – whose authority St. Paul had recognized – yet it should be denied to illegal commands. What then if failure to obey actively led to use of force by

the "power" in order to "make good those illegall commands?" Was
resistance then legitimate? Burroughes, said Ferne, had concluded that
while the power must not be resisted, the "illegall will of the man may."
Ferne agreed that conceptually – "in conceit" – the power and the
person, and the power and its abuse (or the illegal will) could be
separated, and argued that the obedience required could be calibrated
accordingly: active obedience was due to the power and its agent but
could be denied to the illegal will. Such "conceit" risked casting the
perplexed conscience still deeper into perplexity.[76]

The "satisfaction" Ferne promised to conscience became clearer
when he moved from obedience to resistance. There, distinctions between power, person, and illegal will did not matter: "in resistance wee
cannot sever them, for the resisting of him that bears the power, though
unlawfully commanding, is a resisting of the power also." Power in the
abstract cannot be the object of obedience or resistance; that object is
concrete, and it is the magistrate who bears the power: "Though the will
and command be illegal, yet because he that bears the power lawfully,
uses that power (though illegally) to compasse that will and execute that
command, the power it self is resisted in resisting him that so uses it."[77]
There was thus no way in which resistance could be legitimate, and
Ferne clinched his argument by an example that must have unsettled his
Christian opponents:

That power and soveraignty ... employed to compasse ... illegal commands
was a power ordained and settled in them. When *Pilate* condemned our Saviour
it was an illegal will, yet our Saviour acknowledges in it *Pilates* power that was
given him from above ... The truth is, the lawfull power is resisted, when armes
are taken against Princes abusing that power to the compassing of unlawfull
commands.[78]

The conclusion was inescapable. Even had King Charles's commands
been unlawful, by virtue of the power he embodied he should be
obeyed. But there was more to it: "*Conscience* that knows He has by Law
a power to command assistance for the defence of Himselfe and protection of His Subjects, will easily conclude it a Legall power and command, not only not to be resisted, but also to be actively obeyed, as all
Legall & ordained powers ought to be."[79] Not only was resistance
forbidden, but active obedience was required. When Ferne identified
the royalist cause with "Conscience" he closed the opening he had
elsewhere allowed for non-obedience to an illegal command. Both
royalists and parliamentarians appealed to law as a weapon in the war

on hard questions, but one side concluded that obedience must be absolute, the other that resistance was mandated. Here, regardless of prior commitments in religion or politics, conscience faced a stark choice.

The complexities of choice help us to understand the actions of some of those clergy whose courses, once war came, at first appear puzzling. As ministers they were purveyors of casuist solutions to hard questions, but in the translation of theory to practice they themselves shared the anxieties of lay consumers of casuist comfort like Hodgson and Campion. And as with laymen, the outcomes were sometimes unexpected. Samuel Hoard, whose refutation of the Calvinist doctrine of predestination ("the opinion which I have forsaken") and embrace of Arminianism caused a stir among his godly colleagues in the 1630s, remained in his comfortable living until his death. Flexibility, a prudent silence in print, and, probably, the support of his influential patron the Earl of Warwick, outweighed earlier doctrinal partisanship. He did not become a royalist polemicist.[80] He was more fortunate than the principled, abrasive, quarrelsome Daniel Featley of Lambeth and Acton, for whom choice seems to have been preempted by events and his own personality. He was a fervent anti-papist, an opponent of Laudian innovations before the wars, and a member of and speaker in the Westminster Assembly. He also conformed to the prayer book and provocatively wore a surplice, which aroused the fury of undisciplined soldiers and the suspicion of parliament. He was imprisoned and lost, as he said, liberty, library, and livelihood. Yet if Featley adhered to principle in his support for episcopacy, he hardly chose the king. If he opposed much in the Caroline church, he surely did not – as his career in the 1630s might have suggested – choose parliament.[81] Such cases remind us both of the difficulties of predicting alignment in the 1640s on the basis of leanings in the 1620s and 1630s, and of the frequent opacity of grounds of choice.

In other cases the reasons for choice seem transparent, yet were not *immediately* based on positions taken on large divisive issues in church or state. Instead they addressed the legitimacy of acting in accordance with predilections formed by those positions. Here the case of Edward Symmons is illuminating, for it reveals both a progression from anti-Laudianism to vocal royalism, and a further evolution and adaptation of doctrines of resistance and obedience to the fluctuating fortunes of war. In the 1630s Symmons had been Stephen Marshall's ally. When he later followed a different path from his old friend, much of his justification took the form of a continuing public dialogue with Marshall, whose status as one of the parliamentary clerical grandees bestowed added public resonance. Their printed exchanges were intended not merely as personal vindications but as calls to readers to follow them in right choices.

Symmons declared that his conscience could not "concurre in this way of resistance with some of his Brethren"; he could not commit the sin of rebellion.[82] He rejected Marshall's arguments for the ultimate supremacy of parliament, he found the idea of the hereditary guilt of English monarchs absurd and insisted on the king's "innocency," and he thought that it was a minister's duty to preach "Peace and obedience."[83] He deplored ministers who – like Marshall – preached war, and he refused to "preach to promote the warre (as they call it) for the Parliament." In all this, although warmongering ministers declared him "an Apostate," he was constant in his opinions, "still the same man, obstinate in my way."[84] Symmons's refusal to preach war had two grounds: the proper role of the minister, and the proper placement of authority in the state. The first was applicable to himself and his clerical peers: "Sirs, I am a Minister of the Gospell of Peace, and 'tis against my calling and my conscience to [preach ... warre], the Kings expresse command also being to the contrary."[85] As for response to authority in the state, the way to a satisfied conscience for cleric and layman alike was through obedience, as Symmons's chapter headings made clear:

1. The King being the Supreme Magistrate hath immediate dependence upon God, to whom onely he is accountable.
2. Authority is a sacred thing, and essentiall to the Kings Person.
3. The Subjects duty and the Soveraignes Excellency.
4. The lawfulnesse of resisting the Kings personal will by force of Armes disavowed.

Resistance, he concluded, was contrary to the way of God and his laws, to the gospel, and to the practice of Christianity.[86] Yet Symmons also, briefly and obliquely, raised a thorny question: what authorized authority? The ultimate answer of course was God, but there remained a problem as to how God showed his authorization and how men could know when the recipient of the divine imprimatur had changed. This issue went beyond the debate that opposed direct divine mandate to contract between king and people; it raised the possibility of legitimacy bestowed by usurpation or conquest not only in the remote past but here and now, and of the validity of non-monarchical forms of government. Indirectly it opened a door to the claims made by parliamentarians.[87]

In a sermon preached and published in 1644 Symmons returned to many of these themes, but with significant changes of emphasis that reflected the complexities of real war. Unlike the *Loyall subject* of 1643, which was directed to all the king's subjects, this *Military Sermon* was preached at Shrewsbury to Prince Rupert's army. It was intended to hearten and confirm in their course of action soldiers who had already taken arms for their king. Much remained unchanged, from the sinfulness of rebellion – a "sinne not onely against piety, but even against nature it selfe" – to exhortation to moral reformation, and to the sermon's organization and style.[88] Yet there were also subtle shifts. The proper role of ministers, for example, now appeared in a different light. Although he "could never yet speake the language of *Kill, Slay, and Destroy*, which the Ministers of the Rebells side are so skilfull in," his sermon was nonetheless intended to animate the troops of one side against those of the other. To urge them to conduct themselves mercifully and honorably in battle as befitted their "Loyall Hearts," and to deplore their moral failings, was not to undermine their killing function. The wickedness of the enemy's cause validated their own, for the enemy committed the ultimate blasphemy: "a King is the Image of Christ as God, and to rebell against a King is to strike at the face of Christ as God." Symmons now conceded difficulties he had previously passed over, although they did not change his conclusions. He admitted, for example, that among the enemy there were men who were merely misled, and some who were positively good; the realities of war between old friends, allies, kin, and neighbors led him to distinguish between misguided "assisters in" and hardened "contrivers of" rebellion.[89] He also recognized that insistence on obedience led the soldier to hard places in real war if he faced an "illegal" or unjust command. Symmons's response, however, was an uncompromising Nuremberg defense. Soldiers' commissions were granted by God through his medium the king, "*the mouth of God* unto His Subjects"; they therefore had a "*right Commission [which] makes a Lawfull Souldier.*" From this it followed that

a right Commission makes the warre it self lawfull to the Souldier, although it were undertaken by the Prince upon unjust grounds: for the Subjects duty is, to minde his owne call rather then the cause, for though in matters of Religion we disclaime, and abhorre the Doctrine of blinde obedience, yet in matters of State, and order, we professe allowance of it ... things above us, belong not to us.[90]

Symmons, as good Protestant and old anti-Laudian, might claim consistency on matters of religious conscience, but by 1644 it had grown harder to reconcile an independent conscience in religion with a submissive conscience in the state. His solution was to insist that the loyal subject must not be a "Busie-Body" in matters above his competence.[91]

As war and unsettled peace dragged on, the message of the flood of works, printed and spoken, that we have been considering grew less reassuring, less convincing, less relevant. Symmons, like other authors, had hoped otherwise: "[W]e see fighting doth but increase the fire, happily 'tis writeing which may quench the flame."[92] Instead the controversy over subjects' right to resist and duty to obey resolved itself into "Bookes written against Bookes, and Conscience pretended against Conscience. In this perplexed condition, What shall the people doe? What shall they resolve?"[93] The fame and persuasive power of Marshall's inflammatory sermon, "Curse ye Meroz," which proved the error of withholding one's hand from blood, showed the vanity of Symmons's trust in the reconciling power of the written word. Delivered some sixty times up and down the country and published in six editions between 1641 and 1645, it was effective as well as popular.[94] Symmons encountered soldiers who fought for parliament because the sermon had convinced them that it was their duty to do so; yet he also reported that they proved open to counterargument.[95]

Symmons's satisfaction may have been misplaced, for the casuists' skills could become self-defeating as observers saw them deployed with equal dexterity by both sides, in book pitted against book and conscience against conscience. Yet if casuistry contained the seeds of self-destruction it was nevertheless the form in which public moral questions continued to be addressed in the war years, and through which right choices in cases of "intricate doubts" could be sought, found, and acted upon. The pastoral oracles who solved the village's hard questions relating to promises, marriage, and money were the counterparts in the domestic sphere of the controversialists and casuists of the greatest public "perplexity" of the age, whose clients ranged from Symmons's common soldiers to gentry and officers like Campion and Hodgson. In the humane conclusion to his study of Marvell, John Wallace recognized "the thousand ways in which . . . antagonists can be alike," as well as the existence of a point on which conscience demanded divergence – the "singular" conviction that constituted "where it stuck." Hodgson, it seems, never doubted the rightness of the actions to which what he "read and heard" led him at that point of divergence. For many, however, the absence of any clear divine mandate in England's affairs, the dangers of social disorder, and the multiplicity of arguing voices perpetuated "perplexity," and led some to the sense of "defeat and resignation" that Wallace found in Marvell's last years.[96]

The flood-tide of casuistry receded, but it did not die. Its traces survive in Thomist and Kantian moral theory, and the methods of case divinity echo in the exemplary fictions so useful to moral philosophers; in public issues too, from Nuremberg to Bosnia, the moral distinctions and methods of casuist argument intermittently return in recognizable form. From the later seventeenth century, however, its literature and practice increasingly addressed the secular and private, the subject less the hard questions of public policy and events than those of private conduct in private relations. Nor did the clergy lose their function as pastoral advisers, but their advice grew more private in scope and their claims to authority – now shared with secular advisers – more muted. Arthur Dent and William Ames were displaced by *The Athenian Mercury* and, as Keith Thomas has pointed out, sincerity of motive came to pre-empt correctness of conclusion as justification for action.[97]

In the decades after the Restoration, it has been suggested, politeness and civility came to be preferred to moral absolutes in resolution of disputes. The civility of the age can be exaggerated, but nonetheless Englishmen were lucky in that they were never again – even in 1688 – presented with as stark a need for choice as that which had confronted them in 1642. Their political and religious preferences could be accommodated without recourse to the agonizing decision of whether to resist and engage in war. For a short period in the 1640s the methods of casuistry employed by ministers to resolve private anxieties came to dominate debate over the public issue of war or peace, obedience or resistance, as they and their readers and hearers faced that "colossal case of conscience."[98] In their assumption that the premise of all argument must be that power in the state derived from God they did no more than express the orthodoxy of their age that the world and all in it emanated from and was ruled by him.[99] When they addressed the particular decision that confronted Englishmen – whether or not it was legitimate to take up arms – they turned away from commitment to particulars of religious reformation or preservation, or particular political grievances, to the nature of authority in the state, to its proper exercise, and to the ways in which it could be won and lost. The clerical literature of the casuistry of war or peace in England foreshadows the secular political theories of a less clerical age. It also, by casting the issues in terms of moral duty rather than political rights, required not only that Englishmen choose, but that they act in support of their choice.

CHAPTER 6

Thomas May and the narrative of Civil War

J. G. A. Pocock

Poet and historian, Thomas May was born in Sussex in 1595 and died in London – under circumstances much derided – in November 1650.[1] Beginning with the contemporary satire *Tom May's Death*, attributed to Andrew Marvell,[2] a special degree of venom was displayed towards him, and the story grew up that he had hoped for the laureateship on Ben Jonson's death in 1637, and had turned parliamentarian, and historian, out of disappointment when the bays went to William Davenant instead. To much later times there has persisted a tradition of dismissing his *History* as mere hack work, propaganda written to the specifications of his employers, and it can still be said that May as a literary and historiographical figure has received little serious study.[3]

This chapter will attempt to remedy this neglect. The more one knows of the Civil War parliament, the more one doubts whether it knew its own mind well enough to instruct a mouthpiece; the well-worn adage that history is written by the winners depends on the assumption that the latter know what they have won and why they wanted to win it, and of few can this be said with less conviction than of the apparent victors in the English Civil Wars. Whatever May's motives or the sources of his income, it is possible that he found himself uninstructed and even perplexed as to the history he was expected to write. What is certain is that his *History of the Parliament* opens with the frank declaration that it is very difficult to write the history of a civil war in which one is involved, because one knows only half of the story, and proceeds to the premise that to write the history of such a civil war as that which broke out in England in 1642 is a task altogether without precedent. There is a case for regarding Thomas May as perhaps the very first to instruct English historians in the problems they must confront to all futurity, once that civil war had broken out; and as with Andrew Marvell, his destiny was his choice,[4] even if he did not quite know what destiny he was choosing. He wrote as a member of his own

public, who knew what it was to face terrible choices they had not
desired to make.

The Subject of this work is a Civill War, a War indeed as much more then
Civill, and as full of miracle, both in the causes and effects of it, as was ever
observed in any Age; a Warre as cruell as unnaturall; that has produced as
much rage of Swords, as much bitterness of Pens, both publike, and private, as
was ever knowne; and divided the understandings of men, as well as their
affections, in so high a degree, that scarce could any venture gaine due
applause, any reason give satisfaction, or any Relation obtaine credit, unless
amongst men of the same side. It were therefore a presumptuous madnesse, to
think that this poore and weak Discourse, which can deserve no applause from
either side, should obtaine from both so much as pardon, or that they should
here meet in censure, which in nothing else have concurred.[5]

May registered his *History of the Parliament of England* with the Stationers, as published by the parliament's authority. We have no record
that he was instructed to write it, or when he commenced writing,[6] but
the volume which these words introduce did not appear until 1647 and
carries its narrative no further than the middle of 1643. In the passage
just quoted, there is much that is conventional; May is drawing upon,
and will cite, both ancient Roman and modern European authors who
have written about the difficulty of writing about a civil war when one is
in the midst of it; but we should not lose sight of the possibility that May
is not operating a convention so much as articulating his own perplexity
at finding himself in a civil war, when by definition the conventions of
shared speech have broken down. How this happened, and how a
conflict that "divided the understandings of men" moved from being a
war of pens to being a war of swords, is the narrative problem he has
begun to address. From this initiative a partisan explanation, an un-
equal distribution of guilt, will in due time emerge, but that is not the
initial problem. The historian – a role May has begun fully to assume –
must first face the problem that it will be very hard for his history to find
readers who will not reject it; from which it must follow that his history
will, for the same reasons, be very hard to write.

He must start by asking himself what purpose his narrative is meant
to serve. We very soon see that the function of history, under ideal
circumstances, is still for May the classical and almost bardic one of
recording the glorious deeds of heroes for the delight of their descend-
ants; but that under conditions of civil war this aim cannot be realized.
There are two sets of reasons for this. Tacitus, though he wrote a
generation later than the civil wars he narrated, had still to reckon with

readers descended from protagonists whose deeds had not been glorious but conducive to the unnatural condition of civil war itself.[7] It is far harder for May, writing while the unnatural actions are still going on and he himself cannot escape the role of a participant, or at least a dependant protected by one side. He must ask himself whether the historian, writing at such a moment that he must anticipate the memory of posterity, has any business to be where he is.

And I could have wished more then my life (being my self inconsiderable) that for the Publike sake, my Theame could rather have been the prosperity of these Nations, the Honour and happiness of this King, and such a blessed condition of both, as might have reached all the ends, for which Government was first ordained to the world: Then the description of Shipwracks, Ruines and Desolations. Yet these things truly recorded and observed, may be of good Use, and benefit Posterity in divers kinds. For though the present Actions, or rather sufferings of these (once happy) Nations, are of so high a marke and consideration, as might, perchance, throw themselves into the knowledge of Posterity by Tradition, and the weight of their owne Fame: Yet it may conduce to the benefit of that knowledge, to have the true causes, originall and growth of them represented by an honnest Pen.[8]

Why should the historian volunteer to substitute himself for the normal processes of social memory? Part of the answer seems to be that tradition is equal to the conservation of fame, meaning the memory of glorious deeds; but when the deeds have proved disastrous, conducive to ruin, desolation, and the unnatural condition of civil war, memory must be supplemented by explanation, and the pen of the historian is required to reflect as well as to record. From the Herodotean function of saving the deeds of the Greeks and barbarians from oblivion, May must pass to the Thucydidean function of providing a *ktēma es aeí*, an explanation of disaster which may be valuable to posterity; it is not glory but disaster which perplexes the mind and calls for a narrative that does more than preserve. Under conditions of historical miscarriage, memory by itself is not enough.

For the truth of this plaine and naked Discourse, which is here presented to the publike view, containing a briefe Narration of those Distractions which have fallen amongst us, during the sitting of this present Parliament; as also some Passages, and visible Actions of the former Government (whether probably conducing to these present calamities or not, of which let the Reader judge) I appeale only to the memory of any English man, whose yeares have been enow to make him know the Actions that were done; and whose conversation has been enough publike, to let him hear the Common Voice, and Discourses of

People upon those Actions; to his memory I say, do I appeale, whether such Actions were not done, and such judgements made upon them, as are here related. In which perchance some Readers may be put in minde of their own thoughts heretofore; which thoughts have since, like *Nebuchadnezzars* dreame, departed from them.[9]

May elaborates the concluding sentence; in times of the breakdown of government, the dissolution of civil ties, and the outbreak of domestic war, the reader may need the assistance of the historian in remembering his own experience and his own subjectivity. It is less than seven years since the parliament began to sit, but so much has happened in that time that he may have difficulty in remembering, not merely what happened but how he felt about it when it happened. His former experience and his former self may seem as strange to him as last night's dream, and he may need prompting from the historian to remember them at all; but he must remember them if he is to understand, and to follow in narrative, the origins of his present predicament. It may be worth asking whether a Roman historian could have written like this, and whether May is not indebted here to his awareness – which we shall see was intense – that the conflict of king and parliament had been conducted by the printing and reading of declarations, before there was a resort to armed violence.

Under Thucydidean or Tacitean conditions, the explanation of causes must supplement, but does not replace, the commemoration of deeds; but both activities are exposed to the difficulty that in war, and most poignantly in civil war, it is hard to see the other side of the hill. The historian – let alone the subject – knows only what has been done on the side where he himself is, and this affects not only his narrative but his judgment as to the springs of action. May cites the case of a Catholic and a Protestant (a Flemish and a Hollander) historian of the wars in the Netherlands[10] as illustrating the point.

But where Warre continues, people are inforced to make their residence in severall Quarters, and therefore severall, according to the places where they converse, must their information be concerning the condition and state of things. From whence arises not onely a Variety, but a great discrepancy for the most part in the Writings of those who record the passages of such times. And therefore it has seldome happened, but that in such times of calamity and Warre, Historians have much dissented from each other.[11]

Not only do the two Netherlanders give "a contrary censure concerning the occasion of that Warre"; the historian's ideal function, the commemoration of worthy actions, is similarly disturbed.

How much valour the English Nation on both sides have bin guilty of in this
unnaturall Warre, the World must needs know in the generall fame. But for
particulars, how much Worth, Vertue, and Courage, some particular Lords,
Gentlemen, and others have shewed, unlesse both sides do write, will never
perfectly be known. My residence hath bin, during these Wars, in the quarters, and under the protection, of the Parliament; and whatsoever is briefly
related of the Souldiery, being towards the end of this Book, is according to
that light which I discerned there. For whatsoever I have missed concerning
the other Party, I can make no other Apology then such as *Meteranus* (whom I
named before) doth in the Preface to his History, *De Belguis tumultibus*, Whose
words are thus: *Quod plura de Reformatorum, et patriae defensorum, quam de Partis
adversae rebus gestis exposuerim; mirum haudquaquam est, quoniam plus Commercii, et
familiaritatis mihi cum ipsis, et major indagandi opportunitas fuit. Si Pars adversa idem tali
probitate praestiterit, et ediderit; Posteritas gesta omnia legere, et liquido cognoscere magno
cum fructu poterit.*[12] In like manner may I averre, that if in this discourse more
particulars are set down, concerning the actions of those men who defended
the Parliament, then of them that warred against it; it was because my
conversation gave me more light on that side to whom, as I have endeavoured
to give no more then what is due, so I have cast no blemishes on the other; nor
bestowed any more characters, then what the truth of Story may require. If
those that write on the other side will use the same candour, there is no feare
but that posterity may receive a full information concerning the unhappy
distractions of these Kingdoms.[13]

There is more here than a conventional claim to impartiality. May
(and van Meteren) are telling us what it is like to write history in a civil
war, and emphasizing that civil war is such that its history must be
written by both sides. And in May, consideration of the historian's role
in civil war is leading on to consideration of the nature of civil war itself.
It is because civil war is an unnatural condition that its history must be
written in terms of its origins. To perform glorious deeds is natural to
men, and they call for commemorative narration rather than explanation. It is the unnatural whose causes, origins, and occasions must be
sought out and combined in a narrative of the obscure, the unexpected,
the arcane, and the crooked; a civil history is a very different thing from
a natural history, and narrative in the latter is confined to commemoration. Historical poetry, whose theme is or should be glory, is by no
means incapable of narrating the crooked ways of men and the inscrutable ways of God; but to write history in the midst of civil war is to write
a half truth, which can be completed only when the adversary completes
his half-true narrative of causation as well as action, and therefore calls
for prose. May must now proceed to consider the structure of his
necessarily complex narrative, in which a history of causes and origins is

the reverse of Whig or commemorative; it exists to narrate disaster, to explain how the unnatural happened.

> This I must adde, that to inform the world of the right nature, causes and growth of these Distractions, it will require that the Discourse begin from precedent time: which I shall indeavour to deduce down to the present with as much brevity, as the necessity of unfolding truth can possibly admit.
>
> Neither is it needfull to begin the Story from times of any great distance; or to mention the Government of our most ancient Princes; but from that Prince (fresh in the memory of some yet living) who first established the Reformed Religion in this Kingdome, and according to that, settled a new interest in the State: which was most behoofefull and requisite for her Successors to follow, and much conducing, besides the glory of Almighty God, to their owne Honour, Power, and Greatnesse.[14]

Clarendon could have had May in mind when he remarked that, unlike others, he saw no need to go back to the reign of Elizabeth in search of the origins of the Civil Wars.[15] Both writers were in the grip of the neoclassical assumption that the past must be presented as a digression from a history which sought to relate a present unity of time and space; but there was also a rhetorical and political necessity dictating their choice of interpretative strategies. Like other historians and protohistorians who had lived through the events of the 1640s and sought to narrate them, they were possessed by the experience of civil war: of a civil war among Englishmen, who had neither expected nor desired it and wanted above all things to know how they had come to be involved in it. They took it for granted, as did so much in the political language of the time, that the English kingdom was or had been marked by an exceptionally high level of natural, civil, and ecclesiastical unity, and that the disintegration of this unity was what made the war of the 1640s a "civil" and "unnatural" conflict. It was this – we shall note May's use of the phrase "the dissolution of this government" – which had to be explained, and the strategy adopted by every historian was to go back in time to a point where the unity of the kingdom could be exhibited, its structure explained, and a beginning made in uncovering those flaws which had subsequently destroyed it. How far back one went had much to do with one's decision as to what had held the kingdom together and what had broken it up in civil war. Clarendon looked no further than the 1630s because he intended to identify a limited number of mistakes and malpractices which had destroyed the Caroline peace. May went back to the reign of Elizabeth for reasons we are about to consider. James Harrington, the most macrohistorical of all, went back to the ultimate instability and subsequent transformation of feudal monarchy, itself the product of the disintegration of the Roman empire and the Roman republic.[16] What was anglocentric in all this was less the undeniable chauvinism of Englishmen toward their British others, than the assumption – itself a response to the agonizing experience of unwanted civil war – that an English civil war must have English causes, and that an English history must be constructed which would contain those causes within itself.

In search of a moment or structure of stability which contains the causes of its own deconstruction, May proposes to go back, not to the ancient constitution ("the Government of our most ancient Princes") but to the Elizabethan legislation which "established the Reformed Religion" and "settled a new interest in the State." By using "Reformed" rather than "Protestant" he may be indicating that the theology of the Elizabethan church was Calvinist, though certainly not that its government was or should have been Presbyterian; and when he speaks of religion becoming "a new interest in the State," we must beware of supposing that he is reducing religion to a mere component of the state's structure. Our own secularism encourages this assumption, but May is saying, not that religious considerations are subordinate to political, but that in Elizabethan England the two were equal and became inseparable, so that it was a disaster when the two were allowed to be separated once more. Charles I, we shall hear, was misled by his bishops into furthering this separation, and it grew into a calamitous breach between the king and his parliament, between his natural and political persons. The "interest" established by Elizabeth was not maintained by her successors; this was the root cause of the civil war in which May finds himself living and of which he is a historian. It is not the history he would have preferred to write;[17] it is the history of why he is a historian at all. The disappointed laureate – if he ever existed – is the speck of grit in the body of the oyster, but the pearl is shaped by the waves which have torn the oyster from the rock.

So far, religion as an "interest in the state" – a phrase which May repeatedly uses – need denote no more than the duality of the Henrician "empire," in which the king ruled as supreme head in both church and state; we catch sight of the debate as to whether he exercised his spiritual jurisdiction as king in parliament or out of it. But the "interest" is established by Elizabeth rather than Henry, and it is the interest of the "Reformed" religion; Calvinist theology may be integral to that interest, and the "Arminian" assault on it the cause of its disruption. But May's attention is focused on "interest" in a more Rohanesque sense;[18] it is matter of policy as well as doctrine and discipline.

That Reformation engaged the Queene in a new Interest of State, to side with the Protestants against those Potent Monarchs of the other Religion, which seemed at the beginning as much danger and disadvantage to her, as it proved in conclusion security and Honour; so impossible is it for any disadvantage to prevail over them that helpe the Lord against the Mighty...[19]

But Queene ELIZABETH had woven the interest of her own State so inseparably into the cause of Religion it selfe, that it was hard to overthrow one without the ruine of the other. And God, who had given her so much grace and courage as to rely wholly upon him, did with that Almighty hand, not onely hold her up from sinking, but lift her above the heads of all her enemies.

By what degrees and means she atchieved the great actions of her reigne, and brought so much prosperity to her Nation, it is not the scope of this discourse to relate at large (for her History is not the Worke in hand) but only in briefe to declare that before her death she was the happy instrument of God to promote the Protestant Religion in all parts...

All which she accomplished by the justice and prudence of her government, by making the right use of her Subjects hearts, hands and Purses in a Parliamentary way...[20]

The image of Elizabeth as the Protestant Deborah, actively supporting the Calvinist churches in Scotland, France, and the Netherlands, may have been largely an invention of the 1620s, and May was certainly not the first to suggest that James I's weakness, Buckingham's mismanagement, and Charles I's positive desertion of the Protestant cause had soured relations between kings and parliaments between 1621 and 1629; but he was among the first to present this narrative as relating the origins of a civil war, recently broken out and still going on. Under James:

Thus was the King by degrees brought, not onely to forsake, but to oppose his owne interest both in civill and religious affaires, which was most unhappily seene in that cause (as the Duke of ROHAN observed) wherein, besides the interest of all Protestants, and the honour of his Nation, the estate and livelihood of his owne children were at the height concerned, the Palatinate business.

From hence flowed a farther mischeife; for the King being loath perchance that the whole people should take notice of those waies in which he trod, grew extremely disaffected to Parliaments, calling them for nothing but to supply his expences, dissolving them when they began to meddle with State Affairs, and divers times imprisoning the Members for Speeches made in Parliament, against the fundamentall privileges of that high Court.[21]

Under Charles, especially after 1629,

What Counsells had then influence upon the Court of England, might be the amazement of a wise man to consider; and the plaine truth must needs seeme a paradox to posterity; as that the Protestant Religion, both at home and abroad, should suffer much by the Government of two Kings; of whom the former in his own person wrote more learnedly in defence of it; and the latter in his owne person lived more conformably to the Rules of it, than any of their Contemporary Princes in Europe. But the Civill affaires of State were too ill managed, to protect, or at least to propagate true Religion; or else the neglect of Religion was the cause that Civill Affaires were blessed with no more honour and prosperity. The right waies of Queen ELIZABETH, who advanced both, had been long ago forsaken, and the deviation grew daily farther, and more fatall to the Kingdom.[22]

The evil counselors have begun to cast their shadow, but the mystery of state remains structural and independent of personality. It is a significant comment on the history of English historiography that a modern reader is probably more disposed to contest May's argument than to inquire how it came into being; how far is May its architect, how far is he carrying on a discourse already in existence, how many years has it taken to reach the form it has for him between 1645 and 1647? What seems clear is that the failure to conduct an effective support of the Calvinist princes and churches is being presented as the tip of the iceberg, both symptom and cause of a deeper failure to maintain the Protestant structure of the English state; and that this in turn is destabilizing the unity between crown and parliament, on which both government and liberty depend.

But these Gentlemen, who seemed so forward in taking up their own yoake, were but a small part of the Nation (though a number considerable enough to make a Reformation hard) compared with those Gentlemen who were sensible of their birth-rights, and the true interest of the Kingdome; on which side the common people in the generality, and the Country Freeholders stood, who would rationally argue of their owne Rights, and the oppressions that were layed upon them.

We hear the voices of 1647, the year in which these words were published. The common people may be heard from in their own history; their voice may be a rational one. Nevertheless:

the sins of the English Nation were too great, to let them hope for an easie or speedy redresse of such grievances; and the manners of the people so much corrupted, as by degrees they came of that temper, which the Historian speaks of his Romans, *ut nec mala, nec remedia ferre possent*, they could neither suffer those pressures patiently, nor quietly endure the cure of them.[23]

This is not just conventional piety, though it is surrounded with much conventional rhetoric. The search for a remedy against oppression has led to the greater evil of civil war, just as the rhetoric of non-resistance predicted, and May is in process of finding out how this happened. He has already told us that his explanation will necessarily be both partisan and partial. So far we know of it only that it entails a failure to maintain the unity of church and state of which disregard of parliamentary liberties seems to be a consequence. From the parliamentary disasters of 1628–9 May proceeds to the rise to power of the higher clergy, who condemned most things done by the Protestant churches of Europe and not a few things done by Henry VIII and Elizabeth I, "especially after they had gotten in the yeare 1633, an Archbishop after their owne heart, Doctor LAUD."[24] May is clear that these Arminians were not crypto-Papists, but he is sure he knows the reason.

The Archbishop of *Canterbury* was much against the Court of *Rome*, though not against that Church, in so high a kinde; For the Doctrine of the Roman Church was no enemy to the Pompe of Prelacy; but the Doctrine of the Court of *Rome* would have swallowed up all under the Popes Supremacy, and have made all greatnesse dependant upon him: Which the Archbishop conceived would derogate too much from the King in Temporalls (and therefore hardly to be accepted by the Court) as it would from himselfe in Spiritualls, and make his Metropoliticall power subordinate, which he desired to hold absolute and independent within the Realme of *England*.[25]

This is not a paranoid reading, but the catastrophe is at hand. Laud's policies are about to provoke the Covenant rebellion in Scotland, "the first coale ... which kindled since into so great a combustion, as to deface, and almost ruine, three flourishing Kingdomes."[26] The origins of the War of the Three Kingdoms, however, lie in England, in the failure to maintain the state's interest in the cause (and the doctrine) of European Protestantism, which has opened the way for the clergy to press their claims to authority beyond what the Elizabethan settlement will bear; beyond the unity of church and state which is the deeper interest of both.

[F]or from the Clergy this fire began, though the State was not innocent. The tyranny of Civill Government moved the same pace that the ambition of Prelacy did: And the Kings Councell had gone so farre, as they could not be content, that the people were patient, unlesse they could take away all possibility for the future, of the peoples redresse.[27]

It is a classic account of how excessive power drives itself, but the origins are in the clergy, not the council. May is sure how the move against

Scotland originated, but it is a matter of the mysteries of state, not the wickedness of individuals.

> The Archbishop of *Canterbury* was a maine Agent in this fatall worke; a man vigilant enough; of an active, or rather of a restlesse minde; more ambitious to undertake, then politick to carry on; of a disposition too fierce and cruell for his Coat; which notwithstanding, he was so farre from concealing in a subtle way, that he increased the envy of it by insolence. He had few vulgar and private vices, as being neither taxed of covetuousness, intemperance, nor incontinence; and in a word, a man not altogether so bad, as unfit for the State of *England*.[28]

The flaw of state has occurred in England. King James's failure to support the Palatines and the Calvinist cause has opened the door, first to favorites and counselors indifferent to the king's unity with his subjects – the parliamentarian reading of the 1620s is already well in place – second, to the thrust of the non-puritan clergy[29] toward the independence of their authority in an independent kingdom. This double offensive has reached the point of provoking the Scottish rebellion, the first flame of the War of the Three Kingdoms. However, whether writing at the command of authority or at his own volition, Thomas May is the historian of the English parliament summoned at the end of 1640, and he has reached the end of the prehistory which explains how that parliament came to meet. The failure of Charles I's campaign against the covenanters, and the unconcealed reluctance of his English subjects to support the bishops against their Scottish brethren,[30] compels him to summon a parliament and ensures that it will meet in a mood to remedy the flaws of state which have brought things to this condition. These flaws, once again, are English; there is no suggestion, and it could hardly have entered May's head, that weaknesses in the structure of the Scottish state could have precipitated crisis in both kingdoms. The Scottish crisis of 1637 is presented as the result of a rash move by the English bishops and the king – a king, May might have said, after their own heart – and it is the English parliament which must meet to mend matters.

The central fact, the central *explicandum*, the central mystery of state, in May's history – as, it is reasonable to suppose, in his personal and political experience – was the outbreak of war between Englishmen and this is the next theme he turns to consider. He assumes without discussion that the origins of so English a disaster must be the English themselves; however crucial the roles of the other kingdoms, Englishmen did not fight each other for Scottish or Irish reasons, but for reasons of their own. And May's explanatory structure is already in place. There is an English "state" – he uses the term – long established in existence; and whatever fissures have been allowed to open up in it, civil war is the result of its intimate unity no less than of that unity's disruption. The English war is unnatural because Englishmen are, as well as have been, naturally members of one body; more unnatural, therefore, than wars between kingdoms subject to a multiple monarchy. The second book of the *History of the Parliament* is devoted to the origins of that war, its outbreak located at the moment "when the Parliament's Ordinance for the militia, and the King's Commission for the Array were put in execution,"[31] and its explanation deduced from the coincidence of the Grand Remonstrance and the news of the Irish rebellion.

At that time began that fatal breach between King and Parliament to appear visibly, and wax daily wider, never to be closed, until the whole Kingdom was by sad degrees brought into a ruinous War.
From henceforth no true confidence appeared between him and that high Court; every day almost contributed somewhat to the division, and Declarations upon divers occasions were published to the world; of which, with frequent intermixtures of gracious expressions from the King, and affectionate professions from the parliament; yet the substance was matter of expostulation, and many intervening actions (which we shall endeavour to expresse particularly) did so far heighten them, and sharpen by degrees the stile, till those Paper-protestations became a fatall Prologue to that bloudy, and unnaturall War, which afterward ensued.[32]

May is showing himself aware that his narrative has changed course and structure. The flaws of state which began in the time of James I have carried his history through the rebellion of the Scottish covenanters, and explain why it was necessary to call an English parliament in 1640, and what actions that parliament might feel obliged to undertake. They do not suffice to explain why king and parliament found themselves so far estranged that civil war was the outcome; and May is setting up the history of that crisis in what Hobbes called "diffidence" as in part a history of language: a history Thucydidean in the sense that words change their meaning and the language in which the parties profess their confidence in one another becomes the instrument by which that confidence is destroyed. It is also a history of print, and its existence complicates the historian's task in two ways. First, he is writing in the midst of a print culture which challenges the primacy of his own narrative; there is no need, says May, to rehearse all the speeches made by Pym, Rudyerd, Grimston, Bagshaw, and Clotworthy when parliament first met, because they have all been printed and the reader has access to them.[33] Secondly, these printings are not merely documents and sources of information, but actions and events in the story to be recounted; which is no doubt why Rudyerd's speech is nevertheless given in full.[34]

There are two mysteries of state for which May must account in order to explain the occurrence of civil war in England: how it was that the king was led first to attempt force against the parliament, and then to withdraw his person from it, leaving a space which could be filled up only by rumors, plots, fears, and mistrust; second, how it was that the king, having played such a part in creating a civil war that no one wanted, was nevertheless able to find an army, and a party, willing to fight for him. To choose these as the questions needing answers was, of course, to begin imposing a certain structure on events; but they were questions that could not be answered merely by extrapolating from the post-Elizabethan flaws of state that had provided May with his narrative of November 1640. New mysteries of state, new arcana of human conduct in politics, would have to be explained; and it was in the logic of May's understanding of the historiography of civil war that they should be stories told as having more than one side. He tells them together, from the moment at which, in his judgment, they both began.

So great it was, that we can hardly call it the Triall of the Earle of *Strafford* only; the Kings affection toward his People and Parliament, the future successe of this Parliament, and the hopes of three Kingdomes depending on it, were all tryed, when *Strafford* was arraigned.[35]

How farre the Earle of Strafford did in his lifetime divide the Kings affections from his People and Parliament (which was part of his Charge) I cannot surely tell; But certain it is, That his Tryall and death (which has made me insist the longer upon it) did make such a division in that kinde, as, being unhappily nourished by degrees afterward, has almost ruined the three Kingdomes.

The length of his Tryall, whilest two Armies at an heavy expence were to be paid, and other businesse at a great stand, did divide some impatient people (at least in some degree) from the Parliament; The manner of his condemnation divided the Parliament in it selfe; and the eager pressing of his death did discover or cause a sad division of the King from his Parliament.

Nine and fifty Members of the House of Commons dissented in Vote from the rest, upon the Bill of Attainder; Upon which some indiscreet persons (for so I must needs describe them, though it was never knowne who they were, or by whose notice it was done) the next day set up a paper upon the Exchange, with the names of those nine and fifty, and a Title over it, *The names of those men, who to save a Traytor, would betray their Country.*

They that were thus posted up, supposing this to be done or caused by some of their House, were much provoked at it, many of them growing by degrees disaffected to the Parliament, (not all, for there were among those dissenting Gentlemen very wise and learned men) and upon that unhappy distraction that fell out about a yeare after, forsooke the Parliament . . .

The worst consequence of all was, that the Kings heart did upon this occasion appear to be quite alienated from the Parliament.[36]

May is certainly not writing panegyric or apology, at this point, for the side he has chosen to take. The first overt blame of the king as guilty of civil war occurs at his discussion of the Triennial Act, and even there may be chiefly an indication of the hardening of attitudes.

And where it was objected, That no King ever granted the like before; they answered, It was evident, that no King before ever made so great a necessity for a Parliament to require it . . .

It was nevertheless probably then thought by all, that the King would not have assented to that Act, if at that time the freshnesse of those forementioned grievances in the peoples hearts, and the present discovery of that odious Treason, of bringing an Army against the Parliament, had not made it unsafe for him to deny.

That opinion was more confirmed by the following Actions, since time, and the inconstancy of some Lords and Gentlemen, had raised him a Party. When that knot, which by Law he could not againe untie, he indeavoured to cut a sunder by the Sword; as was afterwards observed in the Parliaments Declarations.[37]

The more Charles veers toward a solution by violence, the more urgent it becomes to know how he acquired a party; not only is this mysterious in itself, but the turn toward civil war could not have happened without it. Book 1 of the *History* concludes with five pages of reflection on the causes of defection from the parliament to the king, which May considers so important that he anticipates his narrative to bring it in, at a point where he has not reached the Irish rebellion. He discusses first the attack upon the bishops, which had raised fears among all those of the younger clergy whose hopes lay in preferment; second, "[a]nother thing which seemed to trouble some, who were not bad men . . . that extreame License, which the Common People, almost from the very beginning of the Parliament, tooke to themselves, of reforming, without Authority, Order, or Decency, rudely disturbing Church Service, whilest the Common Prayer was reading, tearing those Bookes, Surplices, and such things . . ."[38] The common people, we remember, knew rationally enough when their rights were being infringed;[39] but this is another matter. The distinction between civil and religious grievances recurs when May looks ahead to recall that within a year of the autumn of 1641 a part at least of the people were willing to join in war against the parliament, though at the point which his narrative has reached this was unthinkable. John Aubrey records that May had a close friend, Sir Richard Fanshawe, a yet more minor poet, and: "Mr. Emanuel Decretz (Serjeant Painter to King Charles Ist) was present at the debate at their parting before Sir Richard went to the King, where both Camps were most rigourously band[i]ed."[40]

It is possible that May is enlarging this parting of friends – occurring on the artistic margins of what had been King Charles's court – into a general debate among the previously parliamentarian gentry, when he writes:

I remember within the compasse of a yeare after, when the Civill War began to break out over all the Kingdom, and men in all companies began to vent their opinion in an argumentative way, either opposing or defending the Parliament Cause; and Treatises were printed on both sides: Many Gentlemen, who forsooke the Parliament, were very bitter against it for the proceedings in Religion, in countenancing, or not suppressing, the rudenesse of people in Churches (which I related before) acting those things, which seemed to be against the Discipline of the English Church, and might introduce all kindes of Sects and Schismes... They also affirmed, That Lawes and Liberties having been so much violated by the King, if the Parliament had not so farre drawn Religion also into their cause, it might have sped better; for the Parliament frequently at that time, in all their expressions, whensoever they charged the corrupt Statesmen of injustice and Tyranny, would put Popery, or a suspition of it, into the first place against them. I remember, when the Warre was begun, among those little Treatises, which were then published, as many there were without any names to them, I found one, in which the case is thus expressed, to recite the words of it.[41]

May says he is remembering a time of paper war and personal choice, conducted both in print and in the hearts of men. The pamphlet which he proceeds to quote at length, and in italics, has not been identified, and there is internal evidence which may date it as late as 1643;[42] but he thinks it important to introduce its argument before he has reached November 1641. The text he excerpts insists that allegations of crypto-popery against Charles I could never be proved – there was, as we should say, no smoking gun – and were bound to backfire, weakening the parliament's infinitely stronger, and indeed unanswerable, case against him for violating the laws and liberties of his kingdom.

From whence may follow a strange conclusion; That the Kings dealing so much with Rome, to the disadvantage of the Protestant Religion, should now turne to his own advantage in a Protestant Kingdome. And we may make this as paradoxicall a supposition, That if the King had never done anything prejudiciall to the Protestant Religion, he would have found fewer Protestants this Parliament to take his part.[43]

May and his source are not being cynical; they are pursuing the *arcana imperii*, the crooked timbers of human behavior, which ensue because religion and civil government in England are bound up inseparably in a single interest of state, so that when their unity breaks down they are doomed to become entangled. The religious aspect of monarchy, the text continues, should never be discussed apart from its civil, and it has been a disaster

that frequent naming of Religion, as if it were the onely quarrell, hath caused a great mistake of the question in some, by reason of ignorance, in others of subtilty; whilest they wilfully mistake, to abuse the Parliaments Cause, writing whole volumes in a wrong stated case;[44] *as, instead of disputing whether the Parliament of England lawfully assembled, where the King virtually is, may by Armes defend the Religion established by the same power, together with the Lawes and Liberties of the Nation, against Delinquents, detaining with them the Kings seduced Person: They make it the question, Whether Subjects, taken in a generall Sense, may make Warre against their King for Religions sake?*

Such was the sense of many Gentlemen at that time, which adhered to the parliament. But to proceed in the Narration.[45]

It is possible to read May as writing his *History* less at the dictation of parliament in 1646–7 than in continuation of his debate with Fanshawe several years earlier. Certainly he represents the outbreak of civil war as the outcome of innumerable debates like this, occurring all over the kingdom (that is, the kingdom of England). At the same time, however, the passage doubly quoted – if May is not inventing the text to speak for him – seems to affirm the position which May chose to take in opting for the parliament; that its war was not against the king but against his evil counselors; against the king only in so far as he had placed himself in the hands of those counselors; against the king in his natural person so long as it was unnaturally separated from his political person, which could be manifested only in unity with his parliament. May thought it so important to articulate this doctrine that he anticipated his narrative by one or even two years to do so.

Book II of the *History* returns to the later months of 1641, when "the Sequel within a short time proved worse, then the wisest men could imagine, or the most jealous possibly suspect; though jealousies and fears were then grown to a great height, and the Parliament of *England* less than ever, assured of the Kings real affection to them."[46]

Published in 1647, these words offer a retrospect of a time when things happened faster than the emotions could respond to them, so that, though Charles I is emerging as the central blameworthy figure, the mysteries of state, the uncontrollable character of history, are providing the theme of the narrative. A chapter later, having reviewed the arguments for and against the Grand Remonstrance, May sums up in humanist but Tacitean language: "For mine own part, I will make no judgment at all upon it; nor can we truly judge by the successe of things. But such an unhappy Genius ruled those times (for Historians have observed a Genius of times, as well as of climates, or men) that no endeavours produce the right (though probable) effects."[47]

He proceeds to the words, already quoted, about the paper war which followed the breach between king and parliament, and preceded the war of swords. All this has been preceded by a section on the outbreak of the rebellion in Ulster,[48] in which May does not on the whole present the need to raise forces for Ireland as precipitating a crisis in confidence between king and parliament, thus leading to the competing attempts to call out the militia which were the actual occasion of civil war. This catastrophe occurs in an English setting and is the result of an English act: the king's attempt to arrest the five members and Lord Mandeville, followed by his withdrawal from Westminster and parliament. Here, if anywhere, the evil counselors should be identified; but even Lord Digby, whom it would be easy to blame for both the attempt on the five members and its failure, is somewhat downplayed.[49] It is as if the real danger arose from the vacuum of power itself, the physical space between king and parliament growing wider as the king moved north, which could be filled only by fear and mistrust, the fantasy and then the reality of violence. The paper war now moves to the center: "for about this time, and for three months after, such Messages, Remonstrances, Petitions and Answers grew so voluminous upon all occasions, as might, recited *verbatim*, make a large History."[50]

Such verbiage makes May's history harder to write; as documentation, it is more verbose than his narrative can accommodate, while as action, it both constitutes and conceals the reality of what is happening. To Clarendon, and to his readers,[51] the exchange of state papers represented the attempts of the "constitutional royalists" who now gathered about the king to convert the space of separation into a space of negotiation; but to May, this *ralliement* was itself part of the problem, since it divided the parliament and made civil war possible. His narrative proceeds to Queen Henrietta Maria's departure for France with the crown jewels, intending as the parliament afterwards contended to use them to raise an army,[52] and to the king's attempt upon Hull (counseled by Digby). It is this which moves the parliament, in one declaration which May reports at length,

> to inform the King, that his Interest in Towns, Arms, or the Kingdom itself, is not of that kinde that private men have interest in their Goods, to sell or dispose of at pleasure; but onely as entrusted to him for the good of all: in performance of which trust, none but the Parliament, while it sitteth, are or ought to be his Counsellors and directors: that there can be no good or useful disputation, where the Principles are not granted: and it was even heretofore taken (say they) for a certain Principle, That the Parliament sitting is the onely Judge of what is dangerous to the Common-wealth, and what useful, as likewise what is lawful in these cases; which the King, by advice of no private Counsel whatsoever, ought to control or contradict: which Principle till the King will be pleased rightly to apprehend, Disputations and Declarations are endlesse, and no true understanding between him and his people can be begotten.
>
> Of all these things if a Reader desire to be satisfied in particular, he may finde the questions all fully stated by the Parliament, and the King's desires expressed by himself in two large Declarations: one called the Parliament's third Remonstrance, dated the 26. of May, 1642; and the Kings Answer to that Remonstrance.[53]

The more Charles I's separation from parliament grew into a theater of possible civil war, the more parliament was moved to tell him that he had no being out of parliament, and to approach the doctrine that parliament might act against him in his own name and might even claim to be him in his political person, though his natural person were against it. The kingdom of England could lay claim to such unity that rebellion by the kingdom was metaphysically impossible, though rebellion by the king was moving from unthinkable to possible. May had reached the brink of the doctrine of parliamentary sovereignty proclaimed by such bold spirits as Henry Parker;[54] and there are two questions to be asked concerning it. The first is how far May regarded it as justifying his own choice of the parliament's side in the Civil War, how far as among the occasions of that war. The second is how far May was party to its invention in the summer of 1642 and elaboration over the years following, and how that process originated and proceeded. Certainly, this had never been said before; how far is May looking back from 1647 on its invention, and how far, as it was formulated, did it seem to consist of beliefs which those involved had held since time whereof their memories ran not to the contrary? The creation of a discourse is a complex historical problem, which the word "invention" does not solve by itself.

Meanwhile, the action of the paper war had replaced the problem of the evil counselors; it occurred because the king had begun to gather a more formidable, because more principled, set of advisers. After the attempt upon Hull, Charles continued to seek to provide himself with a guard, and the parliament to respond out of fear for its own safety.

But the Kingdome was not much affrighted with any Forces which the King could so raise; nor could any other attempt of his in the Northern parts, make the people fear a Civil War, until they saw that great defection of the Parliament Members, which began before the end of *April*, and continued for the greatest part of that *May*, for at that time did the Lords one after the other, and sometimes by numbers, abandon the Parliament sitting, and go to the King at *York*, insomuch that in a very short space, those Lords became the greater number; and their departure began therefore to seem less strange, then the constant sitting of the rest... Within the same compasse of time, many of the house of Commons, though no great number, in respect to those who continued in that house, did likewise so far break that trust which was reposed in them, as to forsake their seats in Parliament; some of them, as was reported, invited by Letters from the King, and others of their own accord.[55]

If not the "evil counselors," these defectors are the "delinquents" of later parliamentary language. May does not do much toward identifying them, remarking of a further defection after the reverses of early 1643 that their names "are here spared, because this latter revolt must needs carry the face of a crime; as being no matter of opinion or conscience, by which the first justified themselves."[56]

The motives of the 1642 defectors are discussed in the usual humanist *pro et contra*; as they were men of character and distinction, some thought them justified by London intimidation, while others held that just such men were liable to be seduced by ambition. But the debate itself was a historical reality. "Such discourses were frequent in all companies at that time, for different affections did at all meetings beget such argumentative language."[57] If Aubrey is to be relied on, May was speaking from his own experience; certainly he wishes us to see the outbreak of civil war as consisting in such debates occurring in the lives of individuals everywhere. Without the defections of April and May there could have been no civil war, since the king would have lacked a party; and further, by dividing the parliament, they compelled a choice between parliament and king which individuals must make for themselves. Parliament's central claim, that the kingdom in parliament constituted a unity of persons which nothing could dissolve, was subverted by their actions, and one is left wondering how far May was persuaded by it. These are the circumstances in which he brings forward resolutions passed in both Houses – or what was left of them – whose language governs his writings for the remainder of his days. "*That it appears that the King, seduced by wicked Counsel, intends to make War against the Parliament . . . That whenever the King maketh War upon the Parliament, it is a breach of the Trust reposed in him by his People, contrary to his Oath, and tending to the dissolution of this Government.*"[58]

Charles I was to be tried and executed for making war against his parliament and people; the words "dissolution of government" were to lie at the center of English political debate down to Locke's *Second Treatise of Government* and the fall of James II. May, publishing his *History* in 1647, did not know that the first event was about to occur; dying in 1650, he could not have imagined the second and third. In the above quotation, he recorded parliament's proclamation that a state of civil war was imminent; less to justify his own choice than to narrate a moment at which choices had to be made everywhere. "For now the fatal time was come, when those long and tedious Paper-conflicts of Declarations, Petitions and Proclamations, were turned into actuall and bloody Wars, and the Pens seconded by drawn swords."[59] In the next chapter we hear how

the Parliaments Ordinance of *Militia*, and the Kings Commission of *Array*, were justling together almost in every County: the greatest of the English Nobility on both sides appearing personally, to seize upon those places which were deputed to them either by the King or by the Parliament. No Ordinances from the One, or Proclamations by the Other, could now give any further stop to this general and spreading Mischief. God was not pleased that one Chimney should contain this Civil fire, but small sparks of it were daily kindling in every part of the Land.

Let it not therefore seem amisse, if in the first place I make a brief Relation into what posture every particular County, or most of them, had endeavoured to put themselves, during that time, which was since the twelfth of *July*, when the first apparent denouncing of War began, and the General was elected in Parliament; till the three and twentieth of *October*, when it broke out in a fierce and cruell Battel. But let not the Reader expect any full or perfect Narration of this, which would take too great a time, and prove as tedious as unnecessary. The onely reason why I have entered into it, is to inform the Reader what Lords and Gentlemen did first appear in action on either side in those particular Counties, that in the progresse of the Story he may be better acquainted with those names, whose Actions proved of so high concernment in the future War. Nor can any perfect Judgements be made of the affections or condition of any one County in this brief Narration of so short a Time: for scarce was there any

City or Shire, but endured in processe of time many Changes, and became altered from their first condition, either by unconstancy of affections, or else enforced to take a new side, as they were threatned by approaching Armies of either party, when the War grew to a greater height.[60]

The *History* has returned to its starting-point: the ideal function of recording the deeds of worthies and the real difficulty of doing this in time of civil war. It has been necessary to narrate the origins of that war, and it is here characterized as a war of localities, breaking out every-where as the demands of royal and parliamentary officers compel every man to declare himself where he is; if this is "the dissolution of this government," the government is strong enough in its dissolution to compel choice universally, and since it is divided into two heads or persons, the innumerable narratives of local conflict can still be included in the greater narrative of war between Oxford and Westminster. The paper war is far from over; Book II concludes with seven pages of charge and countercharge about Ireland, six about the king's proclamation of his opponents to be rebels;[61] but Book III begins with the gathering of field armies. May comes as close as any contemporary does to descri-bing the war as "the second Essex rebellion" when he says of the parliament's general setting out from London:

Great was the love and honour which the people in generall bore to his Person, in regard of his owne vertue, and honourable demeanour; and much increased by the Memory of his noble Father, the highest example that ever yet I read, of a Favourite both to Prince and people; of whom that was most true, which VELLEIUS PATERCULUS speaks with flattery and falsehood of SEJANUS, *In quo cum judicio Principis certabant studia populi*; The peoples love strived to match the Prince his judgment.[62]

Unless the allusion is double-edged, May should have had uncomfort-able dreams of an angry Elizabeth. King Charles meanwhile has no general better than the Palatine brothers, soldiers of fortune whose forays make him as many enemies as friends,[63] but transforms the entire war by his triumphant appearance on the Welsh marches, where

with such skill had the King managed his affairs there, and so much had fortune crowned his indeavours, that before the middle of *October*, which was about three weekes after his first coming to *Shrewsbury* with an inconsiderable Body of an Army, he was growne to a great strength, consisting of about six thousand Foot, three thousand brave Horse, and almost two thousand Dragoneers.[64]

This is the climax of the process by which the king ensured civil war by building himself a party and an army. We should like to know more of the thousands who gathered to him at Shrewsbury, but May tells us little; he would have said that he was not there and had no opportunity to speak with them. The armies meet in a great field of action.

At the famous Battell of *Edgehill*, the great cause of English Liberty, (with a vast expence of blood and Treasure) was tryed, but not decided, which did therefore prove unhappy, even to that side, which seemed victorious, the Parliament Army.

For though the Kings Forces were much broken by it, yet his strength grew accidentally greater, and more formidable than before; to whom it proved a kinde of victory, not to be easily or totally overthrowne.

For the greatest Gentlemen of divers Counties began to consider of the King, as one that in possibility might prove a Conquerour against the Parliament; and many of them, who before as Neuters had stood at gaze, in hope that one quick blow might cleare the doubt, and save them the danger of declaring themselves, came now in, and readily adhered to that side, where there seemed to be least feares, and greatest hopes, which was the Kings Party; for on the Parliament side, the incouragements were onely publike, and nothing promised but the free enjoyment of their native Liberty; no particular honours, preferments, or Estates of Enemies; and on the other side, no such totall ruine could be threatened from a victorious Parliament, being a body as it were of themselves, as from an incensed Prince, and such hungry followers, as usually go along with Princes in those waies.[65]

This is how things go in civil war. King Charles won at Edgehill by fighting it at all; but whether he owed his success to his legitimate or his illegitimate authority is another matter. Parliament's setbacks in politics, despite successes in the field, are soon followed by formidable and revolutionary political action. "For things were growne beyond any precedent of former ages, and the very foundations of Government were shaken; according to the sense of that Vote, which the Lords and Commons had passed a yeare before, *That whensoever the King maketh Warre against the Parliament, it tendeth to the dissolution of this Government.*"[66]

That resolution had transformed the English Civil War, rather as the Declaration of Independence, working in a contrary direction, was to transform the rebellion of the American colonies. Once it had proclaimed the indissoluble, and in the medieval sense, mystical unity of king and parliament, the war could never again be a baronial rebellion like those "of former ages." The unity had been proclaimed because it was being broken, and parliament was in arms as the king's political person, defending his government against his natural (and seduced) person bent on dissolving it. This opened the door to charges of an unlimited extent against "the man Charles Stewart"; for the present,

however, the parliament must give itself unlimited authority to preserve
and reform the government he threatened.

Three things of that unusuall nature fell into debate in one moneth, which was
May, 1643, and were then, or soone after fully passed; one was at the beginning
of that moneth, concerning the Assembly of Divines at *Westminster* . . .[67]
    The case seemed of the same nature with that of *Scotland*, in the yeare 1639,
when the Scottish Covenanters (as is before mentioned in this History) upon the
Kings delay in calling their Nationall Synod, published a writing to that
purpose; That the power of calling a Synod, in case the Prince be an Enemy to
the truth, or negligent in promoting the Churches good, is in the Church it
selfe.[68]

And as if that were not momentous enough, the parliament proceeded to order the making of a new Great Seal, to replace that carried
by the Lord Keeper to the king at Oxford; at which infringement of the
highest totems of monarchy

the people stood at gaze, and many wondered what might be the consequence
of so unusuall a thing. Some that wholly adhered to the Parliament, and liked
well, that an action so convenient and usefull to the present state, was done by
them, looked notwithstanding upon it, as a sad marke of the Kingdomes
distraction, and a signe how irreconcileable the differences might grow be-
tweene the Parliament and the Kings Person . . . But before this businesse was
fully concluded, another thing, which seemed as great a signe how wide the rent
was growne, fell into debate in the House of Commons . . . The matter was
about charging the Queene of High Treason . . . upon which within few
Moneths after, she was impeached of High Treason by the House of Commons, and the Impeachment carried up by Master PYMME to the House of
Peers, where it stuck for many moneths, but was afterward passed there also;
and may be further discoursed of in the due time.[69]

That time, however, never arrives. The narrative of military events is
resumed, through parliament's many defeats in early 1643, to the
recovery of its fortunes at the relief of Gloucester and the first Battle of
Newbury – already described in print by its parliamentary though not
yet by its royalist participants.[70] The military face of things begins to
change, and the transformation of state to keep pace with it. At the time
of the Gloucester campaign the king arrives at his Cessation of Arms in
Ireland, of which "there may be a large Discourse in the continuation of
the History; as also of the Covenant which the Parliament, and that part
of the Nation which adhered to them, about this Time entered into with
their Brethren of *Scotland*, for maintenance of the Religion, Lawes and
Liberties of both Kingdomes. FINIS."[71]

There was no continuation of the *History of the Parliament* under that title, or in the form of the successive and separately paginated "books" or installments, of which it had so far consisted. What May published in 1647 had reached the year 1643, and it is accurate to say that he there stopped producing the *History*, and that his next historical publication, the *Breviary of the History of the Parliament of England*, did not appear until 1650 and is constructed along different lines. We may therefore say that his work was interrupted in 1647, and ask ourselves why this occurred. Pending further research, we are obliged to speculate. An obvious suggestion is that the disturbed political conditions of the years 1647–50 had something to do with it. If – and it is not certain – May saw himself as writing "for" the parliament, or some specific group within it, he might well have wondered during those years how he could best serve his patrons, what they wanted, whether they held power, or even consisted of the same persons.

It may be important, at this point, to recall the powerful and sensitive language used by May at the outset of the *History*, where he remarks that the memory of one's former thoughts may prove as strange as Nebuchadnezzar's recollection of his dreams of the previous night. He had written of an English traveler's opinion: "that there was greater need to remember our own Countrymen, then to inform strangers of what was past; So much (said he) have they seemed to forget the things themselves, and their own N[o]tions concerning them."[72] It is a striking comment on what it may be like to write a classical history, preserving for posterity the events which have occurred under one's observation, when the events are unprecedented, unpredicted, unnatural, and unbelievably strange, and when one is writing for a print culture in which rapid publication ensures that one's readers have experienced the same events, occurring at the same speed. It was exacting enough – we may be disposed to add – to ask oneself and one's readers to recollect the formation in 1643 of the Solemn League and Covenant from the standpoint of 1647, when the army was marching on London and beginning to purge the membership of the parliament; to write the history of the New Model Army, through 1644, 1645, and 1646, while oneself experiencing the Agitators and the Levellers (not that May ever mentions them), the Second Civil War and the king's trial and execution, may well have seemed more than May could demand of himself or bring himself to demand of others. This must remain conjecture; what is certain is that his next and last historical work surveys the latter series of events, down to but not including the last, and is written in the state of mind induced by the experience of them.

A Breviary of the History of the Parliament of England. Expressed in three Parts ... appeared in 1650. It described itself as "*Written in Latine by T.M. and for the generall good translated out of the Latine into English.*" The Latin version which preceded it[73] was clearly intended for readers beyond England or the British kingdoms; like Milton's *Defensio Populi Anglicani* it was addressed to the network of readers in Latin Europe, and it would be interesting to know if there are any traces of its reception in Amsterdam, Paris, or Venice. No attempt is made here to compare the Latin and English texts, though this might be worth doing. May is unlikely to have undertaken the Latin work if he had not been commissioned to do so; he, like Milton, may have been serving the post-regicide regime in some secretarial capacity. The translation, undertaken "for the general good," is aimed at an English readership, which has lived through the events it narrates; even if commissioned by the same masters, therefore, it has a different impact, and must be read with a different ear, from a Latin text – no matter how close the translation – written for, and read by, a public of erudite Europeans who had beheld the English revolution, no doubt with mystification and horror, from a short but significant distance. We should try to read the *Breviary*, as we read the *History*, as it appeared on the London bookstalls, and was there picked up by readers some of whom bound and preserved it.

The full printed title declares that the *Breviary* is:

Expressed in three Parts:
1. *The Causes and Beginning of the Civil War of England.*
2. *A short mention of the Progress of that Civil War.*
3. *A compendious Relation of the Original, and Progress of the Second Civil War.*

We shall see that it does indeed stop at the exact point where the third objective has been achieved; and we should remember that it was published in the year of a third war against Charles II in Scotland. May has declared an intention of summarizing his previous *History* – this is one reason for calling the present work a breviary and of going beyond it to the end of 1648.

There is to be a narrative of two English civil wars, but there has also been war in all three kingdoms.

And though the condition of *Scotland* and *Ireland* were during that time no whit happier, (which being subject to the same King, were exposed to the same Calamity) our discourse especially shall be of *England*, as the noblest Kingdom and the Royall seat; from whence the distemper might first arise, and be derived to the rest: And wonderfull it may seem how great the distemper of that Government was, which ingendered so great a disease! how great the malignity of that disease, to which a Parliament was not sufficient Medicine.[74]

Since England is the imperial kingdom, the ills of the three kingdoms must arise from flaws in the English state. The distemper of the English government was so great that even a parliament could not cure it. The meeting of a parliament produced not reform but civil war; parliament's victory in that war could not resolve it but was followed by another. These mysteries of state can be recounted in ways that apportion blame to several parties; but the equation between the words "King" and "Calamity," and the word "malignity" that soon follows, indicates which way the wind is blowing. The paragraph that continues without a break introduces language harsher with regard to Charles than any we have heard before. "Forty years old was King *Charles*, and fifteen years had he raigned, when the Parliament was called: so long had the Laws been violated (more then under any King), the Liberties of the people invaded, and the authority of Parliament, by which Laws, and Liberties are supported, trodden underfoot; which had by degrees much discontented the *English Nation*."[75]

The duration of misgovernment is carefully identified with the duration of this king's reign. It could still be ascribed to evil counselors, but far back in the *History* May had ominously singled out a passage from Machiavelli making princes responsible for the advice they receive and observing that they often get the advice they are known to want.[76] The evil counselors begin to disappear, or rather to appear as a necessary fiction.

The Parliament shewed a great and wonderfull respect to the King, and in many expressions gave him humble thanks for calling them together, without any reflection upon his Person for what had passed in former misgovernment; but since no cure could be made without searching wounds, and that grievances must be recited, they resolved so to name them, as to cast the envy of them upon evill Counsell, and still mention the King with all honour and reverence possible, as will appear to any that read the printed Speeches, which at the beginning of that Session were made in the House by men of Eminency.[77]

Of the bill to make Parliament indissoluble without its own consent:

This Bill was a thing, that former Ages had not seen the like of, and therefore extremely was the Kings Grace magnified by those that flattered, but much condemned by others, who hated Parliaments and Reformation, complaining that the King had too far put the staffe out of his own hands. But many men who saw the necessity of such a thing, without which no money upon the publike faith could be borrowed, did not at all wonder at it, saying, That as no King ever granted the like before; so no King had ever before made so great a necessity to require it; but some men were of opinion that it was not of security enough to make the Kingdome happy, unless the King were good; for if he were ill affected, he had power enough still to hinder, and retard them in any proceeding for the good, and settlement of the Common-wealth and so by time and delayes lay a greater Odium upon the Parliament, for not satisfying the peoples desires, then if they had not had that seeming power to have done it: Which proved in the conclusion too true, when the King by such protraction of business, not at all concurring with them in the main, had raised a party to himself against them, to cut asunder that knot by the sword which by Law he could not unty.[78]

This echoes language used in the *History*,[79] but the image of a king who is not good has been abruptly introduced; a king alienated less by other men's actions, by the promptings of those around him, than bent from an early time on making war against the parliament. The rioting around Westminster "howsoever it were meant, produced of ill consequence to the Commonwealth, and did not so much move the King to be sensible of his grieving the People, as to arm him with an excuse for leaving the Parliament and City..."[80] The king's malignity, however, does not explain how he gathered a party:

But nothing made the Kingdom fear a War until that great defection of Parliament Members, who left their Seats, and went to the King at York... This revolt of so many Members of both Houses was generally looked upon, as a thing of most sad consequence, and likely to produce no effects, but lamentable and wicked; as to nourish and encrease the King's disaffection to Parliament; to encourage his distance from it, and attempts to subvert it; to secure the Irish Rebels, to subvert the dignity of that high Court, and make the King, by this diminution of their number (as he did in his following Declarations) call them a faction, a pretended Parliament, and such like names.[81]

Not the actions, still less the actors, but their effects are "wicked"; nevertheless the passage is part of the rhetoric which presented these defectors as "malignants" and made them an issue in all subsequent peace negotiations (on which May does not dwell). Without them there could never have been a civil war; but even while tending in his recast narrative toward making Charles I guilty of an intent to make war against the Parliament, May does not lose sight of the fact that many took his side spontaneously, and others accidentally or involuntarily.

But immediately after this time, the Kings Commissions of Array were sent down into every County (though often declared by the Parliament to be illegall) and were obeyed in many places more than the Parliaments Ordinances for the *Militia;* by reason that so many Lords and Gentlemen adhered to him now against the Parliament. But there were scarce any Counties free from contention, betwixt the Commissioners of the one and the Ordinances of the other; which struggled together, with great Nobility, and Gentry on both sides; neither had the Kings Proclamations, nor the Parliaments Ordinances obedience from all, only as far as the now drawing swords enforced it.[82]

The narrative of civil war is now launched, and carries Book 1 through Shrewsbury and Edgehill to Brentford and the winter quarters of 1642. The next book opens with May's reminder of what it is like to be a historian conducting such a narrative.

The beginnings of the Civil War, together with the Series of causes whence it sprung, as likewise the degrees by which it grew, have been already briefly and clearly shewed; The things which remain to be unfolded are of so great a weight, of so various a nature, and of so many pieces; that scarce any Historian (I might say History it self) is sufficient to weave fully together so many particulars; my entention therefore is to make only a short mention, not a full Narration, of that Variety.

For the War went on with horrid rage, in many places at the one time; and the fire once kindled, cast forth through every corner of the land not only sparks but enduring flames; insomuch as the kingdom of *England* was divided into more Wars then Counties; nor had she more fields then skirmishes, nor Cities then Sieges; and almost all the Palaces of Lords, and great Houses were turned everywhere into Garrisons of War; they fought at once by Sea and Land; and through all *England* (who could but lament the miseries of his Country) sad spectacles were of plundering, and firing Villages; and the fields, otherwise wast and desolate, were rich only, and terribly glorious in Camps and Armies.[83]

The heightened rhetoric conceals that May is not here saying that we must wait for the other side's histories to know the full truth; perhaps he no longer expects the war to end in such an eclogue. The narrative proceeds through battle, political actions, and negotiations – with Montrose's arrival there is war in Scotland[84] – until Charles gives himself up at Newark, "either to make peace upon his own conditions, or kindle a new war,"[85] and the surrender of Oxford and Astley's army mark "the end of this fierce War."[86] There is momentarily a British dimension – "The Scots alleaged that he was no less King of Scotland then of *England;* and that therefore their Kingdom had some right to the disposing of him; the English affirmed that his person was to be disposed by the authority of the Kingdom in which he then was."[87] But the problem is determined by the Scottish withdrawal. English history now takes a new turn.

... the Civil War being ended, a dissention more then Civill arose among the
Conquerors, which seemed therefore more sad to all good men, because it was
between those, who before had with most united affections and desires, thrown
their lives and Fortunes into the hazard against a Common Enemy: whom the
same cause, the same fervour of reforming Religion, and restoring Liberty; and
the same Prayers had linked together in the nearest bond of conscience.

By this division, under the names of *Presbyterian* and *Independent*, still encreas-
ing, the minds of men began beyond all measure, to be embittered against each
other; one side complained that the Covenant was broken: the other, that it was
not rightly enterpreated by them, nor so, as that it could any way be a
vindication of the cause undertaken, or the publike Safety; on both sides were
men of great reputation.[88]

The original conflict had been a civil war because it too was "more
then Civill,"[89] but May had been able to explain it as the result of an
error in the reason and interest of state. This dissension will not result
directly in war between the two factions, but will be exploited by the
king and the Scots to produce a civil war in which the factions desire
different outcomes; nor is May able to explain it as an English quarrel of
state. It may be that he has not told us enough about the Solemn League
and Covenant, or the deliberations of the Westminster Assembly, to
make it clear why Englishmen should be disagreeing about a new
interest of state and religion; while the idea that they were not disagreeing about their own solutions to the problem, but about those which the
king and the Scots might oblige them to accept in a negotiation, is not
quite thinkable. May is not prepared to say what all this was about.
"These dissentions of Presbiterian and Independent (because the motives and intentions of men are not enough known) our purpose is to
touch with more brevity than the actions of open War, and plain
hostility, though they also are here shortly mentioned."[90]

The plain fact is that it is the Presbyterian faction who are led to begin
"Calumnies" against the army, who respond by demanding both their
pay and a voice in the settlement of the nation. They further, "upon
what design, or what jealousies I leave to judge,"[91] remove the king from
Holmby; there ensue the intimidation of the parliament by the London
rioters, the army's march through London to deliver them, and the
temporary depression of the Presbyterian faction. But Book III shows the
consequence to have been the certainty of a second civil war, not arising
from the division into Presbyterians and Independents but promoted by
the king from Carisbrooke with the aim of exploiting that division. That
the Presbyterians, in "their hatred against the Independents . . . desired
that liberty, might be quite taken away by the King, rather then

vindicated by the Independents,"[92] is less of a mystery of state than the continued strength of the king, who

though set aside, and confined within the Isle of *Wight*, was more formidable this Summer, then in any other, when he was followed by his strongest Armies. The name of King had now a farther operation, and pity of the Vulgar gave a greater Majesty to his Person. Prince Charles also ... was able to raise (as will afterwards appear) not onely Tumults but Wars.[93]

Since the future Charles II played no part in the Second Civil War, this reads like a promise to write a history of the war of Dunbar and Worcester which May was never to fulfill. Immediately, however, he is acknowledging the continued power of the king's sacred authority, while regarding Charles I's exercise of it as altogether malignant. The Second War, like the First, breaks out all over the country, but not because rival commissioners are compelling choice; a series of spontaneous local royalist movements – in London, Surrey, Kent, Wales, Yorkshire – is confronted by local detachments of a dispersed New Model:

Which Army, as when it was conjoyned, in one year, *Anno Dom.* 1646, it quite vanquished and broke all the Kings flourishing strength, and reduced the Kingdom to the obedience of Parliament: so at this time with no less fortitude than felicity, being divided into parts, in all corners of the Kingdom it continued victorious; so that fortitude and fortune might seem in that Army (as the soul in an humane body) to be all in the whole, and all in every part.[94]

May is writing panegyric, but who is the victor – which of parliament and army is the soul and which the body – might admit of some doubt.

These Victories obtained every where by the Parliament, though some of them may seem small, yet will appear great, and worthy of commemoration to all those who consider how much the Common-wealth, if but one of these fights had miscarried, had been endangered; and the Parliament itself, weighing the number and variety of their hazards, may the better acknowledge the continuance of God's providence, and his very hand with them. By these little victories also a way was made for higher Trophies, and an absolute subjugation of all their enemies, which about this Time miraculously happened.[95]

The miracle is provided by Hamilton's Scottish invasion, and it is not more a miracle than a mystery of state, revealed when we consider the divisions in both kingdoms. "The chief Citizens of *London*, and others, called Presbyterians (though the Presbyterian Scots abominated this Scotish Army) wished good success to the Scots, no less than the Malignants did. Whence let the Reader judge of the Times."[96]

Has he forgotten them already, and is he judging himself? After Cromwell's victory at Preston and Fairfax's at Colchester:

It was worthy of noting, that that English Army, which were by the religious Party of *Scotland* called a Bundle of Sectaries, and reviled by all opprobrious names, should now be acknowledged by the same Scots to be the instrument of God, and vindicators both of the Church and Kingdom of *Scotland*. The greatest Peers of *Scotland* also did ingenuously confess their rashness and Error the year before, for accusing this Army as Rebellious, for acting the very same things in *England*, which now themselves were enforced to act in *Scotland*, for preservation of that Kingdom.[97]

If May's eye was already on the preliminaries to Dunbar, as he wrote in 1650, he may not have understood the dynamics of covenanting politics as clearly as he believed. In 1648, however, a greater English denouement was in preparation.

This great change in the councell of *Scotland* had been to be wondred at, if the change that then happened in the English Parliament had not been a greater miracle. Who would not be amazed at this, that Cromwell, for vanquishing a Scotish Army, by which he delivered *England* from the worst of miseries, should be acknowledged there the Preserver of Scotland and not here allowed the Preserver of *England*; and that the same Victory of his against Scots, should please the Presbyterian Scots for Religions sake, and for Religions sake displease the Presbyterians of *England*; *Oedipus* himself cannot unriddle this; especially if he judge according to reason, not according to what Envy, Hate, and embittering Faction can work.[98]

A reason of state which perceived exactly how interests of state and religion were entwined in both kingdoms taken separately might have been equal to Oedipus' task; but May is perhaps the first, certainly not the last to perceive that the word "Presbyterian" was hard to employ informatively in the politics of the House of Commons. The English miracle is about to occur. An ungrateful parliament renews addresses to the king, who,

during this Treaty, found not only great reverence and observance from the Commissioners of Parliament: but was attended with a Prince-like retinue; and was allowed what servants he would choose, to make up the Splendour of a Court...

But while this Treaty proceeded, and some Moneths were spent in debates, concessions, and denyals: Behold another strange alternation happened; which threw the King from the height of honour into the lowest condition. So strangely did one contrary provoke another. Whilest some laboured to advance the King into his Throne again upon slender conditions, or none at all: others weighing what the King had done, what the Commonwealth, and especially what the Presbyterian friends might suffer, if he should come to Raign again with unchanged affections, desired to take him quite away. From hence divers and frequent Petitions were presented to the Parliament, and some to the Generall *Fairfax, That whosoever had offended against the Common-wealth, no person excepted, might come to judgment.*[99]

If this is a miracle, it is a mystery of state; if it is a revolution, it is a turn of Fortune's wheel. The petitions continue, until they are endorsed by the Council of Officers.

But by what means, or what degrees, it came at last so far, as that the King was brought to tryall, condemned and beheaded; because the full search and enarration of so great a business would make a History by it self, it cannot well be brought into this Breviary, which having passed over so long a Time, shall here conclude. FINIS.[100]

Once again, May breaks off at a point where we are left wondering whether he intended a continuation and why he did not supply one. This time, we know the answer to the latter question; May died in November 1650. *Tom May's Death* insists that he died drunk, and John Aubrey, a less hostile witness, concurs: "Came of his death after drinking with his chin tyed with his cap (being fatt); suffocated."[101] It could well be true; nevertheless the derisive history of Tom May has begun. The text of the *Breviary* suggests that he did intend a continuation, and that it would have been a history of the king's trial and death strongly inclined to the view that Charles I was guilty as charged. Would it have been in Latin, intended like Milton's for a foreign audience? This raises the further question by whom it would have been commissioned: by the Council of State, or by some faction within the Rump Parliament? Had May, the sometime translator of Lucan, become a republican as well as a regicide in his sympathies? The question is not pursued here.

It has been one aim of this chapter to establish that Thomas May was, and is, not a negligible man. As a historian, he has several claims on our attention. He was one of the very first to attempt – if he did not complete – a serious history of the Civil Wars, written according to the historiographical canons of the time, as these were modified by the profound shock of civil war itself. The question of which side he was on – though his partisanship hardened in his later writing – was, as he knew and said, marginal to the deeper problem of how history could and must be written in time of civil war; and here he not only displayed classical and

Tacitist historiography under seventeenth-century stress, but began
instructing English historians as to the problems they must confront in
the times to come, once the War of the Three Kingdoms and the
English Civil War had broken out. We read texts with an eye to the
construction of the discourses of which they form part; and here May,
with his consciousness of how quickly one's thoughts could change and
be buried in one's memory in times of the confusions and revolutions of
government, warns us against supposing that we can be present at the
first invention of a discourse, or at any moment when its construction
can be said to have been completed. Perhaps we need to consider how
events challenge the human capacity to construct discourse, and even
impose themselves on the discourses constructed to meet them. Not only
the events selected by Thomas May as crucial in constituting the English
Civil Wars, but the historiographical problems with which he saw that
they faced him, are – though his interpretations are not – those with
which the most modern of revisionists are still dealing: why was there in
England a war at all? How did Charles I find a party to fight for him?
Did English events determine the course of things in the Three Kingdoms? He knew, as his contemporaries did, what they needed and we
still need to know; problems that continue to challenge historians "by
Tradition, and the weight of their owne Fame."[102]

CHAPTER 7

Samuel Parker, Andrew Marvell, and political culture, 1667–73

Derek Hirst

Establishing what we mean by the phrase "political culture" seems more than usually problematic for the England of the later 1660s. In that time of confusion, the failure of a unitary body politic to survive the shocks of civil war and revolution became ever more apparent. Mounting ecclesiastical trench-warfare between resentful Anglicans and non-conformists of varying degrees of remorse ran parallel to a sequence of military and political disasters, with the Dutch in the Medway in 1667 and the Earl of Clarendon in flight. A resurgent aristocratic culture flourished amid theatrical grandeur, while a burgeoning market-place testified to the emergence of what is often called a middle class. Over all hung the apocalypticism of plague and fire. Such developments, we may assume, had their own internal energies – energies that sometimes seem so autonomous that it is easier to talk of a series of local or sectional cultures than a shared political culture.

Yet however diverse those developments and energies, they overlapped temporally. They must therefore have inflected one another, and have left traces of their encounters and transactions. It is the assumption of this chapter that only a broad reading across the textual register of a moment allows us to recognize such traces and inflexions, and thus to reconstitute what can plausibly be termed a political culture – however partisan and fragmented that culture may sometimes seem. N. H. Keeble has recently argued cogently for a "literary culture of nonconformity"; but was it as separate as he suggests when he claims that the "nonconformist writer ... [was] a distinctive literary persona"?[1] Partisans frequently sought to differentiate themselves from the world, but that is no reason for us to take them wholly at their (occasional and partisan) representations. Men and women live neither by bread nor by party alone. There is much to learn, of politics, religion, and culture alike, from partisan representations;[2] but we now know that even in a narrowly defined political life divisions were usually fluid.[3] If we allow

ourselves to read outside the self-selecting categories of sources, we may
find there was traffic between imaginative literature and the polemics of
religion, between the audiences of the theater and the meeting-house,
between the literary patron and the political partisan. Such traffic may
provide new evidence not just of the meaning but also of the dynamics of
political culture.

The years around 1670 witnessed what has been called the first
Restoration crisis. At the heart of that crisis lay a controversy over
conscience that extended from the disasters of the Anglo/Dutch War
and the fall of Clarendon in 1667 to the defeat with the Test Act of 1673
of Charles's policy of Indulgence to religious dissenters.[4] The long-term
efforts of the bishops and their allies to impose a tighter discipline than
that Charles had appeared to promise in the Declaration of Breda took
on a new urgency in these years as competing groups sought to interpret
the providential signs of plague, fire, and humiliation in the Dutch War.
The Conventicle Act, the first of the repressive measures of 1665–7,
added heavy penalties to non-conformist worship; the Five Mile Act two
years later took the new holy war to the non-conforming clergy by
barring them from corporate towns.[5] Such stringent measures triggered
a two-fold reaction: dissenter pamphleteers campaigned for a relaxation
of sanctions against a minority whose loyalty and productivity they
trumpeted,[6] while in parliament there were attempts in 1668–9 to gain
relief for moderate and respectable non-conformists, either through
comprehension within a broader Church of England or through a
measure of toleration outside it.[7] The Anglican counter was immediate
and powerful. Most obviously, the second Conventicle Act of 1670 –
"the Quintessence of arbitrary Malice," in Andrew Marvell's words[8] –
replaced the lapsed 1665 statute with a broader measure. As provocative
in the eyes of many dissenters was the Anglican onslaught in press and
pulpit. This countered demands for leniency by detailing and polemiciz-
ing the responsibility of the non-conforming conscience for England's
woes, past and present. Civil war, revolution, and regicide had been the
work of enthusiasts; and, eager conformists warned, the strains of
enthusiasm could still be heard in meetings and conventicles, its texts
encountered in the bookshops and streets. By the end of the 1660s there
had developed a thoroughgoing Anglican critique of non-conformist
discourse, the means – it was alleged – by which old evils were perpetuated.

For Restoration dissenters, as for the godly preachers of an earlier
generation, the task was to communicate with "spirit and power" the

immediacy of the religious experience. Such communication necessarily involved rhetorical skills, of voice and metaphor. The fabric may once have been "homespun," as befitted the "plain style" that was the vehicle of choice for godly expositors, but preachers and other dissenters had often settled into patterns that invited the accusation of "canting" leveled by critics.[9] The anxiety occasioned by these developments is palpable in the writings of that elevated Quaker, William Penn. Penn felt driven to begin his major work of 1669 with an apologia: "My matter, stile and method speak not the least premeditation or singularity, but that simplicity and truth which plainly show the affectionate sincerity of my heart, best wishes for your true happiness..."[10] Penn's discomfort seems to have stemmed not simply from the political and social burdens borne by "enthusiasm" in the aftermath of a failed revolution, but also from a widespread intellectual disdain for the techniques of representation deployed by "enthusiasts." For in these years, Latitudinarians were busily resituating the conscience closer to the intellect.[11] The controversy had its moments of lasting value. Thomas Sprat's *History of the Royal Society* (1667) famously conjures metaphor and political evil in a broad cultural and social program, while Milton's three great poems, that embedded style firmly in the conscience, were published in these years between the Fire and the Test Act. But neither Sprat nor Milton sounded the dominant notes.

Simon Patrick, future Bishop of Ely, set the terms of much of the contest over the politics of style in his 1669 tract, *A Friendly Debate between a Conformist and a Nonconformist*. One of the first salvos had been by the Independent leader John Owen in *A Peace Offering* (1667), a work that showed considerable interest in the problem of communicating and representing truth.[12] Patrick seized on the challenge, inveighing relentlessly against non-conformist discursive techniques. In so doing, he advanced a pointed assessment of the concerns of his foes, whose anxiety to communicate with "spirit and power" he recognized;[13] their claims to spiritual experience were, he maintained like Hobbes before him, inherently untestable.[14] Taking his cue from Owen's own language, his attack focused not on epistemology but on representation: the means the dissenters used to assert their claims were fundamentally illegitimate, mere pulpit tricks. The godly preachers' insistent deployment of "melting Tones, pretty Similitudes, riming Sentences, kind and loving Smiles, and sometimes dismally-sad Looks," were a "Puppet-play," aimed to move the "Senses and Imaginations" of the audience rather than their "Reason and Judgement." As he argued this, Patrick came very close to a sociology of hearing: "the better sort of Hearers are now out of love with these things."[15]

Patrick provoked his foes on two fronts. Polemic by what professed to be dialogue was of course a familiar ploy; but when non-conformist nerves were already sensitive, Patrick's decision to couch his plea for reason and judgment, his denunciation of appeals to the emotions, in the avowedly fictive form of an imagined debate rubbed them raw. The content of the "debate," friendly or otherwise, offered further provocation. At one level, as Patrick Collinson has recently reminded us, any sermon "must be properly appreciated, not as some kind of text . . . but as performance."[16] In times of religious contest, charges of hypocrisy and showmanship were therefore bound to be polemical mainstays. But in denouncing pulpit theatricality Patrick also turned on his enemies their own complaints against that other bugbear of the 1660s, the playhouse.[17] The ensuing cries of foul play testify to his success. The presbyterian Samuel Rolle retorted sourly, "Who so *mimical*, so *Theatrical* in a Pulpit, as some amongst your selves? Of whom it is said, that it is as good to hear them preach, as to see a play."[18] John Owen similarly lamented Patrick's exploitation of poetic form and literary artifice in an encounter Owen judged but "Dramatick or Romantick," while John Humfrey – a more searching political thinker than most of the other protagonists – politely if pointedly regretted that "Religion should be brought as it were on the Stage, and made Comical in the *Friendly Debate*."[19]

Patrick's friends too could see advantage in locating the struggle to control the conscience in the polemics over the stage. The controversy excited by Patrick was slight compared to the storm aroused by the exuberant Samuel Parker, future Bishop of Oxford, whose *Discourse of Ecclesiastical Politie* was published in 1670. While, as we shall see, Parker's attitude to the controversy over the stage was complex,[20] he left no doubt by his extended metaphors of his desire to put the dissenters there. The "fanatics," in his analysis,

derive all their religious motions and phantasms from the present state and constitution of their Bodies, and move only upon the stage of Fancy, and according as sanguine or melancholy are predominant, so the Scene alters. Sometimes their bloud runs low, their spirits are weak and languid, melancholy reeks and vapours cloud and overwhelm their Fancies, and then the Scene is all Tragedy, and they are immediately under *spiritual desertions* and troubles of Conscience . . .[21]

It was no wonder that Owen, dismissing "the last Act" of the "Tragical Preface," claimed to see in Parker the playwright as much as the man of

God; or that Humfrey should have thought to provide stage-directions for Parker's final dispatch: "So let us leave that Hero to his Victory, in the *Sella Curulis* of his own Imagination. Sound Drums and Trumpets. *Exit* the brave Author: One carrying off the Slain. *Vox Episcopi plaudite.*"[22] And most famously, Andrew Marvell's *The Rehearsal Transpros'd* (1672), with its nod to Buckingham's play *The Rehearsal*, insistently conflated Parker with the playwright "Bayes." Marvell's, we may now appreciate, was not the singular gesture it is sometimes thought. Like many other gestures in the controversy, less sustained and successful though they were, it reflected and manifested Restoration sensitivities to the stage and to ecclesiastical style alike.

A broad jockeying for cultural position was in progress. If Owen excoriated Patrick for his exploitation of poetic form and literary artifice to depict a debate "Romantick" as well as "Dramatick," Samuel Rolle went further, denouncing Patrick and his allies for "a Romance way of preaching and writing Divinity, as if they meant to Evangelize Sr. Philip Sydney, and thought that all Divinity might well be planted within the Compass of his Arcadia."[23] Rolle's jibe makes clear the magnitude of the issues of literary decorum that confronted the warriors for conscience at the close of the Restoration's first decade. Patrick and Parker charged that neither style nor conscience could be freed from the burdens of the past, and it seems likely that at least some non-conformists agreed. If John Milton sought to justify God's ways to man in works that vindicated literary style almost as insistently as they did divine providence, Samuel Rolle sneered at partisan abuse of Sidney's legacy by – surely deliberately – conjuring the memory of the encounter of Milton's *Eikonoklastes* with *Eikon Basilike.*[24]

As the nation's rifts seemed to open once more, most dissenters strenuously disclaimed any "enthusiastic" heritage. They strove instead for some piece of a middle ground that they were trying hard to establish and define through style as much as tenet. The late Richard Ashcraft observed that around 1670 a suggestive clustering of non-conformist works appeared blazoning "reason" in their titles.[25] The ubiquity of the claim, and the posture, did not always make for clarity of polemical strategy, as we might infer from the single greatest publishing event of these years. Between 1670 and 1672 John Eachard's *The Grounds and Occasions of the Contempt of the Clergy and Religion* went through eight editions. Eachard directed his stance of intellectual superiority at the pulpit foibles of the inadequately educated; and, to judge by the reception, he struck a chord. What we ought to find instructive is the difficulty of readers, then and now, in establishing Eachard's partisan affiliations. His book was denounced, variously, by John Owen and by George Herbert's publisher;[26] even Anthony à Wood, that astute observer of academic print politics, was taken aback when he found Eachard, the apparent scourge of pulpit folly, closeted with the high-priest of intransigence, Samuel Parker, at one of the Archbishop of Canterbury's dinner parties.[27] But whatever Eachard's covert politics, his overt injunctions to urbanity secured him an eager audience.

The traffic between style and conscience might even be called the defining polemical issue of the middle years of Charles II's reign. It drew from Ferguson "the plotter" a 700-page defense of metaphor;[28] and of course it elicited from Andrew Marvell one of the most successful polemics of the reign. Style was also the issue in the opening words of the preface to Parker's *Discourse of Ecclesiastical Politie*. Parker's tone was far from Penn's, and among his purposes was the defense of Patrick's use or abuse of literary forms. Keeble has recounted Parker's eager participation in the debate Patrick had initiated;[29] but he does not note the tell-tale character of the non-conformist protests at Parker's own rhetorical ploys and railings. As one critic observed disdainfully – and with the obvious sympathy of both Owen and Humfrey – had the *Discourse* "been condited to the present Gust of the Age, by Language, Wit, or Drollery, it might have found some entertainment in the world[, b]ut downright dirty Railing, is beneath the genius of the Times."[30] The role of such condemnation in spurring Parker to return to the fray with his *Defence and Continuation* is clear. Parker's renewed and lengthy defense of Patrick's choice of the debate form, and his further excoriation of John Owen's metaphor and "cant," render unmistakable the links among expressive form, decorum, and church discipline.[31]

Marvell's general strategy in *The Rehearsal Transpros'd* seems clear enough. As Keeble has argued, he undoubtedly sought to identify the "farcical inconsequentiality" of Parker as churchman with Buckingham's fictional "Bayes," a composite of Dryden and Davenant, as dramatist.[32] We might surmise that Marvell was moved to select an oddly theatrical title and motif for a devastating ecclesiastical satire not merely by contempt for Parker's churchmanship or by the opportunist desire to attach the controversy over conscience to the equally heated squabbles over the stage. Literary rivalry was of course also involved, since in his tribute to Milton's *Paradise Lost* Marvell showed his distaste for Dryden, coupling reference to the "bays" of glory with derision for those who wrote in rhyme.[33] And we could go further. It was the universal assumption – one that Patrick and Parker had themselves made manifest – that arms and arts marched in concert. Milton clearly sought to establish a certain religious, and perhaps political, position on the highest of literary ground; we might assume that Marvell's objectives were not unconnected. At the very least, charges of partisanship and scurrility might be deflected by the posture of literary competition.

Yet such argument cannot adequately explain the title nor the repeated swipes in Marvell's text at "Bayes," that ludicrous composite. These are after all the most immediately visible gestures in a work which in all other respects is fiercely engaged in partisan politics. That the puzzle has remained so long unexamined, let alone unanswered, stems from a modern intellectual bias: historians, political and literary alike, have often focused on a writer's overt arguments, especially when those arguments have seemed principled. But other signals might better identify the direction in which an argument is pointing. We have Marvell himself, or rather Archbishop Laud mediated by Marvell, as our authority for an approach that would look more widely. Toward the end of *The Rehearsal Transpros'd* Marvell recited Archbishop Abbot's testimony that his successor at Canterbury, and nemesis, Laud, "made it his work to see what Books were in the Press, and to look over Epistles Dedicatory, and Prefaces to the Reader, to see what faults might be found."[34] Historians might learn from that great scholar of the politics of texts to suspect the packaging as well as the substantive content.

There is a further problem in the assumption that Marvell folded Parker into Dryden-as-Bayes simply in order to combine an argument by analogy with some literary oneupmanship. In the years around 1670, an important juncture in the complex history of the relations of the Church of England with its critics, Dryden and Marvell stood in important respects much closer together than did Dryden and Parker. The ideological point of conflating the latter pair might therefore have been lost on readers had they had no other signals by which to steer. Indeed, the author of one dissenter elegy of 1669 seems to have had only positive feelings for the court's poet, proclaiming defiantly, "one Scene of Dryden springs more noble fire" than all the works of Simon Patrick.[35] It is essential to locate Dryden on the political map if we are to understand how and why he came to be folded into Parker; but the difficulty of such an enterprise is manifested by an incident recounted by one of Parker's foes. One day in the winter of 1669–70 a mother and her ten-year-old son, fresh from a performance of John Dryden's *Tyrannick Love*, came across a group of neighbors in the street discussing Patrick's

Friendly Debate and Parker's *Discourse of Ecclesiastical Politie*. The boy's
immediate response to the neighbors' conversation was to register that
the ecclesiastical controversialists and the poet laureate appeared to be
in colloquy, but not perhaps in sympathy. For as the schoolboy critic
noted, it was Dryden's tyrannical male lead, John Lacy, who had
asserted claims over conscience to match those his mother's friends had
found in the churchmen's books.[36] Marvell, manifestly a wide-ranging
reader in the literature of conscience and controversy, could have been
paraphrasing both our dissenting elegist and our theater-going schoolboy in his comment, "One turn of Lacy's face hath more Ecclesiastical
Policy in it, than all [Parker's] Books ... put together."[37]

Warm regard for Dryden the dramatist amongst Parker's foes is
scarcely inexplicable. We readily assume that the prime opponents of a
doctrinaire ecclesiastical establishment were the dissenters and those
who might soon be labeled Deists.[38] Such stalwarts of what was to
become radical Whiggery were part of the constituency at which
Charles II aimed with his 1672 Declaration of Indulgence, and which
James II targeted for very different reasons after 1686. Yet in *Tyrannick
Love*, Dryden, poet laureate, historiographer royal, the dominant figure
of the London stage, upheld the martyr for conscience against the
ruler who sought to tyrannize over conscience. Part of Dryden's plot
was clearly compliment, as the Catholic St. Catherine glanced at
Charles's Catholic wife Catherine of Braganza. But we cannot explain
away so easily the denunciations of priestcraft and assertions of religious relativism in his *The Indian Emperor* of 1666–8 and *The Conquest of
Granada* of 1671–2. In his most popular plays, written in the years of
controversy between the Conventicle Act of 1665 and the Test Act of
1673, the poet laureate repeatedly scrutinized the claims of religious
orthodoxy and controls over conscience. As one versifier claimed in
the summer of 1668, "Playhouse turns to Conventicle."[39] Why then
should Marvell, in his eagerness to destroy that bully of orthodoxy
Samuel Parker, have done so by adding to the discomfiture of Dryden,
perhaps the most visible, and certainly the most fashionable, critic of
intolerance?

The awkwardness and the silences with which historians and critics
alike have covered Marvell's motives stem from their understandable
tendency to read the controversy over conscience in its own ringing
terms. As we have come to learn, conscience could never be seen (as we
tend now to see it) as simply the site of principled commitment. Bridging the public and the private as it did,[40] it all too easily gave rise to the

ad hominem arguments that Marvell and Parker, like most of their contemporaries, vented with such gusto. But while the expression of conscience necessarily involved representation, and invited charges of dissimulation as it became entangled with issues of style and decorum, conscience itself was inextricably bound up with politics, and with contingency.[41] Charles's apparent readiness to protect tender consciences with successive Declarations of Indulgence certainly left Marvell by 1672 rather more favorably disposed toward an indulgent king than he had been five years earlier, at the time of *The Last Instructions*.[42] A king who was less than the nursing-father of the church left Anglican intransigents predictably alarmed. Marvell, equally predictably, did all he could to heighten their embarrassment. But the Anglican bully was more adroit than has sometimes been noticed as he negotiated these difficulties.

Parker poured his vicious and inflated rhetoric on the dissenters in general and in particular on John Owen, formerly Cromwell's chaplain and vice-chancellor under Cromwell of Parker's own university of Oxford. It was from Owen and his ilk, Parker alleged, that all evils in state as well as church flowed. And it was to their defense that Marvell ostensibly sprang – and, as John Wallace showed, with ostentatious moderation and learning as well as wit. Yet Owen was not Parker's only concern, for Parker's various works during the controversy also reveal an interesting tension surrounding Hobbes. Several contemporaries noted, and Gordon Schochet has effectively demonstrated, Parker's ambivalence about Hobbes, at one moment borrowing arguments for the magistrate's jurisdiction over conscience and at another bashing Malmesburian atheism.[43] Anglican unease about the great philosopher had of course been heightened by the fear that the disasters of the mid-1660s might have been providential.[44] Yet Parker's dilemma was more immediate; and it was the manifest inconsistencies in his *Preface* to *Bishop Bramhall's Vindication of Himself*, the work that followed the 1672 Declaration of Indulgence, that Marvell most eagerly exploited, that gave him his greatest opening, and perhaps even occasioned the whole riposte. On the one hand, Charles's Indulgence jolted rigid churchmen like Parker who had in 1670 imagined a devotedly episcopalian Hobbesian sovereign. On the other hand, and just as importantly, Parker had recognized that he had two enemies in view: overtly, Owen and his fellow dissenters, against whom Hobbes could be deployed, at least up to 1672; and covertly – and for reasons that we shall explore – all that was represented by Dryden's fashionable relativism, for which

"Hobbism" sometimes stood as a tag. In Parker's analysis, Hobbism, "as odd as it is, is become the Standard of our Modern Politicks swallowed down, with as much greediness as an Article of Faith, by the Wild and Giddy People of the Age." If he had in mind the enthusiasms of the theatergoers, we might conclude with modern Drydenists that Parker was exaggerating, and that Dryden was really a Pyrrhonian rather than a Hobbist.[45] But Christianity did occupy a distinctly relativist position in the poet laureate's plays,[46] and the audiences seem to have loved it.

Parker's dilemma, and his strategy, is reflected in the structure of his books. While he belabored the dissenters in the texts proper, in the extended prefaces he denounced the ridicule and derision to which the clergy were everywhere subject, as the fashionable made war on "priestcraft."[47] "Making religion ridiculous" became very much a catch-phrase of clerical lament in the years around 1670.[48] The reasons for this, and for the particular character of Restoration wit, are not hard to seek. The many "revolutions in affairs" since 1640 had provided abundant ammunition for charges of hypocrisy against all those claiming to ground their public courses on personal faith; episcopal reassertion since 1660 on the one hand and dissenter regrouping on the other helped give partisan focus to those charges. It scarcely required a classical education to recognize that satire was *the* weapon against fraud and pretension. Parker opened the preface to his *Discourse* by reflecting on his own and Simon Patrick's treatment of their foes, and he pointedly modified the standard defense of true zeal, Christ's assault on the Pharisees. He presented the Savior instead as the first satirist.[49] But while clergy of all stripes castigated their enemies either for striving to make the true religion ridiculous or for conduct such as ludicrous pulpit techniques that brought it willy-nilly into derision,[50] Parker shot his bolt in another direction. Repeatedly and at length he located the church's problems in that fashionable and witty culture that found its center on the Restoration stage.[51] Such a charge has implications for the wider dynamics of Restoration politics and culture, and for modern theories of cultural exchange. The argument of Parker's prefaces seems to offer comfort to exponents of cultural trickle-down: the fashionable vices and irreligion of the elite corrupted the manners and minds of the ordinary townspeople. These, Parker was confident, formed the constituency of dissent.[52] But Parker insisted that the guilt of the wits and of the poets, playwrights, and romancers who catered to them was primarily political, not moral. Such guilt too might be thought a matter of trickle-down, and Richard Allestree, for example, preaching before the king in 1667 cited the complicity of the elite in the erosion of authorities: "They that hear men droll on God Almighty ... will quickly learn to speak with little reverence of their Superiors."[53] But Parker's thoughts ran along a different track. With his eyes presumably fixed on Milton as well as lesser men, he traced the origins of republican thought and practice firmly to the poets (and not, as Hobbes might have had it, to the philosophers) of ancient Greece. There, "scarce any one could pretend to a little skill in Poetry or Wrastling (their two greatest accomplishments) but he must immediately be an Undertaker for new modelling the Commonwealth."[54] Wrong courses in church as well as state were inseparably connected with wrong cultural values. As Parker insisted, it was not only the clergy who had reason to fear: "The Principles of irreligion unjoynt the Sinews, and blow up the very Foundations of Government: This turns all sense of Loyalty into Folly." Indeed, "At the same time they shake hands with Religion, they bid adieu to Loyalty."[55]

We are now in a better position to appreciate Parker's strategy, and thus Marvell's counter. Parker was certainly, and above all, alarmed at the threat to the Church of England posed by dissenters like Owen who saw in the fall of Clarendon in 1667 an opportunity to appeal to the king for a renewal of Indulgence. But although dissenters might threaten the whole arch of church and state, they scarcely constituted in themselves a present danger. As Parker repeatedly made clear in his prefaces, they were marginalized, confined to disreputable trading and conventicling quarters. The real threat lay in the conjunction of dissenters with atheistical wits and machiavellian or discontented statesmen.[56] Parker's predicament here commands some sympathy. Drawn to Hobbes (at least before Charles's second Declaration of Indulgence in 1672) for the blunt espousal of the magistrate's power of coercion, he was yet repelled by the atheistical air that some found so attractive in the philosopher. The claim that religion is a fraud perpetrated by self-interested clergy "is become," he complained, "the most powerful and fashionable Argument for the Toleration of all ... [T]he Reason, why I have thus far pursued this Principle, is, because 'tis become the most powerful Patron of the Fanatick Interest; and a Belief of the Indifferency, or rather Imposture of all Religion, is now made the most Effectual (not to say most Fashionable) Argument for Liberty of Conscience."[57] The claim that fanaticism found its patron in a dangerously fashionable skepticism was central to Parker's purpose.

The protests of Owen and others at Parker's railings were beside the point, for he was speaking past them.[58] Parker's long engagement with Hobbes suggests as much, for the sage of Malmesbury was scarcely an author dear to the dissenters. Parker railed at and caricatured the dissenters, and thumped the tub endlessly about the social and political rather than ecclesiastical threat they represented, to draw the attention of a polite audience, and to warn it.[59] As he said at the outset, "I never proposed to my self any other aim in this following Discourse, than, by representing the palpable inconsistency of Fanatique Tempers and Principles with the Welfare and security of Government, to awaken Authority to beware of its worst and most dangerous Enemies."[60] In fact, he particularized even further, for what he was most concerned to warn against was a single figure.

However gratifying to churchmen of a certain stripe the Clarendon Code, they could not find even the second Conventicle Act of 1670 wholly reassuring. The king's commitment to the church of his father, called in doubt by the 1662 Indulgence, was scarcely reaffirmed by the ministers who replaced Clarendon after 1667. We do not need to rely on Parker alone to conclude that the most worrisome to the churchmen were not the crypto-Catholics like Clifford and Arlington. The real worry centered on Buckingham, who had worked with Owen in 1668 to try to rally support for a toleration bill in parliament, and who was widely credited with responsibility for the 1672 Indulgence. At the first reading of the Declaration in one London parish church, a member of the congregation was reported to have "cried, *the Devil take George* [Duke of Buckingham]." When Robert Wild closed "Poetica Licentia," his panegyric "upon His Majesties Gracious Declaration," he had his Conformist parody of one of Patrick's "friendly debaters'" lament, "But Oh, the Grandees now about the King, / They, they procured this Licentious Thing. / Some men there be that carry all before 'em; / The D. of Lauderdale is of the Quorum; / And Geo. of Buck. is Dux Malorum."[61]

Parker could therefore have been confident that his signals would be picked up. The general claim of the preface to his *Discourse of Ecclesiastical Politie* that atheism to republicanism was near allied gained political substance in the text. "'Tis not impossible but there may be a sort of Proud and Haughty men among us (not over-well affected to Monarchick Government) who, though they scorn, yet patronize this Humour, as a check to the Insolence and Presumption of Princes." By the time of the third work in Parker's polemical series, his *Preface to Bishop Bramhall's*

Vindication of Himself, the attack on the Duke of Buckingham was not very covert. Lamenting the 1672 Indulgence and asserting the independence of church and churchmen, Parker inveighed against those wits who allied with the sectaries to betray the king. "Atheism and Enthusiasm are apart and by themselves the most desperate and dangerous causes of Misery and Calamity to Mankind; but when they combine Interests and join Forces against a common Enemy, what Government can withstand their Fury? ... Especially if in the third place, it should ever so fall out, that crafty and sacrilegious States-men should join themselves into the Confederacy ..." Parker then went on to point unmistakably at the dissolute duke when he instanced those who would debauch the king, encouraging his "ill Inclinations," even "by the meanest and most dishonourable Services."[62]

That thrust opened the door to Andrew Marvell, who replied to Parker in a work of corruscating wit that, abundant evidence shows, was eagerly read by friend and foe alike. It is no coincidence that Marvell wrote one of the most effective pieces of controversy of his age explicitly in answer to the slightest of Parker's three blasts, his *Preface* to *Bishop Bramhall.* As John Spurr has recently shown, Bramhall was a key figure in the resurgent episcopalianism of the Restoration, so Parker's use of him made his own distasteful episcopalianism all the clearer.[63] It was also the *Preface* that contained the clearest strike at Buckingham. Marvell, with a long history of attachment to the duke stretching back to the 1650s,[64] saw a way to combine the polite gesture of clientage with politics of a very different kind.

We can therefore understand more fully the occasion of Marvell's sally into prose controversy. Parker was driven by the changed conditions of 1672 to abandon his earlier almost Hobbesian espousal of royal power in causes ecclesiastical, and to trumpet instead that doughty ecclesiastical warrior Bishop Bramhall; and he explained to himself and the world this change of course by sharpening his thrusts against Buckingham. Marvell seized this chance not only to expose inconsistency while defending conscience but also to appear on behalf of his patron. It must have been the most congenial of moments. Such espousal of the cause of principle in the course of doing personal service may serve as an object-lesson to those today who seek to detach and distinguish. We might then assume that Marvell chose the form he did, attaching his own work of satire to Buckingham's, in order to make explicit the salute to his friend and to assure himself of the widest audience. But such an argument still does not quite solve the conundrum of Marvell's apparent readiness to involve Dryden, himself a foe of the ecclesiastics, in the charge. Nor does it square with his own explanation of why he chose to call Parker "Bayes."

Much of the account Marvell gave at the start of *The Rehearsal Transpros'd* of what he was about makes perfect sense. Dryden seems to have fit the bill as Marvell drew it up. Parker's penchant for the appearance of anonymity while very publicly cudgeling others paralleled the conduct of the theatrical Bayes in literary controversy. More particularly, in their quarrelsomeness, and in their strident conviction of their respective superiority as stylists, they bore considerable likeness. As Marvell's editor notes, it was through such characteristics that Buckingham drew Dryden-as-Bayes in *The Rehearsal.* There is no mistaking the gusto with which the satirist pursued Parker through the labyrinth of the latter's works; nor is there any doubt of his delight in seconding his patron's ridicule of Dryden. Yet the last item in Marvell's account poses difficulties: "both their Talents do peculiarly lie in exposing and personating the Nonconformists."[65] Such an account would fit Dryden in 1682, at the height of his attack on dissenters and Exclusionists; but not ten years earlier when the object of his criticism seemed to be the High-Churchmen. Since this is the only reference to ecclesiastical issues in Marvell's explanation, and since the whole of *The Rehearsal Transpros'd* revolves around the connection between Bayes and ecclesiastical polemic, it is clear that we need to probe a little further into Marvell's purposes.

Marvell had a third target in view. Apart from some lines of John Ogilby characterizing Bishop Bramhall, the only English poet whom Marvell quotes at length in *The Rehearsal Transpros'd* is Sir William Davenant. More signally, it is not any recent Davenant but the Davenant of *Gondibert*, some twenty years earlier, who is held up to ridicule at both beginning and end of Marvell's text. And that earlier Davenant had had no qualms about "exposing and personating the Nonconformists." It was in the separately published *Preface* to *Gondibert* that Davenant, together with Hobbes, had with "Arrogance and Dictature" sought to impose "stile ... Wit ... Language ... on the world."[66] It was in the *Preface* too that Davenant distanced himself from those who adopted "a pennance of gravity," whose "inspiration is a spiritual Fitt," whose religion consisted like that of the Jews "in a sullen separation of themselves from the rest of humane flesh ... [in] a fantastical pride of their own cleanness."[67] Dryden's *Essay of Dramatic Poesy* laid him open to Buckingham's ridicule as a dictator of style; but Davenant too had sought to lay down the literary law, in the *Preface* to *Gondibert*. And Davenant, much more than the Dryden of 1672, had ridden out to do battle with the self-proclaimed godly.

The figure of Bayes was not therefore simply a contingent means of sending up Parker for his grandiloquence, and of offering a tribute to the patron. The presence of Davenant's *Preface* to *Gondibert* in Marvell's text suggests something far more purposive. The significance for Marvell of the issue of heroic style can be judged from the way he introduced the figure of Parker's Bishop Bramhall, the occasion of the satire. At that point he unleashed dozens of lines of condemnation of the false heroism of romance: "By the Language he seems to transcribe out of the *Grand-Cyrus* and *Cassandra*, but the Exploits to have borrowed out of the *Knight of the Sun*, and *King Arthur*."[68] The words suit Davenant's Gondibert as much as they do Dryden's Almanzor. Marvell's engagement extends beyond Parker's over-writing and buffoonery to include the heroic style as a whole; and the founding text of that style had been *Gondibert* and its *Preface*.

To reconstitute Bayes as the personification of the heroic style is to appreciate the complexity of Marvell's concerns. Certainly he had partisan purposes, since he aimed to make Parker a laughing-stock; and certainly he intended an important service to his patron. But he had as well other work to do. At one level we might confidently imagine literary competition with, or personal animosity for, Dryden; but there was more. Marvell had his own interest – political, personal, aesthetic – in the figure of the hero,[69] and he certainly had his own sense of the proper style.

We might surmise therefore that Marvell folded Davenant/Dryden into the figure of Parker no less eagerly than he folded Parker into the figure of Davenant/Dryden. He hoped in each case to annihilate the one by means of the other: Parker's churchmanship was no less distasteful than was the aesthetic excrescence represented by Bayes. But of course in neither case can we segregate. Parker's churchmanship was compounded with theatricality, while the political and social implications of "Bayes" and his aesthetics had long been apparent. In 1650 Davenant had after all assiduously paid tribute to "Courts and Camps."[70] Though the royal Declaration of Indulgence in 1672 complicated matters, leaving Marvell arguing warily for a tolerationist king whose drift to absolutism he was to condemn five years later in *The Growth of Popery and Arbitrary Government*,[71] on the whole the early years of the Restoration had only clarified the political drift of "Bayes" toward his mentor Thomas Hobbes.[72] Marvell would have felt vindicated had he known that at just the time he was formulating *The Rehearsal Transpros'd* the Earl of Sandwich, President of the Council of Trade and military hero, was arguing that the dissident colony of Massachusetts Bay should be reduced to obedience through saturation with "orthodox bookes, poetry, common Ballads."[73] The poet who was also an MP knew only too well the persuasive force of works of the imagination.

And who is to say that Marvell did not vanquish Bayes on both fronts? On the one hand, the age of the heroic style, whether in poetry or drama, quickly came to an end. And on the other, *The Rehearsal Transpros'd* – which an amused king refused to suppress – perhaps played its part in the swing of opinion in the House of Commons away from Parkerian orthodoxy. In 1670, with discipline ascendant, the House had coupled the passing of the second Conventicle Act against dissenters with an attempt to tax playhouses. In 1673 an attempt to couple the Test Act with relief for dissenters seemed on the verge of success when members were sent home.

The implications of Marvell's attempt to connect the controversy over conscience to the world of the stage and of heroic style are worth pursuing further. The assumption has run fairly widely that the arenas of polite culture and of the non-conformist churches were almost wholly separate, and that those like Milton and Marvell who might have felt some kinship with both were unusual.[74] Into this assumption we have been led not least by the countless partisans who joined the Earl of Clarendon or John Bunyan in arguing that non-conformists turned their fronts against, or their backs on, the world. Richard Ashcraft certainly sought to challenge that presumption insofar as it might apply to John Locke and his friends, but his focus on the radical underground was not primarily directed toward revealing cultural cross-currents.[75] We might learn more from all those who joined Marvell in setting Parker's *Discourse* in a literary context: Owen, Humfrey, the anonymous controversialist who linked his own effort to the "Advice to the Painter" satires of the previous three years.[76] Non-conformity was surely part of a broad literary culture. Milton's verse is not the only warrant for this; so too is the long verse elegy for "Mris. G. E. lately Deceased." That elegy ranges from the spiritual virtues of the lady in question, to Dryden, *Macbeth*, fashionable actors, Patrick's *Friendly Debate*, and pulpit style.[77]

What we might properly call the political culture of the Restoration reveals a host of interconnections, and these complicate any attempt to assess the intent and audience, rather than merely the argument, of a work. The ten-year-old and his mother who could move so easily from Dryden's heroic drama to a street discussion of the leading works of ecclesiastical controversy must challenge academic tunnel vision. Equally arresting is the fusillade of sniping at Dryden's plays that burst from the wits in 1673. Dryden's most prominent work of the moment, *The Conquest of Granada*, gained its notoriety above all from the heroic posturing of its central character, Almanzor, whose unmatchable strength was coupled with an indifference to, indeed a transcendence of, conventional ties to monarchs and faiths. Dryden provided a broad target. And as they drafted Harrington's old discussion group into the very title of the first squib, *The Censure of the Rota*, Dryden's calumniators proclaimed the existence of a political matrix for what might otherwise seem efforts by jealous rivals to debunk the poet laureate and his creations. *The Censure*, which imagined Dryden a member of the republican club of 1659–60, repeatedly accused him of inhabiting a "Poeticall Free-State," fashioning republican utopias whose inspiration derived variously from Columbus and Thomas Hobbes.[78] One defender of Dryden retaliated by branding the Censurer a follower of another old republican, Henry Stubbe. That countercharge itself confirms the existence of a political context; but its manufacturer then complicated the context by identifying Dryden's prime critic as the presbyterian divine, Dr Robert Wild.[79]

With the naming of Wild we encounter a characteristic Restoration alignment. In the 1668 *Essay of Dramatic Poesy* Dryden sourly recognized Wild – a self-consciously witty writer who had made his name by memorializing the triumphs of General Monck – as the most popular poet in London.[80] As we might expect from the Rota episode, Wild's politics were scarcely Dryden's: indeed, he urged his muse repeatedly in the cause of non-conformity, most notably in a verse celebration of the Declaration of Indulgence.[81] Doubtless on the principle that the enemy of my enemy is my friend, Wild also expressed considerable sympathy for Hobbes, beset as the latter was by Anglican monkeys.[82] At one moment, therefore, we find Hobbes cited as the inspiration for Dryden, who was then very much in the eye of cosmopolitan society, and defended by one of Dryden's leading critics, a presbyterian divine and the darling of London's commercial world. Meanwhile, Dryden's superheroes came under attack from both flanks, with churchmen fearing Hobbesian irreligion and others Hobbesian absolutism. Such convolutions make it imperative to look beyond the confines of genre and controversy if we are to grasp the meaning and intent of political argument or literary gesture.

The debate over toleration reveals the permeability of the conventional boundaries dividing secular from profane, high from low. What else was on the bookshelves of all those Londoners Dryden observed consuming the poems of Wild, whom he so despised? Parker – admittedly, no impartial witness – complained in 1673 that mere use of the term "Bayes" was guaranteed to reduce London conventiclers to guffaws.[83] Whether the conventiclers were themselves theater critics or readers of the thousands of pages of controversy over the ways of Bayes is immaterial. By whatever route, they had learned that a road led from the theater to the meeting-house. Conformists and non-conformists were alike accused of introducing the theater to the pulpit, but the traffic also went the other way; indeed, one 1668 versifier was emphatic that "now ... Playhouse turns to Conventicle." Wild's disclaimer, "we Non-Conformists... never going to Plays," must be taken with as much salt as his contention, in the same sentence, that his fellow non-conformists were "never good at" raillery and ridicule.[84] Such non-conformist tastes should not surprise us. It is after all some years since Eamonn Duffy pointed out that one of the leading Restoration publishers of godly chap-books advertised merry and godly titles side by side in the back of his godly wares. The tradition of Martin Marprelate was not dead.[85] The audience Wild addressed was politically aroused, divided in its religious loyalties, and had broad tastes in reading and entertainment. Its very existence helps to explain why Marvell and Parker found it worth their while to write such complex works. The distinctive character of Restoration audiences may explain too Milton's decision to open his *Samson Agonistes*, published in 1671, with a preface that administers some heavy-handed literary correction. His criticism of "the Poets error of intermixing Comic stuff with Tragic sadness and gravity" can be read as lamenting the Restoration vogue for Shakespearian revivals. Such a reading would, however, leave the preface oddly disconnected from the strenuous work of the poem itself. If instead we read the preface as a comment on the tragicomedies and heroic dramas of Dryden and his rivals, the conclusion must be that Milton was intermixing moral with literary correction. His purpose, in that eventuality, would have been not simply to chastise the playwrights of his day for endemic bad taste,[86] but also *their audiences* for being gulled into a misapprehension of the morality of suffering. Chastisement could only have been needed if Milton recognized that those whom he thought capable of listening also formed the audiences for the lamentably mixed genres of the stage.

There are both substantive and methodological lessons in this story. Although religious arguments and religious convictions were crucially important to Restoration politics, it was by no means only religious conviction that drove and shaped religious argument. The cause of toleration in the later seventeenth century cannot be read simply as an aspect of the history of Whiggery, or of dissent, or of rationality. Parker and Marvell, like their less famous contemporaries Wild and Eachard, engaged in some striking maneuvers. The reasons were various, but not the least was the fact that in the public life of their day patronage, partisanship, and style were inseparable. Such interweaving by definition bound together patrons as well as writers. If we can see Marvell pursuing in the same text literary issues and rivalries, the claims of conscience and the demands of patronage, and if we can assume that at least some of his readers were sufficiently informed to catch his multiple purposes, we should ponder the pressures on others caught up in that same fabric. After all, had the audience for Dryden's plays, or Wild's satires, not been so mixed, sophisticated and cosmopolitan grandees like Buckingham or even Shaftesbury would surely have been as fish out of water when they bid for non-conformist support in the metropolis. Few barriers, disciplinary or otherwise, divided the world of politics from the theater;[87] nor were the discourses of stage and meeting-house wholly discrete.

A second point needs to be made, not about the tastes of the audience but about its nature. Protagonists of orthodox godly culture certainly reached out in unorthodox ways in the attempt to include others, using broadsheet and chap-book forms to clothe a strenuous message. Their efforts should not mislead us into assuming that the meaner sort only read beyond the bible and the merry tale when their betters deliberately spoke to, or down to, them. If we are to subscribe to the model of co-optation by the elite, a model that sometimes shades into something like cultural trickle-down, that has recently become fashionable among scholars,[88] we need to ensure that it is more flexible than has hitherto appeared. There are intriguing signs that, at least in London, artefacts of what might seem a culture of elevation had in the first Restoration crisis a surprisingly extensive appeal. That belligerent controversialist Samuel Parker, who had in other respects such sensitive antennae, complained in 1681 that "the Plebeans and Mechanicks ... in the Streets and the

Highways" read and discussed "Lectures of Atheism" out of Hobbes's
Leviathan.[89] If Parker's claim was not an entire fabrication, we may need
to abandon assumptions that the print upheaval of the 1640s was simply
an aberration, and that a top-down focus on subsequent cultural and
political change will suffice. Only a broad reading *across* the texts of these
years will open the full significance of the phrase "political culture" for a
period when the audiences for broadside, playbill, and sermon often
had as much in common as did the authors.

CHAPTER 8

Sidney's Discourses *on political imagoes and royalist iconography*

Victoria Silver

It is usual to observe that there is nothing republican in Algernon Sidney's *Discourses concerning government* that Milton did not better express; nothing institutional that Harrington did not better imagine; no theoretical or polemic point that Locke did not better conceive and argue. Granted such a dearth of originality in Sidney's case,[1] there yet remains an achievement peculiar to his writings which perhaps Locke alone comes anywhere near approaching. This achievement has to do with *ethopoeia* or self-representation, an ineradicable dimension of all political activity, yet somehow hidden from our discussions of political philosophy. Sidney and Locke (and Hobbes a bit more slyly) recognize that political ideas most obviously do not operate in a vacuum, but must make their way through a maze of human habit and history, sentiment and experience, which comprise the very stuff of political practice. That is to say, for any idea of government to be understood and embraced, it must be found personable, sociable – congenial to the beliefs and aspirations, apt and timely to the needs, of the community to which it is addressed. Such civility is properly exercised by the author, whose formulations convey something more than an intellectual position, because the way in which a political argument is conducted not only implicates the character of the person making it but the nature of the society to which we are enjoined.

This is Sidney's singular contribution to the political literature of his age: that in political philosophy as well as in politics, manners maketh man. Thus the *Discourses* are peculiarly directed against Robert Filmer's authorial *ethos*, whose mores of argument in Sidney's view abuse reader and citizen alike. The attack on Filmer's character is undertaken not least because the royalist author of *Patriarcha* had proven himself so adept at image-making on his own party's behalf. More adept perhaps than Sidney, his opponent: for although *Patriarcha*'s stock declined precipitously after Locke published the *Two Treatises* and more or less reinvented the terms of debate, Filmer's little tract has still continued to attract academic interest into this century. By contrast, Sidney's *Discourses* have languished in semi-oblivion until fairly recently; and I would argue that their neglect owes as much to Sidney's own *ethos*, the self-image he projects on and off the page, as it does to current theoretical biases. Because if *Patriarcha*'s politics carry little weight with us except as they document a problem in contractarian theory, we still acknowledge its role in precipitating a great wave of Whig philosophizing, not to mention the uncanny timing of those Stuart propagandists who suavely resurrected Filmer's treatise from the grave. We patronize his primitive categorical logic, with a post-Cartesian prejudice congenial to Hobbes and hostile to Sidney's discursiveness even as it is to Locke's. And however covertly at this distance, we admire the impervious offense Filmer gives to those once-and-future Whig pieties in which we are now thoroughly and complacently versed. But just such current notions of doing political philosophy – whether as propaganda, system, or provocation – tend to inhibit our understanding what in Filmer's argument (as against Stuart policy) fomented such vehement resistance from Sidney in the *Discourses*, a resistance sufficient to conspire in his own conviction for treason against the crown in 1683.

Peter Laslett's introduction to Filmer's writing and Locke's *Two Treatises*, Gordon Schochet and Johann Sommerville on Filmer and patriarchalism, Richard Ashcraft on Locke and dissent have gone far to remedy this omission in our interest and knowledge, as has J. G. A. Pocock's broader analysis of sixteenth- and seventeenth-century republicanism. But not for Sidney, who is usually consigned to a footnote; and this despite the unstinting advocacy of Blair Worden, Jonathan Scott's truly remarkable political biography, and Alan Huston's important account of Sidney's influence on nascent republicanism in England and America.[2] In Laslett's words, Sidney remains the merely "conventional hero" whose "outraged blusterings" and "unreadable text" Laslett typically contrasts with Locke's "quiet irony and smoothly flowing argument," and then dismisses, along with the similarly indigestible because antiquarian James Tyrell.[3] Yet taken together with Laslett's puzzling remark that the debate over *Patriarcha* brought about, somehow unduly for English politics, the execution of one of the participants, the nature of Sidney's dismissal here can be seen as backhandedly justifying his argument against Filmer.

That is because Laslett's scorn would appear to arise largely from a difference in moral taste – in manners. He may exert himself with wit and anthropological solicitude to imagine the mind of a Filmer, comparing the cultural force of seventeenth-century patriarchalism to emperor worship in Japan, and Filmer's mythology of kingship to Nazi invocations of the immemorial "Volk." And after the horror of the Holocaust, and the desolation of world war, he might understandably share Filmer's bleak vision of humanity. But Laslett has no comparable imagination for the different sort of archaism posed by Sidney's example. In his account, Sidney is a displaced Hotspur, a Churchill without a war, whereas Locke's virtue is precisely the unassuming but monumental competence of the Anglo-American middle class, chivvying the Axis powers off the map even as he says Locke "flicked [Filmer] off the ridge of a temporary notoriety into permanent obscurity."[4]

My intention here is to recall how image instructs our political understandings, not only our choice of politicians. David Cannadine has written as much about Churchill himself, whose family scandals and reputation as an aristocratic opportunist dogged him in public opinion to the point of making his political achievements appear anomalous, if not obscuring them altogether.[5] That predicament exposes the not-so-silent factor of morality in political practice, which our formal modeling of politics fails to engage for the simple reason that "doing justice" involves more than rationalizing the relationship of law to property. That is, if the actual character of political obligation were not more than natural, more than legal, more than logical, Filmer would have won the day for royalism.

A REPUBLICAN CRITIQUE OF ROYALIST IMAGOES

Sidney's salutary argument in the *Discourses* is that the way in which we judge political philosophy cannot ultimately separate itself in kind or complexity from the way in which we decide the common good; how best to go about accomplishing it; or who shall lead us to it. In whatever sphere, political representation must observe equity, the principle of fidelity to the particular human fact. In the ancient phrase that Sidney himself invokes, "the proper act of justice is to give to everyone his due,"[6] while injustice is quite simply inequity – an arbitrary, exaggerated, and so disproportionate claim to value:

reason enjoins every man not to arrogate to himself more than he allows to others, nor to retain that liberty which will prove hurtful to him; or to expect that others will suffer themselves to be restrain'd, whilst he, to their prejudice remains in the exercise of that freedom which nature allows. He who would be exempted from this common rule, must shew for what reason he should be raised above his brethren; and if he do it not, he is an enemy to them. This is not popularity, but tyranny; and tyrants are said *exuisse hominem*, to throw off the nature of men, because they do unjustly and unreasonably assume to themselves that which agrees not with the frailty of human nature, and set up an interest in themselves contrary to that of their equals, which they ought to defend as their own.[7] (*Discourses*, pp. 192–3)

Sidney thus imagines politics as a form of personal *ethos* or virtue, that is to say, a practice of moral understanding and action dignifying both governor and governed, and dependent upon the subjective discipline of judgment and choice which *Patriarcha* would make an automatic, almost exclusive prerogative of kings and their cabals, and of course Robert Filmer as author. For Sidney observes that the very liberty of understanding that Filmer exercises in defending royalism he would withhold from every citizen by his argument, and what is more, from every reader by his manner of expressing it: "Hee that oppugns the public liberty, overthrows his own, and is guilty of the most brutish of all follies, whilst he arrogates to himself that which he denies to all men" (*Discourses*, p. 18). As against the explanatory impasse Laslett remarks in contractarian theory,[8] Sidney here describes a contradiction in Filmer's rhetorical position which challenges the moral integrity of *Patriarcha*'s author as well as its argument. The challenge amounts to something more sophisticated and substantial than what Laslett takes to be the *ad hominem* strategy of the Whig controversialists who, he believes, either failed to understand the significance of Filmer's naturalism, or mistook his analogy of kingship to patriarchy for a genuine identity between the two. But Sidney is a better reader of *Patriarcha* than Laslett will allow, precisely because the critical paradigm he brings to that tract is shared in large measure by Filmer himself. For Sidney adopts the model with the greatest currency and intelligibility in his own age, a kind of neo-aristocratics which has its intellectual origins in Aristotle's analyses of Greek public culture. Yet as Jonathan Scott observes, Sidney's political understanding and method of argument are also substantially indebted to Machiavelli's model of contingent politics in the *Discourses* on Livy. Each of these political models draws on the anti-formalist vein of ancient rhetorical theory, passed from the Greek Sophists, Plato and Aristotle, to Cicero and revived in the Italian Renaissance, which sought to address at once the expressive, ethical, and political contingencies of public representation (Aristotle's *Rhetoric* was itself continuously read as a political treatise, not least by Hobbes in *De Cive, De Homine,* and *Leviathan*).9

Indeed, the *Discourses* charge Filmer with committing a kind of rhetorical tyranny, a subjective encroachment upon reader and citizen where the principle of justice is transgressed in the very act of writing. Sidney himself argues the continuity of all political expressions – personal, discursive, and institutional – which is why the *Discourses* hold philosophizing to the same moral standard as any human action. It is thus ironic that Chief Justice Jeffreys would declare at Sidney's trial that *scribere est agere,* writing is doing; for that assumption, taken in a different sense from that Jeffreys intends, guides the argument of those putatively random papers purloined from Sidney's study and employed to testify against him. Such an ethics of argument is entirely to the *Discourses'* point that political models always entail a certain vision of the human person, an *ethos* projected both in devising and in living them out. Yet a danger attends this insight, a danger of which Sidney himself is acutely aware even as he fashions and enacts a counterexample of republican rectitude at his trial and execution. What disturbs Sidney is that a society can come to treat a given political order as irrevocable because it has turned a particular institution or office into its own identity as a people. Such personifying tends to naturalize political order in a manner that Filmer shrewdly exploits for royalism. That is, simple familiarity with our civic imagoes can make them and the political *status quo* for which they stand appear natural and inevitable, when both in Sidney's view should be scrupulously portrayed as artificial and elective.

Thus Sidney would ensure not only our freedom to choose how we will represent ourselves as a people, but also the range of our political imagoes – our subjective liberty to change our institutions and officers, to be represented, in other words, differently from the way we have been. To that end, we must be free to criticize and alter our civic expressions, both personate and institutional, since they are instrumental to our own reform and betterment as a people:

Laws and constitutions ought to be weighed, and whilst all due reverence is paid to such as are good, every nation may not only retain in itself a power of changing or abolishing such as are not so, but ought to exercise that power according to the best of their understanding, and in the place of what was either at first mistaken or afterwards corrupted, to constitute that which is most conducing to the establishment of justice and liberty. But such is the condition of mankind, that nothing can be so perfectly framed as not to give some testimony of human imbecility, and frequently to stand in need of reparations and amendments.

Many things are unknown to the wisest, and the best men can never wholly divest themselves of passions and affections. By this means the best and wisest are sometimes led into error, and stand in need of successors like to themselves, who may find remedies for the faults they have committed, and nothing can or ought to be permanent but that which is perfect.[10] (*Discourses*, p. 461)

In Sidney's account, there can be no perfect political form because there is no perfect human being. Reform and innovation are inevitable and necessary for that reason, while "those who will admit of no change would render errors perpetual, and depriving mankind of the benefits of wisdom, industry, experience, and the right use of reason, oblige all to continue in the miserable barbarity of their ancestors, which suits better with the name of a wolf than that of a man" (p. 462). In other words, when a people are disallowed the free use of their understanding and judgment, their relation to government is rendered irrational – the specious effect of passion, prestige, glamour, and charm, in sum, the magic of idealization as he describes it in his essay *Of Love*:

I could wish that all men would do the like, write and speak what they know in themselves, and leave the judgment to others, whereby we should come to a much more exact knowledge of our own natures, than either we attain unto by reading the painted artificial writings of those that rather aim at setting forth what should be, than what is, and, speaking nothing of themselves but their praises, do rather desire to be thought wise men than to be good, and, aiming at honour more than truth, disguising themselves, delude others; or those who, Ixion-like, embrace clouds, fill themselves with airy-abstracted speculations, that please the fancy but never inform the judgment, both seeking for applause, neither care to benefit themselves or others.[11]

We can be led by our civic imagoes to imagine ourselves in a way both pleasing and remote, a flattering figment of identity to distract us from the social predicament to which government should respond. But once lulled into complacency by these idealizing fictions, we have no desire to understand what is actually the case with us, much less to admit and alleviate the contradictions and inequities of our political practice. As Sidney remarks, any idealization inevitably discounts "what we are in all accidents," the particular human fact to which justice must attend, and which includes our agency as makers of ourselves.[12] For we tend to treat not only our political myths but our political imagoes as sacrosanct, a kind of "second self" that we approach religiously, which is to say that we extend to them an implicit, unquestioning devotion because they allow us perversely to escape the exercise of judgment and responsibility for our social condition.

By Sidney's definition, the facility of civic imagoes in blinding us to our circumstances is fundamentally unethical: it is also the peculiar iconic preserve of the absolute monarch. Once placed above the law, and so beyond any means of critical representation, Filmer's patriarchal king recognizes himself solely in his own propaganda, and is condemned to rule without moral consciousness. The result is a grand egoism exacerbated by the very nature of courts and their creatures, whose *raison d'être* is adoration – the exchange of moral autonomy, even rationality, for a perverse sort of pleasure. To Sidney and many of his contemporaries, the agent and epitome of political corruption is the courtier, who is *servus* to the royal imago in a specially ignoble sense:

for as servile natures are guided rather by sense than reason, such as addict themselves to the services of courts, find no other consolation in their misery, than what they receive from sensual pleasures, or such vanities as they put a value upon; and have no other care, than to get money for their supply by begging, stealing, bribing, and other infamous practices. Their offices are more or less esteemed according to the opportunities they afford for the exercise of these virtues; and no man seeks them for any other end than for gain, nor takes any other way than that which conduces to it. The usual means of attaining them are, by observing the prince's humour, flattering his vices, serving him in his pleasures, fomenting his passions, and by advancing his worst designs, to create an opinion in him that they love his person, and are entirely addicted to his will.[13] (*Discourses*, pp. 254–5)

Most of Sidney's diatribe against kings and courts derives from the ancient topoi of the tyrant and the political parasite;[14] but the organizing idea of addiction, which appears throughout the *Discourses*, is peculiarly Sidney's own, with its implications of self-enthrallment and irrationalism, both of which assume the loss of self in a morass of desire. The courtier surrenders personality for pleasure, so that the only thing distinguishing self is its relentless, amoral pursuit of gratification – a perverted will to power requiring the abasement of character to the fulfillment of brute desire.

Sidney's account of this addiction evokes Michel Foucault's analysis of ancient Greek erotics, which conceives the utter submission of self to pleasure as a profound ethical degradation. Among the Greeks, Foucault observes, "the traditional signs of effeminacy" were not associated with homosexuality or even 'inversion,' but rather with the person "who yielded to the pleasures that enticed him; [for] he was under the power of his own appetites and those of others."[15] Such an individual no longer has moral or rational autonomy but has become enslaved to his appetites – an addiction others can manipulate to their own purposes and pleasure. When applied to politics, this judgment expresses the relationship of political to psychological mastery, where the governor must govern himself if he is not to be governed in turn. According to Sidney's account, such a reversal of sovereignty is the ineluctable fate of the absolute monarch who, surrounded by those whose livelihood depends on their skill at flattery, grows increasingly infantile, even bestial in his own desires (*Discourses*, p. 266) – a "monstrous" consumer of the people, whom he regards as merely the paraphernalia of his projected self:

When a magistrate fancies he is not made for the people, but the people for him; that he does not govern for them, but for himself; and that the people live only to increase his glory, or furnish matter for his pleasures, he does not inquire what he may do for them, but what he may draw from them. (*Discourses*, p. 433)

Gross addiction to self moves the bad magistrate to divert legitimate political prerogative to obtaining private pleasure, and to employ every insidious means of preserving this power of self-indulgence at the public expense. For Sidney, the dilemma peculiarly posed by such a magistrate consists in his ability to make the people themselves complicit in their own abuse – their very survival obliging them to adopt the moral and legal promiscuity of the current regime, with their children becoming habituated to its vices. In such a manner, an entire society grows addicted to its own political malaise, with the creeping abasement of the governed mirroring the self-engendered decadence of the governor (p. 434).[16] Thus addiction, understood as the self's habitual submission to its overmastering desires, can consume not only an individual but through their governor, an entire society, once it discards the moral imperatives of justice and the mutual self-discipline of governor and governed.

A REPUBLICAN INQUIRY INTO ROYALIST ICONOLATRY

In Sidney's view, the absolute monarch is both unwilling and unable to distinguish self from state, with the theological *mysterium* of the king's two bodies understood after the manner of Louis XIV's *L'état c'est moi*.[17] But this is not only a moral and political problem: it is a problem in the theory of representation. The aspect of *Patriarcha* that Sidney analyzes acutely and originally in the *Discourses* is the order of representation presupposed by Filmer's idea that any monarch's claims to identity, authority, and obligation are self-evident, complete, and incontrovertible *because* original and natural. Seen one way, Sidney's argument simply returns us to the fundamental difference between royalist and republican concepts of political order as, respectively, innate or instrumental to the human condition, either divinely given and irrevocable or phenomenal and contingent. But in another way, the distinction is between iconic and ideative images, between a perception of the image as virtually indistinguishable from what it evokes, and the opposed understanding of the image as representative or instrumental. Seen in terms of image-theory, divine right and patriarchal theories of kingship do not conceive government as properly representative at all. The state is itself personate, the effect of an emanation of virtue and power from the person of deity to the person of the monarch. To the extent that the king is thus understood as "participating" in the divine, so his person and his rule are iconic in nature. To this apotheosis of the monarch, court culture testifies in its forms and symbologies, such that royalism approaches idolatry. Government is accordingly single, absolute, and permanent because true, and the king himself a species of religious icon, an image tantamount to God that demands our subjection, not our inquiry.

Conversely, with its theories of tacit as well as original consent between government and the governed, republicanism assumes the artistic, representative, critical nature of politics from its first institution. Unlike royalism's *mysterium* of divine investiture at the beginning of history, the republican myth of social contract is a postulate or hypothesis susceptible to rational interrogation – to trial of its validity as a political assumption.[18] This explanatory model of social contract renders political practice at once intelligible and accountable; government has the delimited status of a human device, an experiment in social representation contingently created to our benefit. Such postulates are not, as Rousseau supposes for Hobbes or Laslett for Filmer, a *mimesis*, an attempt to represent what was or is actually the case. Rather, the social contract serves as an instrumental picture that ensures our liberty of self-assessment. It is a rational myth, an image of political engagement to be tried and modified by the standards of justice and the common good – even as Carol Pateman has recently done for Locke.[19]

And the same is true of every political form allowed and condoned by the contractual picture: "it ought to be consider'd that the wisdom of man is imperfect, and unable to foresee the effects that may proceed from an infinite variety of accidents, which according to emergencies, necessarily require new constitutions, to prevent or cure the mischiefs arising from them, or to advance a good that at the first was not thought on" (*Discourses*, p. 173). Under a republicanism like Sidney's, political representation is contingent both in theory and practice: on the one hand, government must have more than the formal, symbolical coherence of royalism; it must fully and consistently articulate the idea behind its inception, without hieratics or mystery, so that it can be judged and used. On the other hand, political forms must assist in effecting what they express, or they become meaningless, defunct, absurd, or "sottish." These contingencies render the state mutable not only in its institutional form but also in its conceptual shape. And the same is true of the governor, the state's imago or personate representation who, as Sidney observes, may be one, few, or many depending upon practical exigencies and the viccissitudes of the popular will:

natural equality [in persons] continues till virtue makes the distinction, which must be either simply compleat and perfect in itself, so that he who is endued with it, is a god among men, or relatively, as far as concerns civil society, and the ends for which it is constituted, that is, defence, and the obtaining of justice. This requires a mind unbiased by passion, full of goodness and wisdom, firm against all the temptations to ill, that may arise from desire or fear; tending to all manner of good, through a perfect knowledge and affection to it ... Where such a man is found, he is by nature a king, and 'tis best for the nation where he is that he govern. If a few men, tho equal and alike among themselves, have the same advantages above the rest of the people, nature for the same reason seems to establish an aristocracy in that place; and the power is more safely committed to them, than left in the hands of the multitude. But if this excellency of virtue do not appear in one, nor in a few men, the right and power is by nature equally lodged in all ... (*Discourses*, p. 453)

According to Sidney's model, "civil society" embodies no suprahuman reality but rather expresses an entirely human value – the common good – and an idea or principle of implementing that value – doing justice. Its civic institutions and imagoes are accordingly historical, particular and variable insofar as they are found meaningful in these moral and practical terms. When they aren't, then sooner or later they will be replaced or reconstituted because political forms are devices more or less useful, which must meet complex criteria. They must be shown rationally, morally, popularly, and practically viable; or they are meaningless, whatever their formal or legal integrity. Government is thus an instrumental relation between a political form and an intended effect, namely doing justice and ensuring the commonweal. In Sidney's contractarian account, the assessment of that relation lies in the purview of every reasonable person (although women, along with children, the senile and insane, he does not count as such).

He accuses Filmer, by contrast, of hiding all issues of governance behind the screen of *arcana imperii*. "An implicit faith," Filmer argues in *Patriarcha*, "is given to the meanest artificer in his own craft. How much more is it, then, due to a Prince in the profound secrets of government. The causes and ends of the greatest politic actions and motions of state dazzle the eyes and exceed the capacities of all men, save only those that are hourly versed in managing public affairs."[20] To this analogy Sidney replies with some exasperation:

Who will wear a shoe that hurts him, because the shoemaker tells him 'tis well made? Or who will live in a house that yields no defence against the extremities of weather, because the mason or carpenter assures him 'tis a very good house? Such as have reason, understanding, or common sense, will, and ought to make use of it in those things that concern themselves and their posterity, and suspect the words of such as are interested in deceiving or persuading them not to see with their own eyes, that they may be more easily deceived. (*Discourses*, p. 13)

Of course we can choose to relinquish rationality – the paradox and perversion of the tyrant and courtier – or we can cultivate it by means of a truly critical politics. But Sidney would have it that only by understanding and maintaining the instrumental status of political representations can we reclaim human agency itself from sin and thus restore society to something approximating the myth of its original creative freedom. Like most writers of his republican persuasion, Sidney sees any concept of virtue as meaningless without the integral human capacity to discriminate and choose by which we undertake to better ourselves and our world. So the *Discourses* inveigh against "painted artificial writings" or "airy-abstracted speculations" in the political sphere, because these "whimsies" (as Sidney likes to call them there) seek to hide by a delectable or purely formal picture the perturbations and possibilities of human being. The degeneration of politics into corruption and oppression, the moral failure of absolute monarchy, is the consequence of iconolatry both in the king and in the people, whose addiction to the imago of the monarch deprives them equally of self-consciousness.

For Sidney, political representations (whether institutional or personal) have no authority except in their proven effect, understood as justice and the common good. When that effect is not forthcoming, such forms almost invariably grow extravagant and perverse, projecting an image altogether remote from the less pleasing fact in a manner antithetical to Sidney's idea of moral discipline. Moreover, this chronic disparity between office and real agency in the iconic politics of royalism threatens utterly to disable the state, a point Sidney underscores with the improbable image of an incumbent House of Lords, all one hundred and fifty of them, obliged by their titular claims to take the field in their own persons, as the lone bulwark of England's defense (*Discourses*, p. 490).

Once again, the problem is not with the personification of rule, but rather with the status we give political imagoes like king and nobility. If our governors serve as the canon of civic virtue, they should stand in a critical relationship to us, observing in themselves that moral discipline and integrity which Sidney regards as essential to a proper representation of the people. The ancient aristocratic idea is that, in choosing to subject ourselves to the presumptively just governance of our betters, we will learn by emulation comparable virtue as a whole society. Furthermore, in Sidney's contractarian model where informed assent gives representation its validity, the popular sanction of a governor reciprocally sets a standard of performance and public expectation by which that governor's rule will be criticized in turn. So Sidney sees subjection to any political imago as conditional upon its achievement of justice and the common good:

If the nature of man be reason, *detur digniori* ["let it be given to the worthier"], in matters of this kind, is the voice of nature; and it were not only a deviation from reason, but a most desperate and mischievous madness, for a company going to the Indies, to give the guidance of their ship to the son of the best pilot of the world, if he want the skill required in that employment, or to one who was maliciously set to destroy them; and he only can have a right grounded upon the dictates of nature, to be advanced to the helm, who best knows how to govern it, and has given the best testimonies of his integrity and intentions to employ his skill for the good of those that are embarked. (*Discourses*, p. 80)

A REPUBLICAN SATIRE ON ROYALIST ROMANCE

Superficially, the opposition between Sidney and Filmer may seem more nominal than real to the extent that both ideologies are aristocratic in assumption. Yet the issue of representation serves to elicit their defining differences: for Filmer, meaningfulness and validity are innate, automatic to the focal image ordained by God, and accordingly, independent of any particular intent or use. So when Filmer reads scripture, history, or experience, he gauges their significance symbolically, with a few salient images or impressions arbitrarily controlling the sense of every other one, in much the same way that the regal icon subsumes all differences arbitrarily under itself. As John Dunn observes, it is the "frenetic over-assimilation of differences to unity" that gives *Patriarcha* its seeming self-evidence, its plausibility.[21] Sidney charges such symbolic reductions with transgressing against the more prosaic truth. So where Filmer sees the affirmation of one order, one significance everywhere, Sidney anticipates a different emphasis to any one image in each succeeding use. At one level, this is to distinguish a formalist from a rhetorical model of meaning; yet with *Patriarcha* and all such representations of human things, Sidney's concern extends beyond the theory of representation as such to the ethics of its use. He would have it that, by translating the actual vagaries of political enterprise into categorical identities (on the same principle that incarnates the state in the king's very person), Filmer's argument cunningly elides equally salient differences of circumstance and quality on which the meaningfulness of representation depends. This expressive injustice inexorably promotes moral and political inequities, since it is only by fidelity to the particular fact that we can distinguish its quality and precise nature: by such means, we can discriminate actual from figurative fathers – *pater* from *pater patriae* (*Discourses*, p. 41) – and still more crucially, the government of a Moses from a Caligula (p. 398).

The prime intention of the *Discourses* is accordingly to anatomize Filmer's inequitable, unjust practice of representation. Rhetorical equity, understood in this way, is not positive but restrictive, an allowance for real and rational differences in words, images, and things:

> To chuse or institute a father is nonsense in the very term; but if any were to be chosen to perform the office of father of such as have none, and are not of age to provide for themselves (as men do tutors or guardians for orphans) none could be capable of being elected, but such as in the kindness to the person they were to take under their care, did most resemble his true father, and had the virtues and abilities rightly to provide for his good. If this fails, all right ceases; and such a corruption is introduced as we saw in our court of wards, which the nation could not bear, when the institution was perverted, and the king, who ought to have taken a tender care of the wards and their estates, delivered them as a prey to those whom he favoured. (*Discourses*, pp. 64–5)

In his own devout paternalism, Sidney conceives the status of a father as unique and inimitable except in one way – when those who propose to assume this relationship evince its distinctive moral character in their every action toward the child. Significantly, Sidney does not call the quality of the relation "love" but rather "kindness" or "taking care," emphasizing the public, evident expression of paternity as a disposition that intelligibly and practically seeks the child's welfare in all things. Moreover, he goes on to observe that no natural father deserves the name, much less the legal authority of one, if he fails in the obligation to provide such care. Sidney thus holds the name of father accountable to that general criterion of meaningfulness which opens his argument here, namely moral validity, where wisdom appears not only in professing the right but rightly performing it.

But in disallowing Filmer's symbolical extension of "father" to the person of the king, as an image at once inapt, unjust, and immoral, Sidney exemplifies his whole theory of representation. For the figure *pater patriae*, once translated into an actual prerogative under law, gives the king paternal authority *ipso facto*, without holding him to the moral and effectual standard of paternal care. It ignores outright the displacement of terms intrinsic to any tropological usage, instead assigning to this analogy the scope and force of an actual identity irrespective of the circumstances which, in Sidney's opinion, ought properly to condition any paternal claim, whether natural or artificial.

In thus attending to the equity or justice of Filmer's representation, Sidney challenges the grand organizing principle of *Patriarcha* – that formal supremacy predicates moral and political excellence. He demonstrates that the seeming naturalism of *Patriarcha*'s claims for kingship is the figment of its discursive practice, which has been called literalist when it is more properly allegorical. For by symbolic assimilation or synonymy, Filmer tends to give certain concepts a primacy and power which allow them freely to subsume anything under an allegorical identity, regardless of other, more salient circumstances that might give that thing another meaning or value. By just such a categorical imperative, Filmer manages to abstract all scripture's elder or authoritative or prominent males into kings and dynasts, with Abraham becoming the real and immediate, as against figurative and prophetic, monarch of all he surveys. As one might expect, Sidney responds to this sudden elevation of the patriarch by pointing out every evident circumstance that obtrudes between Genesis' representation of Abraham and Filmer's account of him as "lord paramount":

To say the truth, 'tis hard to speak seriously of Abraham's kingdom, or to think any man to be in earnest who mentions it. He was a stranger, and a pilgrim in the land where he lived, and pretended to no authority beyond his own family, which consisted only of a wife and slaves. He lived with Lot as his equal, and would have no contest with him, because they were brethren. His wife and servants could neither make up, nor be any part of a kingdom, in as much as the despotical government, both in practice and principle, differs from the regal. If his kingdom were to be founded on the paternal right, it vanished away of itself; he had no child: Eliezer of Damascus, for want of a better, was to be his heir: Lot though his nephew, was excluded: He durst not own his own wife: he had not one foot of land, till he bought a field for a burying place: His three hundred and eighteen men were servants (though according to the custom of those days), or their children; and the war he made with them, was like to Gideon's enterprize; which shews only that God can save by a few as well as by many, but makes nothing to our author's purpose. (*Discourses*, p. 24)

The thrust of Sidney's precisely prosaic reading of Genesis is to criticize, by extension, any representation of a thing that disregards its particular existence. Yet Sidney acknowledges that the force of facts alone cannot counter Filmer's allegorizing, which capitalizes on the very term king "as if there were a charm in the word" (p. 508). It has this charm not because Filmer's theory taps into some deep, residual mystique popularly attending that office, as Laslett suggests. Sidney himself knows better: if there is any mystique to *Patriarcha*'s politics, it is the calculated "dazzle" of that different sort of word-magic which sublimes the testimony of history and text into symbol, and thus seemingly substantiates Filmer's claims for kingship. In other words, by a kind of lexical dissimulation, certain habitual expressions, certain usages of custom and law, lose any circumstantial meaning and, with it, their original capacity to analyze and so affect the actualities of political practice. Like the appellation "father," they become mere ciphers in Filmer's hands.

Indeed, human history is reduced in *Patriarcha* to a single analogy of kingship to patriarchy ceaselessly amplified, in something like Foucault's account of a culture only superficially various, whose ever-expanding similitudes disguise a fundamental impoverishment of ideas and political possibilities together.[22] For his part, Sidney refuses to believe that human experience is devoid of innovations in which we are able to adapt political representation to the vicissitudes of our situation. There is, he argues in the *Discourses*, a versatility of understanding and practice to human being, as well as a versatility of circumstance, which Filmer's political allegory would entirely suppress. Instead, in the guise of systematic politics, Filmer's model transforms the historical and

cultural variety of human political behavior into the enchanted iter-
ations of myth. And as Sidney recognizes, the advantages of myth are
considerable. Myth depicts the apparent order of things as a *fait accompli*
that can be amplified but never altered by explanation. And Filmer's
allegory of patriarchal kingship orchestrates just this impression of an
unchanging and so inevitably recurrent social problem and its formal
solution in the political icon of absolute sovereignty. By such formaliz-
ing of the loosely customary analogy of kings to fathers and gods,
Patriarcha's allegorizing itself creates an aura of givenness or fate about
royalist politics sufficient to deflect public and even rational inquiry.

Most of Sidney's animadversions upon Filmer have to do with just
such an attempt to conceal or evade the moral entailments of representation. Filmer's dissimulations include his preference for an axiomatic
argument, which preempts proper warrant for any assertion; a symbolic
exegesis that denies any circumstance but the superficial point of comparison; the concatenation of its own peculiar categories without regard
for their actual force in human experience; its fragmentation of other
texts and histories to allow perverted and so deceptive extracts; its
sensationalism, which invariably represents the most extreme case as
necessary and ineluctable. Such maneuvers explain why Sidney concer-
tedly accuses Filmer of trying to addict the reader's judgment to his
"fables," "fictions," or "figments": disfiguring the complex motives and
circumstances occasioning political activity, reducing them to a specious
logic; fostering a ritualized, aesthetic understanding of the relations
between power and order so as to falsify the exigencies of government;
and imposing the wishful coherence of narrative upon the inevitable
discontinuities of political history.

In sum, Sidney portrays *Patriarcha* as inventing a kind of nominal
world, a political phantasia exceeding even "the extravagance of fables
and romances" (*Discourses*, p. 32), in which the "court-language" of
royalist apology reconceives the whole range of human experience so
that, under the pretext of expounding sovereignty and its obligations, we
may be brought to accede in absolutism and civic passivity (p. 28). It is
this idealizing rage, this categorical departure from the particular,
which in Sidney's view permits Filmer plausibly to convert "whimsies"
and "chimeras" into necessities, "romance" into history, "fancy" into
law, "implicit faith" and "madness" into rationality, and to present the
"enslavement" or "addiction" of self to idols as the proper exercise of
civic liberty. So Sidney observes that "'Tis usual with impostors to
obtrude their deceits upon men, by putting false names upon things, by

which they may perplex men's minds, and from thence deduce false conclusions" (*Discourses*, p. 383). By his account, *Patriarcha* owes less to intellectual tradition or political practice than it does to the extravagances of court propaganda, inasmuch as Filmer's theory does little more than promote and elaborate the splendid facade, the glorious impostures, by which royalism has always worked to aggrandize power for king and court.

Against these tactics, Sidney brings what Laslett deplores – the prolix because atomical, circumstantial, and forensic argument of the *Discourses*. He conspicuously disavows systematic in favor of contingent, differential meanings, by way of a close, sustained reading of *Patriarcha* that distinguishes in detail between what the tract contends and what its own evidence will allow. While he makes Filmer out to be a promoter of fictions, Sidney himself refuses to countenance, much less inhabit, the royalist romance fabricated by *Patriarcha*'s argument. His distaste for Filmer's "absurdities" is signaled by the critical irony that informs almost every sentence of the *Discourses*, mocking what Sidney regards as a pattern of promiscuous and illicit conflation – of incumbent power with legitimacy, of glamour with virtue, desire with judgment, coercion with consent, bondage with obligation. Such perverse valuations can be nothing but unjust in practice, because politics for Sidney consists not in the imposition of formal identities but the drawing of right distinctions. Inasmuch as the soul of Filmer's royalist romance is credulity and fascination, irony is Sidney's means of disenchantment. It performs a relentless *reductio ad absurdum* on *Patriarcha*'s spectacles and illusions, as here where the judgments of Tacitus are satirically counterposed to Filmer's:

Tacitus did not understand the state of his own country, where he seems to be ashamed to write the history of it, *Nobis in arcto & ingloriosus labor* ["My labor is restricted and inglorious"]; when instead of such glorious things as had been achieved by the Romans, whilst either the senate, or the common people prevailed, he had nothing left to relate, but *saeva jussa, continuas accusationes, fallaces amicitias, perniciem innocentium* ["savage commands, endless accusations, false friendships, destruction of the innocent"]. They enjoy'd nothing that was good from the expulsion of the Tarquins to the reestablishment of divine absolute monarchy in the persons of those pious fathers of the people, Tiberius, Caligula, Claudius, Nero, Galba, Otho, Vitellius, &c. There was no virtue in the Junii, Horatii, Cornelii, Quintii, Decii, Manlii; but the generous and tender-hearted princes before mentioned were the perfect examples of it: Whilst annual magistrates governed, there was no stability; Sejanus, Macro, and Tigellinus introduced good order: Virtue was not esteemed by the ancient senate and people; Messalina, Agrippina, Poppaea, Narcissus, Pallus, Vinius, and Laco knew how to put a just value upon it: The irregularities of popular assemblies, and want of prudence in the senate, was repaired by the temperate proceedings of the German, Pannonian and Eastern armies, or the modest discretion of the Praetorian bands: The city was delivered by them from the burden of governing the world, and for its own good frequently plunder'd, fired; and at last, with the rest of desolated Italy, and the noblest provinces of Europe, Asia, and Africa, brought under the yoke of the most barbarous and cruel nations. By the same light we may see that those who endeavour'd to perpetuate the misery of liberty to Rome, or lost their lives in the defence of it, were the worst, or the most foolish of men, and that they were the best who did overthrow it. (*Discourses*, pp. 148–9)

Sidney's point here is to confront the reader with all those particulars of Roman political history which, factually and morally, contravene the symbologies, the formal categories, of *Patriarcha*. But this irony does more than ridicule Filmer's account: it also introduces and discriminates among the moral consequences of discursive as well as political representation, to which Filmer himself is resolutely oblivious. Implicitly, Sidney indicts as absurd and unjust *Patriarcha*'s greatest attraction – its formal plausibility – since its author "thinks that the impudence of an assertion is sufficient to make that pass, which is repugnant to experience and common sense" (*Discourses*, p. 280). But irony liberates us from such confusions of form with validity and value. The persuasiveness of the *Discourses* derives from just this persistent effect, and the distinction in authorial ethos it implies. For Sidney wittily associates royalism with a peculiar absurdity of thought and a moral atavism that would induce us again to subjugate ourselves to the images of our own hands, and thus defraud us of judgment and assent at once (p. 39).

The demonstration of absurdity exerts a restraint on the credulity with which we assume the beliefs and dogmas, conventions and necessities which otherwise govern our lives.[23] Sidney's play with the absurd is thus a moral instrument in the best tradition of satire. The human condition he specially deplores in the *Discourses* is our self-subjugation to political imagoes, where the compulsion to approve and adhere to a government is not just imposed from without but inflicted from within, because we have for whatever reason eschewed the personal and public discipline of moral reflection and judgment. Of course, this is a predicament peculiarly exemplified by both the courtier's and the sovereign's addiction to the arbitrary, luxurious exercise of absolute rule, since Sidney sees courtiers (among whom he explicitly counts the author of

Patriarcha) identifying with the regal icon out of sheer voluptuous abandon. The ignoble and licentious service of "court-creatures" expresses their submission not so much to the person of the ruler as to the attendant pleasures of rule, thus rendering their politics at once irrational, servile, and egoistic. Moreover, their addiction entails an utter disregard for the subjective, moral dimension of any person, whether ruler or ruled. Indeed, Sidney finds self-subjugation precisely vicious because it requires a person or a whole society to will their own debasement, by choosing a political imago whose emulation will corrupt and exploit, not benefit them.

Accordingly, the satire he directs at *Patriarcha* expresses profoundly the aversion of an aristocrat for a despot – a despot whose means of justifying personal rule is to eclipse the whole subjective life of politics, from which every privilege and obligation properly derive in Sidney's aristocratic model. He refuses to accept the notion – fundamental to Filmer's iconic politics – that governance must be imposed as against elected. And as both Jonathan Scott and Alan Huston argue, this refusal derives from his belief in the fundamental intelligibility and dignity of human being, which Filmer does not share as that court-creature and merely titular nobleman Sidney abominates. His rhetoric in *Patriarcha* does more than pander to tyrants: in Sidney's estimation, its every interpretative and verbal maneuver exemplifies them.

It is on the basis of this presumptive reciprocity among political, moral, and literate practices that Sidney's own method in the *Discourses* is applauded, and by no less a judge than Coleridge: "Read Algernon Sidney," he says, "his style reminds you as little of books as of blackguards. What a gentleman he was!"[24] What seems gratuitous to Laslett in Sidney's attack on Filmer is precisely the effect of gentlemanly disdain – the disdain of one privileged person for another who has conducted himself indecorously, indecently, unworthily. In Sidney's sketch of Sir Henry Vane, the aristocratic ethic – elaborated in conduct books from the Tudor age on[25] – exhibits its moral claims, namely, a disciplined selflessness and generosity, or *noblesse oblige*. The virtue of the English gentleman had to be instrumental, not simply formal or decorative in the Italian mode: as Ruth Kelso observes, "The gentleman then should live not for himself, but for others; to the neglect even of his own interest and of his own inclinations, mindful that from him must come all the felicity or calamity that befalls his country."[26]

A REPUBLICAN IMAGO AND ROYALIST JUSTICE

To readers of the *Discourses*, it will come as no surprise that when the Rye House Plot thrust him yet once more upon the public's notice, Sidney used the occasion of his trial and execution to project an image justifying not only himself but the Good Old Cause for which he had fought, as well as republicanism more largely. To that end, he fashioned himself along just these gentlemanly lines, winning the admiration of contemporaries for his "quality," his sense of honor, and sympathy for his seemingly untoward sufferings. Furthermore, in tacitly opposing the crown's intemperate prosecution to his own ostentatious sang-froid, Sidney's defense and especially his final words to the court exemplified the abiding argument of the *Discourses* – that personal politics cannot afford to neglect the moral dimension.

As events transpired, Sidney exchanged ignominy with his judge – Lord Chief Justice Jeffreys, "The Hanging Judge" of the Bloody Assize after Monmouth's rebellion – and he did so in a manner nicely illustrating his own theory of political imagoes. Captured in sailor's dress trying to escape the London mob and sent to languish in the Tower, Jeffreys fell victim to those political vicissitudes his own royalism would deny. For his reputation underwent a revolution too, with this avatar of Stuart justice condemned to figure forever as a bogey in the popular mind: gnawing a bloody bone in Lyme Regis; sharing a Surrey house which each had owned with the ghost of John Bradshaw (President of the Court that sentenced Charles I to death); taking his evening drink at Wapping Wall so as to view the weltering bodies of pirates; appearing unmistakably, if anonymously, from out of his portrait to gibbet a susceptible young man in a story of Bram Stoker's.[27] By contrast, the erstwhile traitor Algernon Sidney has garnered the reputation of a martyr to British liberty, thus proving the perpetual saliency of such imagoes to our political understandings.

As Jeffreys averred during the proceedings, Sidney's conviction was itself never in doubt. Rather, Jonathan Scott has suggested that the really remarkable thing about Sidney's trial is the self-discipline, the aristocratic *mesure*, shown by one who had been to that moment an incorrigibly passionate and impetuous man.[28] In his display of *ethos*, Sidney's character appeared so impressively at odds with the onus of the charge against him that it immediately forced the question of his trial's legitimacy, and for centuries exculpated him from his probable collusion in the Rye House Plot. The motive for this unwonted self-control can arguably be traced to his own and Jeffreys's unspoken acknowledgment that how Sidney was perceived by the public would significantly affect how his death sentence was understood: whether, as Charles no doubt intended when he refused Sidney a pardon, it would mark the boundaries of a subject's legitimate dissent; or whether, as Sidney proposed by his extraordinary circumspection, it would define the limits of a magistrate's legitimate authority. The inverted reputations of judge and accused surely vindicate Sidney's reading of the political scene, while testifying to the durable impact of this republican imago, to which Keats also bears witness:

There is of a truth nothing manly or sterling in any part of the Government. There are many Madmen in the Country, I have no doubt, who would like to be beheaded on Tower Hill merely for the sake of éclat, there are many Men like Hunt who from a principle of taste would like to see things go on better, there are many like Sir F. Burdett who would like to sit at the head of political dinners – but there are none prepared to suffer in obscurity for their Country – the motives of our wo[r]st Men are interest and of our best Vanity – We have no Milton, no Algernon Sidney.[29]

What Keats deplores here is a sort of ravening egoism that substitutes for moral engagement in the ruling classes, the notional "best" of his nation: treason as a display of personal genius; a fastidious aestheticism as the impetus behind political reform; high office as a social coup. The result is a politics of mere celebrity – of "éclat," spectacle, sensation, brilliance – which attends only to the superficies and epiphenomena of government, oblivious to what Keats himself understands as the soul of right rule: namely, the moral imperative to seek the public's welfare over one's own.

   It is this gentlemanly principle that Sidney dramatizes at his trial, while Jeffreys makes every effort to exhibit and impugn what he clearly regards as the defendant's willful obstruction of the crown's justice and the king's law. Where Jeffreys is peremptory in ruling, Sidney remains civil in dissent; where Jeffreys grows impatient and insulting, Sidney appears witty and debonair; where Jeffreys bullies or disregards, Sidney reasons scrupulously from point to point; and where Jeffreys would take the moral high ground as sentence is handed down, reproaching the defendant equally for the sins of ingratitude and sedition against his king, Sidney deftly appropriates it for himself, orchestrating his own republican apotheosis:

SIDNEY. Then, O God! O God! I beseech thee to sanctify these sufferings unto me, and impute not my blood to the country, nor the city, through which I

am to be drawn; let no inquisition be made for it, but if any, and this
shedding of blood that is innocent, must be revenged, let the weight of it
fall only upon those, that maliciously persecute me for righteousness sake.
L.C.J. I pray God work in you a temper fit to go unto the other world, for I see
you are not fit for this.
SIDNEY. My lord, feel my pulse, [holding out his hand] and see if I am
disordered; I bless God, I never was in better temper than I am now.[30]

Since Sidney, like his judge, is a political person in this way, not just a
public one – because they face each other as the virtual embodiments of
opposed philosophies of justice and right – their expressions at the trial
are laden with significance, or to our taste, with histrionics: Jeffreys's
imitation of divine nemesis, Sidney's martyr's prayer. But what is
significant about Sidney's defense, both here and in the posthumously
published *Apology* and *Paper*, is its almost exact consistency with the
Discourses' analysis of representation. That is to say, Sidney's conduct
does more than accomplish the private and expedient vindication that
Scott and Huston so insightfully analyze. For the very same arguments
of particular, contingent, and delimited authority and power Sidney
expounds in those professedly random papers, soon to become the
Discourses concerning government, are introduced at his trial as the lawful
restraint he would place on the crown's evidence against himself. Thus
he translates his personal jeopardy into a vivid threat against the nation
as a whole:

SIDNEY. Truly, my lord, I do as little intend to misspend my own spirit, and
your time, as ever any man that came before you. Now, my lord, if you will
make a concatenation of one thing, a supposition upon supposition, I
would take all this asunder, and shew, if none of these thing are any thing
in themselves, they can be nothing joined together.
L.C.J. Take your own method, Mr. Sidney; but I say, if you are a man of low
spirits and weak body, it is a duty incumbent upon this court, to exhort you
not to spend your time upon things that are not material.
SIDNEY. My lord, I think it is very material, that a whimsical imagination of a
conspiracy should not pass for a real conspiracy of the death of the
king...[31]

In thus emphasizing the circumstantial nature of the evidence against
him, or more specifically, the extent to which it must first be rhetorically
invented as proof, Sidney exposes the role of representation in the case
against him. That the court, in the person of Jeffreys, will not reflect
upon the manner of its own evidence and procedure is of course a
symptom of its royalism to Sidney – a show of iconolatry, the inability to

discriminate between our representations and our actualities. Even as justice is not merely formal but particular in his view, so the political authority of a government is contingent upon its practice of equity, giving to every person what is due. That is where politics has its life and legitimacy, even as justice for Algernon Sidney lies in the circumstances, the character of the evidence against him, to which he would draw the attention of an obdurate court. But Jeffreys dismisses his every objection, selectively observing precedent and bending each circumstance to advance a judgment already formed. And to the extent that the evidence used to convict Sidney receives no equitable or impartial representation from Jeffreys, but is rendered arbitrarily conclusive to suit the predilections of his royal master, so the court serves as a cipher for tyranny.

For when Jeffreys directs the jury, in default of the requisite second witness, that *scribere est agere* – that the *Discourses* testify to an overt act of treason although they say nothing about Sidney's precise intent, the particular elements of his alleged crime, or the means to be employed in committing it – he specifies and so deforms the character of Sidney's expressions. He thus bears out however perversely the implicit thesis of Sidney's writings: that political philosophy has a life off the page, a moral entailment not only in the justice of its representation but in the humanity of its practice. Jeffrey Reiman captures this informing principle of the *Discourses* when he observes that "Morality is reason's passion,"[32] which is why Sidney himself insists that the justice of any representation, including the image he fashioned for himself, must be carefully weighed before it is embraced:

The Lord forgive these practices, and avert the evils that threaten the nation from them. The Lord sanctify these my sufferings unto me; and though I fall as a sacrifice unto idols, suffer not idolatry to be established in this land . . . Grant that I may die glorifying thee for all thy mercies, and that at the last thou has permitted me to be singled out as a witness of thy truth; and even by the confession of my opposers, for that Old Cause in which I was from my youth engaged, and for which thou has often and wonderfully declared thyself. (Sidney's *Paper*, handed to the Sheriff on the scaffold)[33]

Notes

INTRODUCTION

Unless otherwise indicated, all quotations in this Introduction are drawn from the chapters indicated.

1 John M. Wallace, *Destiny His Choice: the Loyalism of Andrew Marvell* (Cambridge, 1968). For similar work by Wallace, see "Cooper's Hill: the Manifesto of Parliamentary Royalism, 1641," *English Literary History* 41 (1974), 494–540.

2 We might think in particular of Alasdair MacIntyre, *After Virtue* (Notre Dame, IN, 1981); and Judith Shklar, *Ordinary Vices* (Cambridge, MA, 1984).

3 Lawrence E. Klein, *Shaftesbury and the Culture of Politeness* (Cambridge, 1994); Bernard Mandeville, *Fable of the Bees* (1714).

4 See especially John Bossy, "Moral Arithmetic: Seven Sins into Ten Commandments," in *Conscience and Casuistry in Early Modern Europe*, ed. Edmund Leites (Cambridge, 1988), pp. 214–34.

5 Quentin Skinner, *The Foundations of Modern Political Thought* (2 vols., Cambridge, 1978), vol. 1, pp. 213–43; Brendan Bradshaw, "Transalpine Humanism," and Howell A. Lloyd, "Constitutionalism," in *The Cambridge History of Political Thought 1450–1750*, ed. J. H. Burns (Cambridge, 1991), pp. 95–131, 254–83.

6 Markku Peltonen, "Bacon's political philosophy," in *The Cambridge Companion to Bacon* ed. Markku Peltonen (Cambridge, 1996), p. 297; and see more generally, Ian Box, "Bacon's Moral Philosophy," *ibid.*, pp. 260–82. For Tacitism, see Peter Burke, "Tacitism, Scepticism, and Reason of State," in *Cambridge History of Political Thought*, pp. 479–98.

7 See Quentin Skinner, "Thomas Hobbes and the Renaissance *studia humanitatis*," below, and Victoria Silver, "Sidney's discourses on political imagoes," below. Hobbes's other Cavendish patron, the Duke of Newcastle, was also exercised by the relations among virtue, *virtu*, and political action: see Conal Condren, "Casuistry to Newcastle," in *Political Discourse in Early Modern Britain*, ed. N. Phillipson and Q. Skinner (Cambridge, 1993), pp. 167–9.

8 John Milton, *The readie and easie way* (1659); James Harrington, *The art of lawgiving* (1659), and *Aphorisms political* (1659).

9 Important recent discussions of the representations and self-representations of the godly are Ralph Houlbrooke, "The Puritan Death-bed, c. 1560–c.1660," and Peter Lake, "'A Charitable Christian Hatred': the Godly and Their Enemies in the 1630s," in *The Culture of English Puritanism, 1560–1700*, ed. Christopher Durston and Jacqueline Eales (London, 1996). Still useful on the conception of the pious individual is Sears McGee, *The Godly Man in Stuart England* (New Haven, CT, 1976).

10 On Herbert, see Stanley Fish, "'Void of storie': the struggle for insincerity in Herbert's prose and poetry," below.

11 See perhaps above all John M. Wallace, "John Dryden's Plays and the Conception of an Heroic Society," in *Culture and Politics from Puritanism to the Enlightenment*, ed. P. Zagorin (Berkeley, CA, 1980), pp. 113–34.

12 The interconnections of public and private in popular ideology remind us that the preoccupation with public virtue was no mere aristocratic fetish. See David Underdown, *A Freeborn People* (Oxford, 1996), and Susan D. Amussen, *An Ordered Society* (Oxford, 1988). For ridicule and defamation, see Laura Gowing, "Language, Power and the Law," in *Women, Crime and the Courts in Early Modern England*, ed. Jenny Kermode and Garthine Walker (London, 1994), pp. 26–47; Alastair Bellany, "Railing Rhymes and Vaunting Verse," in *Culture and Politics in Early Stuart England*, ed. Kevin Sharpe and Peter Lake (Stanford, CA, 1993), pp. 285–310; Thomas Cogswell, "Underground Verse and the Transformation of Early Stuart Political Culture," in *Political Culture and the Culture of Politics*, ed. Susan D. Amussen and Mark A. Kishlansky (Manchester, 1995), pp. 277–300.

13 John Milton, *Eikonoklastes* (1649), ch. 7.

14 See Jackson I. Cope, "Sir Kenelm Digby's rewritings of his life," below.

15 Richard Cust's recent study of Sir Thomas Wentworth suggests that Wentworth had available to him in the 1620s two quite distinct vocabularies, of "patriot" and courtier, with their associated literary models and legitimations, and that he consciously chose between the one and the other. Yet Cust also shows the way Wentworth was politically constrained by the persona he adopted. Richard Cust, "Wentworth's 'Change of Sides' in the 1620s," in *The Political World of Thomas Wentworth, Earl of Strafford*, ed. Julia F. Merritt (Cambridge, 1996), pp. 63–80.

16 J. G. A. Pocock, "Thomas May and the narrative of Civil War," below.

17 See Barbara Donagan, "Casuistry and allegiance in the English Civil War," below.

18 See Derek Hirst, "Samuel Parker, Andrew Marvell, and political culture, 1667–73," below.

19 See Richard Strier, "'I am Power': normal and magical politics in *The Tempest*," below.

20 For an example (with some reflections on the methodology) of a close reading of two famous historical "documents," see Richard Strier, "From Diagnosis to Operation: The 'Root and Branch' Petition and the Grand Remonstrance," in *The Theatrical City: Culture, Theatre and Politics in London,*

1576–1649, ed. David L. Smith, Richard Strier, and David Bevington (Cambridge, 1995), pp. 224–44; for an example of the political significance of literary allusions, see Hirst's references to the career of Sir Philip Sidney's *Arcadia* in the Restoration, below, p. 149.

1   "'I AM POWER'": NORMAL AND MAGICAL POLITICS IN *THE TEMPEST*

For help with this chapter, I am especially grateful to Homi Bhabha, Kenneth Graham, Derek Hirst, Jeff Masten, William Veeder, and Frank Whigham; to insightful audiences at Harvard, New Mexico State University (Las Cruces), Occidental College, University of Alabama (Tuscaloosa), University of Texas (Austin), and Yale; to participants in the Shakespeare Association seminar on servants, in the Faculty Renaissance Seminar and in the Graduate Workshops on "Empire" and on "the Renaissance" at the University of Chicago.

1 See Richard Strier, "Faithful Servants: Shakespeare's Praise of Disobedience," in *The Historical Renaissance: New Essays in Tudor and Stuart Literature and Culture*, ed. Heather Dubrow and Richard Strier (Chicago, 1988), pp. 104–33; expanded in Strier, *Resistant Structures: Particularity, Radicalism, and Renaissance Texts* (Berkeley, CA, 1995), ch. 7.

2 See Thomas Kuhn, *The Structure of Scientific Revolutions*, second edn. (Chicago, 1970), chs. 2–5.

3 Rob Nixon, "Caribbean and African Appropriations of *The Tempest*," *Critical Inquiry* 13 (1987), 557–78. [Dominique] O. [Octave] Mannoni, *Psychologie de la colonisation* (Paris, 1950); Aimé Césaire, *Une Tempête* (Paris, 1969). For translations, see *Prospero and Caliban: The Psychology of Colonization*, trans. Pamela Powesland, 2nd edn. (New York, 1964) (hereafter cited as "Mannoni, *Prospero and Caliban*"), and *A Tempest*, trans. Richard Miller (New York, 1992).

4 For instance, Thomas Cartelli's "Prospero in Africa," in *Shakespeare Reproduced: The Text in History and Ideology*, ed. Jean E. Howard and Marion F. O'Connor (New York and London, 1987), pp. 99–115, sees the play's complicity in colonial discourse as part of its meaning, but does not see its usefulness to anti-colonialist discourse as having this same status. Ania Loomba, *Gender, Race, Renaissance Drama* (Manchester, 1989), pp. 145–6, also points out the dissymmetry in Cartelli's analysis.

5 For the claim that the moments when it seems to problematize or contest colonialist discourse constitute or reveal the play's "political unconscious," see Paul Brown, "'This Thing of Darkness I acknowledge mine': *The Tempest* and the Discourse of Colonialism," in *Political Shakespeare: New Essays in Cultural Materialism* (Ithaca, NY, 1985), pp. 48–71, especially p. 69. For the play as in systematic bad faith, see Lorie Jerrell Leininger, "Cracking the Code of *The Tempest*," in *Contemporary Critical Approaches to Shakespeare*, ed. Harry R. Garvin (Lewisburg, PA, 1980 [*Bucknell Review*, 25]), pp. 121–31.

6 For a parallel position, both substantively and methodologically, with regard to *The Tempest*, see Harry Berger, Jr., "Miraculous Harp: A Reading of *The Tempest*" (1969), in *Second World and Green World: Studies in Renaissance Fiction-Making* (Berkeley, CA, 1988), p. 150. For the general position, see Strier, *Resistant Structures*, pp. 166–7 and 204ff.

7 Unless otherwise noted, references are to *The Tempest*, ed. Frank Kermode (London, 1962); hereafter "*The Tempest*, Kermode, ed." Where indicated, I have departed from Kermode's text for fidelity to the Folio (the sole text), for which I have used *The Norton Facsimile of The First Folio of Shakespeare*, ed. Charlton Hinman (New York, 1968), pp. 19–37.

8 *King Lear*, in *The Norton First Folio*, Through Line Number (TLN) 1866–8.

9 For "Knowing naught (like dogges) but following," see *King Lear*, TLN 1153.

10 For Buchanan, see *De Jure Regni apud Scotos, or, A Dialogue, concerning the due Privilege of Government in the Kingdom of Scotland* (1689), pp. 57–8.

11 See Baldesar Castiglione, *The Book of the Courtier*, trans. Charles S. Singleton (New York, 1959), pp. 289–92, and note 1 above.

12 See William Strachey, *A True Repertory of the Wreck and Redemption of Sir Thomas Gates, Knight upon and from the Islands of the Bermudas: His Coming to Virginia and the Estate of that Colony Then and After*, in *A Voyage to Virginia in 1609*, ed. Louis B. Wright (Charlottesville, VA, 1964), pp. 10 and 12.

13 I have rejected the emendation of "present" to "presence" that Kermode accepts. See Stephen Orgel's comments on this in his edition of *The Tempest* (Oxford, 1987), p. 98 (hereafter cited as *The Tempest*, Orgel, ed.).

14 On the theory of Renaissance magic, and the importance in the theory of control over "daemons," see Kermode's Introduction and Appendix B (*The Tempest*, Kermode, ed.); and, *inter alia*, Robert H. West, *The Invisible World: A Study of Pneumatology in Elizabethan Drama* (Athens, GA, 1939).

15 Orgel, "Introduction," (*The Tempest*, Orgel, ed.), p. 25.

16 *Doctor Faustus*, "B-Text," 1.i.115–17, in *Doctor Faustus, A- and B-Texts*, ed. David Bevington and Eric Rasmussen (Manchester and New York, 1993). The "A-Text" version of these lines is slightly different, substituting "subjects" for spirits "of every element" (A: 1.i.124). The literal meaning is clearer in "B," but the political pun is richer in "A," and the connection to subjection is worth noting.

17 I have borrowed the useful term "magian" from Harry Levin, "Two Magian Comedies: *The Tempest* and *The Alchemist*," *Shakespeare Studies* 22 (1969), 47–58.

18 Compare Peter Hulme, *Colonial Encounters: Europe and the Native Caribbean, 1492–1797* (London and New York, 1986), pp. 127–8.

19 Mannoni, *Prospero and Caliban*, pp. 32, 203–4. It is important to note that Mannoni never denies the importance of economics to colonialism. His claim is that "the colonial is not looking for profit only," that he is also seeking and receiving a certain kind of pleasure, which it is essential to take into account "in any attempt to understand what is colonial about a colonial situation" (pp. 32, 204).

20 In *Discourse on Colonialism* (1955), trans. Joan Pinkham (New York, 1972), pp. 39–43, Césaire sees Mannoni as simply a racialist and a colonial apologist; Fanon, on the other hand, in "The So-Called Dependency Complex of Colonized Peoples," begins his discussion of Mannoni's book by saying that "its analytic thought is honest" (*Black Skin, White Masks* [1952], trans. Charles Lamm Markmann [New York, 1967], pp. 83–108). Fanon's critique is more tempered and better taken. Césaire's play (as opposed to the *Discourse*) embodies his positive debt to Mannoni. A Mannoni-like account by Césaire is quoted in S. Belhassen, "Aimé Césaire's *A Tempest*," in *Radical Perspectives in the Arts*, ed. Lee Baxandall (Baltimore, MD, 1972), p. 176.

21 *Black Skin, White Masks*, p. 107. Elizabeth Fox-Genovese and Eugene D. Genovese note that whatever one wishes to say about Mannoni's views of the colonized, he nonetheless "files a more blistering indictment of the colonizers" ("Illusions of Liberation: The Psychology of Colonialism and Revolution in the Work of Octave Mannoni and Frantz Fanon," in *Rethinking Marxism*, ed. W. Stephen Resnick and Richard Wolff [New York, 1985], p. 129). Donald Pease's claim that Fanon found Mannoni's account "contemptible" is a misrepresentation. See "Toward a Sociology of Literary Knowledge: Greenblatt, Colonialism, and the New Historicism," in *Consequences of Theory*, ed. Jonathan Arac and Barbara Johnson (Baltimore and London, 1991), pp. 110, 115.

22 *A Tempest*, pp. 65–6. Pease's claim that in Césaire's play Caliban "persuades Prospero to remain and help in the process of decolonization" is bizarrely inaccurate ("Toward a Sociology," p. 115). Prospero makes the decision for his own reasons and tells Caliban, in the final speech before the epilogue, that "henceforth I will answer your violence with violence" (p. 67).

23 Mannoni, *Prospero and Caliban*, p. 92.

24 Holinshed's *Chronicles* (1587), for instance, were "Of England, Scotland, and Ireland," and of course, "news from the new world" was plentiful throughout Europe in the sixteenth century. For Shakespeare's reading in this material, see (*inter alia*) Kermode, Introduction (*The Tempest*, Kermode, ed.), pp. xxx–xxxiv.

25 *New American World*, ed. David B. Quinn (New York, 1979), vol. v, p. 255b. On the newness and conscious classicizing of this conception, see Quinn, "Renaissance Influences in English Colonization," *Transactions of the Royal Historical Society*, 5th series, 26 (1976), 73–93.

26 On the Spanish innovation, see Helen Nader, "The End of the Old World," *Renaissance Quarterly* 45 (1992), 791–807, especially 799.

27 Prospero, it should be noted, never uses this word. The one use of it in the play (noted by Hulme, *Colonial Encounters*, p. 107) occurs, ironically, in the anti-cultivationist context of Gonzalo's golden age vision (II.i.138).

28 See Stephen Saunders Webb, *The Governors-General: The English Army and the Definition of the Empire, 1569–1681* (Chapel Hill, NC, 1979), pp. 39, 166, and 436–7. I owe my awareness of this important study to Derek Hirst.

29 See Anthony Pagden, *Lords of All the World: Ideologies of Empire in Spain, Britain,*

and France, c. 1500–c. 1800 (New Haven, CT, 1995, pp. 77–9.

30 See Nicholas Canny, "The Ideology of English Colonization: From Ireland to America," *William and Mary Quarterly*, 3rd series, 30 (1973), 575–9, and *The Elizabethan Conquest of Ireland: A Pattern Established, 1565–76* (New York, 1976); see also Webb, *The Governors-General*.

31 Sir John Davies, *A Discovery Of the True Causes Why Ireland was Never Entirely Subdued* (1612), ed. James P. Myers, Jr. (Washington, DC, 1988), p. 165; W. Crashaw, *A Sermon Preached before . . . the Lord Lawarre, Lord Governour and Captain Generall of Virginea . . . February 21, 1609* (1610), D4r.

32 Although Prospero speaks of his "house" at iv.i.186, it is never described or alluded to as a piece of architecture or as one of his own or Ariel's achievements.

33 Kermode has excellent notes on "banks with pioned and twilled brims" (*The Tempest*, Kermode, ed., pp. 97–8 and 173). For this conception of cultivated land as "impenetrably English" and including no new world aspects, see John Gillies, "Shakespeare's Virginian Masque," *English Literary History* 53 (1986), 690.

34 Quoted in Webb, *The Governors-General*, p. 14.

35 Mannoni, *Prospero and Caliban*, p. 105.

36 This is the description of Caliban in the cast list in the Folio (p. 37).

37 Quoted in Philip D. Morgan, *Slave Counterpoint: Black Culture in the Eighteenth-Century Chesapeake and Lowcountry* (Chapel Hill, NC, 1998), p. 100.

38 Mannoni, *Prospero and Caliban*, p. 102.

39 See Pagden, *Lords of All the World*, p. 78: "the Spaniards were overwhelmingly concerned with rights over people, the British with rights in things, in this case land." See also p. 91, on *encomiendas*.

40 Roberto Fernández Retamar, "Caliban: Notes Toward a Discussion of Culture in Our America" (1971), in *Caliban and Other Essays*, trans. Edward Baker (Minneapolis, MN, 1989), p. 16.

41 See Sigmund Freud, *Totem and Taboo*, trans. James Strachey, intro. by Peter Gay (New York, 1989), sec. iii, especially pp. 97–107.

42 *The Tempest*, Kermode, ed., p. 143.

43 Compare Margreta de Grazia, "*The Tempest*: Gratuitous Movement or Action Without Kibes," *Shakespeare Studies* 14 (1981), 255.

44 Prospero has been on the island twelve years (i.ii.53). It seems reasonable to think that we are meant to assume that he heard Ariel's groans and freed him (i.ii.287–92) early in his stay on the island. Ariel was penned in the tree for twelve years also. Why the play is so interested in this particular time-span is mysterious. Surely it is relevant that twelve years is approximately the time needed for a baby (not absolutely newborn) to grow to adolescence.

45 See *inter alia*, *The Tempest*, Orgel, ed., pp. 22–3.

46 Prospero here imagines overgoing Sycorax, as is appropriate for his "more potent" Art, since she used a softer tree (a pine) and one that was already cloven (i.ii.275–9).

47 For "murmuring," see Exodus 16:7, Numbers 14:2, 27, 29, 36; in the New
    Testament, Luke 5:30, John 6:41, etc. The Geneva Bible (1560) and the
    Authorized Version (1611) concur in this translation. English poets of the
    period used the term in this sense; see especially Herbert's "The Bunch of
    Grapes" and Milton's "When I consider how my light is spent."

48 George Lamming, *The Pleasures of Exile* (London, 1960), p. 115.

49 Mannoni, *Prospero and Caliban*, p. 105. Berger remarks on how uncomfort-
    able Prospero is in this dialogue ("Miraculous Harp," p. 169).

50 Compare Menenius on "the great toe of this assembly" in *Coriolanus*, ed.
    Phillip Brockbank (London, 1976), 1.i.154. For a reminder that this image,
    here and in *Coriolanus*, is "open to tonal registers of irony, amusement, and
    teasing," I am indebted to a communication from Lois Kim of the Univer-
    sity of Texas at Austin. I am not sure whether this important point about
    tone alters what Lorie Leininger calls the "crucial" status of the head–toe
    metaphor in the value-structure of the play (see "The Miranda Trap:
    Sexism and Racism in Shakespeare's *Tempest*," in *The Woman's Part: Feminist
    Criticism of Shakespeare*, ed. Carolyn Ruth Swift Lenz, Gayle Greene, and
    Carol Thomas Neely [Urbana, IL, 1980], p. 287).

51 On the lack of industriousness of the Virginia settlers, see Strachey, *True
    Repertory*, pp. 66–8; "A True Declaration of the State of Virginia," in *New
    American World*, ed. Quinn, vol. v, p. 255; and for Lane, see "Ralph Lane's
    Discourse on the First Colony," in *The Roanoke Voyages, 1584–1590*, ed. David
    Beers Quinn (London, 1955), vol. i, pp. 276–80.

52 Berger, "Miraculous Harp," p. 155.

53 On the newness of the Protestant view of labor, the classic statement is Max
    Weber, *The Protestant Ethic and the Spirit of Capitalism*, trans. Talcott Parsons,
    Foreword by R. H. Tawney (New York, 1958), especially ch. 3. Charles and
    Katherine George, *The Protestant Mind of the English Reformation, 1570–1640*
    (Princeton, NJ, 1961), chs. 3–4, see this strand of Protestant thinking as
    especially well developed in England, for which see also Christopher Hill,
    "The Industrious Sort of People," in *Society and Puritanism in Pre-Revolutionary
    England*, 2nd edn. (New York, 1967), pp. 124–44. Jeffrey Knapp's attempt to
    argue that *The Tempest* favors a georgic model of colonialism (see pp. 17–18
    above on the normativeness of this for England) founders on Prospero's
    negative attitude toward labor, which, Knapp rather bemusedly notes,
    "only inchoately approaches the husbandry Virginia requires" (!). *An Empire
    Nowhere: England, America, and Literature from* Utopia *to* The Tempest (Ber-
    keley, CA, 1992), p. 235. On the continuity in the Spanish attitude toward
    labor, see Pagden, *Lords of All the World*, p. 93.

54 See Kermode's note on 1.ii.336–7 (*The Tempest*, Kermode, ed.). Prospero's
    use of the bible seems to have been rather like Bacon's; see *The Advancement of
    Learning*, ed. G. W. Kitchin (London, 1973), p. 39. Césaire's Prospero is a
    new philosopher or "natural magician" along Baconian lines (*A Tempest*,
    pp. 7–8).

55 Compare Brown, "'This Thing of Darkness,'" p. 59.

56 For the controversy over whether this speech is rightly assigned to Miranda (as in the Folio) or should belong to Prospero, see Kermode's note (*The Tempest*, Kermode, ed., p. 32). For the meaning of "race" here, see Kermode (*The Tempest*, Kermode, ed.), pp. xlii–xlvii, but the context brings this usage eerily in line with post-Renaissance racialist discourse. Kim F. Hall (among others) sees "racialism" developing in the Renaissance. See *Things of Darkness: Economies of Race and Gender in Early Modern England* (Ithaca and London, 1995), pp. 6–8, 142–3.

57 Mannoni, *Prospero and Caliban*, p. 106 (and Part II, ch. 2).

58 On incestuous fantasy in the play, see Mannoni, *Prospero and Caliban*, pp. 106–7, and Jeffrey Stern, "The Cause of Thunder: A Psychoanalytic Reading of *King Lear, Pericles*, and *The Tempest*," PhD dissertation, English Department, University of Chicago, 1982.

59 Compare Leininger, "The Miranda Trap," p. 289: "Prospero needs Miranda as sexual bait, and then needs to protect her from the threat."

60 Translation in Sir Arthur Helps, *The Spanish Conquest of America and its Relation to the History of Slavery and to the Government of Colonies* ([1861], intro. M. Oppenheim (New York and London, 1900), vol. I, p. 266 (for the whole document, pp. 264–7); see Stephen Greenblatt, "Learning to Curse: Aspects of Linguistic Colonialism in the Sixteenth Century," in *Learning to Curse: Essays in Early Modern Culture* (New York and London, 1990), p. 29.

61 Michel Foucault, *Power–Knowledge: Selected Interviews and Other Writings*, ed. Colin Gordon (New York, 1980), p. ix, and chs. 5–6.

62 *Une Tempête*, p. 44. For a useful collection of essays by Foucault and others on the topic, see *Power*, ed. Steven Lukes (New York, 1986).

63 The *OED* cites Caliban's line in support of the definition "to overpower, overmaster." This sense is more normal in the period than the *OED* recognizes.

64 On torture in the play, see Curt Breight, "'Treason doth never prosper': *The Tempest* and the Discourse of Treason," *Shakespeare Quarterly* 41 (1990), 25–7.

65 Caliban does not seem to be aware of Ariel. In Shakespeare's play, they never speak to one another. In a remarkable scene of Césaire's play (II.i), they do speak, and discover their kinship within their differences (*A Tempest*, pp. 20–3).

66 For the genealogy of this phrase, see Strier, "From Diagnosis to Operation: The 'Root and Branch' Petition and the Grand Remonstrance," in *The Theatrical City: Culture, Theatre and Politics in London, 1576–1649*, ed. David L. Smith, Richard Strier, and David Bevington (Cambridge, 1995), p. 232.

67 According to Strachey, Paine refused to acknowledge any government in Bermuda after the shipwreck, and replied to the authorities "with such a settled and bitter violence and in such unreverent terms" that Strachey hesitates to quote him directly. Strachey does, however, give the gist of Paine's speech: "let the governor (said he) kiss, etc." (p. 48). Paine is executed, but his speech, especially "with the omitted additions," echoes

through the text. For the "Articles, Lawes, and Orders" of 1611, see *New American World*, vol. I, p. 222.

68 Brown, "'This Thing of Darkness,'" p. 63; Hulme, *Colonial Encounters*, p. 120.

69 Stephen Orgel, "Prospero's Wife," in *Representing the English Renaissance*, ed. Stephen Greenblatt (Berkeley, CA, 1988), p. 226. Orgel repeats and strongly reaffirms this view in the Introduction to his edition, p. 51.

70 Stephen Greenblatt, "Martial Law in the Land of Cockagne," in *Shakespearean Negotiations* (Berkeley, CA, 1988), p. 146.

71 Breight, "'Treason doth never prosper,'" 20, 23.

72 Greenblatt, "Martial Law," pp. 142–3, 150, 152.

73 See John Calvin, *Institutes of the Christian Religion*, ed. John T. McNeill, trans. Ford Lewis Battles (Philadelphia, PA, 1960), III.ii.1–3ff.

74 On "spirits," see, *inter alia*, Herschel Baker, "The Naturalistic View of Man," in *The Dignity of Man* (Cambridge, MA, 1947), pp. 280–2.

75 Breight, "'Treason doth never prosper,'" 11–12.

76 On the competing theologies of penance in the period, see Strier, "Herbert and Tears," *ELH* 46 (1979), 221–47.

77 Césaire, *A Tempest*, p. 33. Greenblatt alludes to this distinction with regard to *Measure for Measure* in "Martial Law," p. 140.

78 This view is ubiquitous in humanist writings. See, among many others, Thomas Wilson, *The Art of Rhetoric* (1560), ed. Peter E. Medine (University Park, PA, 1994), pp. 42–3.

79 In a parallel speech, Prospero sees the "pains" that he has "humanely taken" on Caliban's education as "all lost, quite lost," and claims that Caliban's mind has gotten worse as Caliban has grown (IV.i.188–92). But the context for this judgment is moral (the abortive conspiracy) rather than cognitive. In Césaire's play, Prospero laments that though he has indeed been able to "make a man" from "a brutish monster," he has "failed to find the path to [the] man's heart" (*A Tempest*, p. 66).

80 Leininger, "Cracking the Code," p. 127.

81 Berger, "Miraculous Harp," p. 171.

82 On grace as not medicine but favor, see Strier, *Love Known: Theology and Experience in George Herbert's Poetry* (Chicago, 1983), pp. 139 and 207.

83 I would add that it is not clear that the "acknowledgment" Caliban receives is any more theological than the "grace" that he seeks. Again, the context is entirely practical: "these fellows you / Must know and own" (v.i.275–6).

84 Orgel, "Shakespeare and the Cannibals," in *Cannibals, Witches, and Divorce: Estranging the Renaissance*, ed. Marjorie Garber (Baltimore and London, 1987), pp. 54–5. Jyotsna G. Singh confirms the point by noting that Caliban's desire is specifically and only for male children; see "Caliban versus Miranda: Race and Gender Conflicts in Postcolonial Rewritings of *The Tempest*," in *Feminist Readings of Early Modern Culture: Emerging Subjects*, ed. Valerie Traub, M. Lindsay Kaplan, and Dympna Callaghan (Cambridge, 1996), p. 200. Even in what may be a lustful moment, Caliban's praise of

Miranda to Stephano, Caliban's account stresses her "beauty" (a very high-minded expression of desire) and culminates in a vision of "brave brood" and in another dynastic fantasy, that of Stephano: "I will kill this man: his daughter and I will be king and queen" (III.ii.96–105).

85 See Mannoni, *Prospero and Caliban*, p. 107.

86 For the tendency toward idolatry, see II.ii.117, 140, etc. Caliban's desire to be a "foot licker" would, I think, have been seen as part of this tendency. Shakespeare is drawing on specifically Protestant horror, since foot-kissing was associated with devotion to the Pope. When, in the elegy entitled "Loves Progress," Donne is arguing that the kiss grows more "refin'd" as it moves downward from the face, he notes that it "At the Papall foote delights to bee" (line 84). In *John Donne: The Elegies and the Songs and Sonnets* (Oxford, 1965), Helen Gardner comments on the recurrence of this image in anti-papal propaganda (p. 135).

87 On the inconsistencies in Mannoni, see Fanon, *Black Skin, White Masks*, especially p. 85, and Fox-Genovese and Genovese, "Illusions of Liberation" (note 21 above).

88 The need for strong government in Virginia is a major theme of Strachey's *True Repertory* and of the *True Declaration of the State of Virginia*; for the willingness to use force against the native peoples, see Strachey, *True Repertory*, p. 89; for the quoted phrase, see the *True Declaration*, p. 256 (and compare Caliban's dream "That the clouds ... would open, and show riches / Ready to drop upon me" [III.ii.139–40]).

89 Bourdieu, *Outline of a Theory of Practice*, trans. Richard Nice (Cambridge, 1977), p. 190. Paul Brown ("'This Thing of Darkness,'" p. 60) uses Bourdieu's concept of "symbolic violence" with regard to Prospero's relation to Ariel.

90 Meredith Anne Skura, "Discourse and the Individual: The Case of Colonialism in *The Tempest*," *Shakespeare Quarterly* 40 (1989), 55; Gillies, "Shakespeare's Virginian Masque," 675–6.

91 "A Speach to the Lords and Commons of the Parliament" (1609), in *The Political Works of James I*, intro. Charles Howard McIlwain (Cambridge, MA, 1918), pp. 307–8. For James's disapproval of princes who take an interest in magic and magicians, see David Scott Kastan, "'The Duke of Milan / And his Brave Son': Dynastic Politics in *The Tempest*," in *Critical Essays on Shakespeare's* The Tempest, ed. Alden and Virginia Vaughan (New York, 1997). I am grateful to Professor Kastan for allowing me to see his essay in advance of publication.

92 In this regard, the play can also be seen as arguing for a Protestant marriage – for the one, for instance, that Elizabeth eventually made in 1613 to the Elector Palatine. As Donna Hamilton suggests in *Virgil and* The Tempest: *The Politics of Imitation* (Columbus, OH, 1990), pp. 41–2, the comments on the mistakenness of Alonso marrying Claribel to an "African" (II.i.119–31) seem intended, in the local context, to be an argument against the possible marriage of Elizabeth to the Catholic Duke of Savoy. "African," here,

seems to be a term of cultural distance, since, geographically, Tunis is closer to Naples than Milan is. In acknowledging the force of the "dynastic" reading, I agree with Kastan, "'The Duke of Milan / And his Brave Son,'" but I see this reading as following from the colonial one rather than as deflecting it.

2 "VOID OF STORIE": THE STRUGGLE FOR INSINCERITY IN HERBERT'S PROSE AND POETRY

1 George Herbert, "A Dialogue Anthem," in *Works*, ed. F. E. Hutchinson (London, 1959), pp. 1–4.
2 John Milton, *Paradise Lost*, in *Complete Poems and Major Prose*, ed. Merritt Y. Hughes (New York, 1957), 6.8. Henceforth cited as *PL*.
3 John Milton, "At a Solemn Music," in *Complete Poems and Major Prose*, p. 28. In making this point I do not mean to suggest that Eden is static or without dynamism. It is just that the dynamics – including the possibility of cognitive error and unhappy decisions – unfold within the security of an innocence that is theirs so long as they do not eat the apple. In Eden no action aside from the action of disobeying God's sole command is fatal or irreversible. In fallen life fatality lurks around every corner.
4 Barbara Leah Harman, *Costly Monuments: Representations of the Self in George Herbert's Poetry* (Cambridge, MA and London, 1982), p. 166.
5 *Ibid.*, p. 99, emphasis in original.
6 *Ibid.*, p. 169, emphasis in original.
7 Richard Strier, *Love Known: Theology and Experience in George Herbert's Poetry* (Chicago and London, 1983), p. 252.
8 Joseph Blount Cheshire, ed., *A Priest to the Temple, or, the Country Parson... By George Herbert* (New York, 1908), p. 6.
9 W. Allen Powell, "The Nature of George Herbert's Audience as Revealed by Method and Tone in 'The Country Parson' and 'The Temple,'" *Proceedings of the Conference of College Teachers of English of Texas* 36 (1971), 36.
10 Cristina Malcolmson, "George Herbert's *Country Parson* and the Character of Social Identity," *Studies in Philology* 85 (1988), 246.
11 *Ibid.*, 248.
12 Kristine Wolberg, "All Possible Art: George Herbert's *The Country Parson* and Courtesy," *John Donne Journal*, vol. 8, nos. 1 and 2 (1989), 168.
13 Michael C. Schoenfeldt, *Prayer and Power: George Herbert and Renaissance Courtship* (Chicago and London, 1991), p. 99.
14 Malcolmson, "George Herbert's *Country Parson*," 261.
15 Wolberg, "All Possible Art," 186.
16 Cheshire, ed., *A Priest to the Temple, or, the Country Parson*, p. 231; ch. 6.
17 Rosemond Tuve, *A Reading of George Herbert* (London, 1952), especially pp. 189–90.
18 Ben Jonson, 'To Inigo, Marquis Would-Be a Corollary," in *The Oxford*

Authors: Ben Jonson, ed. Ian Donaldson (Oxford and New York, 1976), p. 465.

19 *Ibid.*

20 Robert A. Lanham, *The Motives of Eloquence: Literary Rhetoric in the Renaissance* (New Haven, CT, 1985), p. 47.

21 *Ibid.*, p. 14.

22 *Ibid.*, p. 47.

23 Herbert, *Works*, p. 445.

24 George Herbert, *The Country Parson, The Temple*, ed. John N. Wall, Jr. (New York, 1984), p. 75.

25 *Ibid.*, p. 79.

26 Michel Foucault, *Discipline and Punish* (New York, 1995), p. 200.

27 *Ibid.*, p. 109.

28 George Herbert, *Latin Poetry*, trans. John Mark McCloskey and Paul R. Murphy (Athens, OH, 1965), pp. 37, 39.

29 John Milton, "An Apology," in *Complete Prose Works* ed. Don M. Wolfe, vol 1 (New Haven, CT, 1953), pp. 941–2.

30 Debora K. Shuger, *Habits and Thoughts in the English Renaissance: Religion, Politics and the Dominant Culture* (Berkeley, CA, 1991), p. 209.

31 William Perkins, cited in Jonathan Dollimore, *Radical Tragedy: Religion, Ideology and Power in the Drama of Shakespeare and his Contemporaries*, 2nd edn. (Durham, NC, 1993), p. xlvii.

32 Sir Thomas More, *Utopia* with *The Dialogue of Comfort*, ed. Judge John O'Hagen (London, 1923), pp. 323–4.

33 Schoenfeldt, *Prayer and Power*, p. 125.

34 "On Narcissism," cited in Jonathan Goldberg, *Voice Terminal Echo: Postmodernism and English Renaissance Texts* (New York, 1986), p. 108.

35 *Ibid.*

36 Shuger, *Habits and Thoughts*, p. 169.

37 Schoenfeldt, *Prayer and Power*, p. 117. I do not, however, follow Schoenfeldt's argument to all of its conclusions. I agree with Richard Strier that Herbert's poetry does not so much display or enact "self seeking courtliness" and "manipulation" as it makes ironic critical use of them (*Resistant Structures: Particularity, Radicalism and Renaissance Texts* [Berkeley, Los Angeles, London, 1995], pp. 111–12). Strier is also correct, I think, when he observes that "Religion in general is something of a problem for New Historicism" (p. 73). On this point see my "Milton's Career and the Career of Theory," in *There's No Such Thing as Free Speech, and It's a Good Thing, Too* (New York, Oxford, 1994), pp. 264–5.

38 Malcolmson, "George Herbert's *Country Parson*," 263.

39 *Ibid.*, 262.

40 *Ibid.*, 263.

3 SIR KENELM DIGBY'S REWRITINGS OF HIS LIFE

1 E. W. Bligh, *Sir Kenelm Digby and his Venetia* (London, 1932).
2 Vittorio Gabrieli, *Sir Kenelm Digby: un inglese italianato nell'età della controriforma* (Rome, 1957) is a full-scale biography that appeared almost simultaneously with R. T. Petersson's *Sir Kenelm Digby: the Ornament of England, 1603–1665* (London, 1956). Gabrieli's account of the Digby marriage is based largely on documents he published partly in an appendix and augmented separately as "A New Digby Letter-Book: 'In Praise of Venetia'" in *The National Library of Wales Journal (NLWJ)* 9 (1955–6), 113–48, 440–62, and 10 (1957), 81–106; and as Sir Kenelm Digby, *Loose Fantasies*, ed. Vittorio Gabrieli (Rome, 1968). The latter is an edition of the British Library Harley MS 6758, a carefully transcribed copy of Digby's early *roman à clef* ("loose fantasies" is the author's own title) with his additions and corrections written in. Sir Nicholas Harris Nicolas had edited the manuscript as *Private Memoirs of Sir Kenelm Digby* (London, 1827 [with bowdlerized "castrations" separately issued in 1828]).
3 Philippe Ariès, *The Hour of our Death* ([1977; trans. 1981] New York, 1991), pp. 377, 393. The same author has recapitulated the subject in *Western Attitudes Toward Death: From the Middle Ages to the Present* (Baltimore, MD, 1974) and in the richly iconographic *Images of Man and Death* (Cambridge, MA, 1985). Several of the poets contemporary with Digby have been placed in a relevant context in Arnold Stein, *The House of Death: Messages from the English Renaissance* (Baltimore, MD, 1986). Stein analyzes Ariès's work sympathetically, but with the proviso that religious particularities were more significant in the Renaissance than the cultural historian takes note of in his overarching structure.
4 H. Aram Veeser, "Introduction" to *The New Historicism*, ed. H. Aram Veeser (New York and London, 1989), p. ix, citing Stephen Greenblatt, *Shakespearean Negotiations: the Circulation of Social Energy in Renaissance England* (Berkeley and Los Angeles, 1988), p. 1.
5 "That many of the texts known to an educated English reader of the seventeenth century would have been encountered in manuscript rather than in print is hardly news ... That some of this material was the creation of professional scribes, whose work was distributed through organized markets, while less widely known, is also a matter of record ... What is lacking to date has been an awareness ... of a larger phenomenon – scribal publication – which had a role in the culture and commerce of texts just as assured as that of print publication," says Harold Love in prefacing his *Scribal Publication in Seventeenth-century England* (Oxford, 1993), pp. iii–iv. In one respect, this chapter may be considered an addendum to Love's study who, while concentrating upon satiric poetry of the post-Restoration decades, says "it will be evident from what follows that the accession of James I precipitated a situation in which, for a variety of reasons, texts of great political and intellectual importance were deliberately reserved for the scribal medium" (p. vi).

6 *Ibid.*, p. 33.
7 I quote from Thomas Walkley's petition to block unauthorized editions from Frank Marcham, "Thomas Walkley and the Ben Jonson 'Works' of 1640," *The Library* 11 (1930–1), 225–9. Cf. Petersson, *Digby*, p. 333 n. 108, and David Riggs, *Ben Jonson: a Life* (Cambridge, MA, 1989), pp. 337–42.
8 *The Poems of Robert Southwell, S.J.* ed. James H. McDonald and Nancy Pollard Brown (Oxford, 1967), pp. xxxv–xxxvi, lxxvii–civ, especially xcii–xcix; I cite from p. xxxv. Louis Martz, *The Poetry of Meditation: a Study in English Religious Literature of the Seventeenth Century* (New Haven, CT [1954] rev. 1962), pp. 103–7, traces in detail the obliteration in both form and intention of one of Southwell's meditational "rosaries" through displacements and excisions "not printed in the early editions, for their hyperbolic praises of the Virgin go beyond anything allowed by even the most conservative Anglican orthodoxy" (pp. 104–5).
9 Bligh, *Digby and his Venetia*, pp. 196–9; Petersson, *Digby*, pp. 139–42.
10 Petersson, *Digby*, p. 134 and p. 338 n. 41.
11 John Aubrey, *Brief Lives*, ed. A. Clark (2 vols., Oxford, 1898), vol. I, pp. 127, 229–30, 232.
12 Bligh, *Digby and his Venetia*, pp. 89–91.
13 Aubrey, *Brief Lives*, vol. I, p. 226; cf. p. 230.
14 *Loose Fantasies* ed. Gabrieli, p. 10. All later citations will refer to this edition by page number. Gabrieli points out how inconsistently Digby maintains a fictional distance between his "narrator" and Theagenes (pp. xxiii–xxiv). Partly on this basis, he concludes with Nicolas that the romance was never circulated, nor meant to be made public (p. xviii), although Digby repeatedly revised it (p. xxiv) with "the best literary expression he was capable of" (p. xviii). The last pages of *Loose Fantasies* constitute the usual ambiguity toward publication that characterizes so many authorial denials of ambition in the sixteenth and seventeenth centuries: "If these loose papers should have the fortune to fall into any man's hands, to the which they were never designed, I desire that this last scrawl may beg pardon for the rest . . . no man hath reason to lose any time in perusing so trivial a discourse of a young and unstayed head . . . I thought fit . . . to say this much in my own excuse, to the end that I may not be thought to have grown unto such a height of immodesty, as to desire that my follies may after me remain upon record. Therefore, whosoever it is that may meet with this . . . convert these blotted sheets into clear flame" (pp. 172–3).
15 *Brief Lives*, vol. I, p. 225.
16 *Ibid.*, p. 226.
17 "Letter-Book," *NLWJ* 9, 448. In the letters Digby refers frequently to his own sexual adventures with a combination of complacency and penitence best captured in this summary: "Vpon my soul and conscience, if the hansomest, greatest, and loueliest woman in the world would haue bin so muche a foole as to haue bin in loue with me, I could not haue loued her againe. *Well I might haue bin courteous to her*, but my loue had no other obiect

but my wife" (452; emphasis mine). See, in addition, *NLWJ* 9, 141, 146, 446; 10, 97; and the letters in Gabrieli, *Digby*, pp. 249, 271, 272. Further citations from the letter-book, "In Praise of Venetia," will appear by volume and page number in the text.

18 Bligh, *Digby and his Venetia*, p. 250, quoting Finch's journal.

19 Aubrey, *Brief Lives*, vol. I, p. 231.

20 *Ibid.*, pp. 226–7.

21 John M. Wallace, "Thomas Traherne and the Structure of Meditation," *English Literary History* 25 (1958), 89.

22 Gabrieli, *Digby*, p. 239.

23 For a detailed account of the popular handbooks (largely Roman Catholic in origin) used in England and their overlapping descriptions of the formal meditation see Martz, *The Poetry of Meditation*, especially pp. 25–107, from which these quotations are taken.

24 Gabrieli, *Digby*, p. 246.

25 *Ibid.*, p. 248.

26 *Ibid.*, p. 249.

4 THOMAS HOBBES AND THE RENAISSANCE *STUDIA HUMANITATIS*

For commenting on drafts I am deeply grateful to Kinch Hoekstra, Susan James, Tom Sorell, and James Tully. To Karl Schuhmann I owe a special debt both for his exceptionally helpful comments and for supplying me with many additional references. For permission to quote from the Hardwick and Hobbes MSS now lodged at Chatsworth I am greatly indebted to his Grace the Duke of Devonshire and the Trustees of the Chatsworth settlement.

1 John M. Wallace, *Destiny his Choice: the Loyalism of Andrew Marvell* (Cambridge, 1968), p. 4.

2 *Ibid.*, especially pp. 54–5, 57, 62–4, 82, 99. Cf. also John M. Wallace, "The Engagement Controversy 1649–1652: an Annotated List of Pamphlets," *Bulletin of the New York Public Library* 68 (1964), 384–405; the discussion of Hobbes's *De Corpore Politico* is at pp. 398–9.

3 See for example Tom Sorell, *Hobbes* (London, 1986), p. 1.

4 See Leo Strauss, *The Political Philosophy of Hobbes: its Basis and its Genesis*, trans. Elsa M. Sinclair (Chicago, 1963), p. 30; Miriam M. Reik, *The Golden Lands of Thomas Hobbes* (Detroit, 1977), especially pp. 25–34; David Johnston, *The Rhetoric of Leviathan: Thomas Hobbes and the Politics of Cultural Transformation* (Princeton, NJ, 1986), pp. 3–25; Richard Tuck, *Hobbes* (Oxford, 1989), pp. 1–11.

5 The exception is Karl Schuhmann, "Hobbes and Renaissance Philosophy," in *Hobbes oggi*, ed. Andrea Napoli (Milan, 1990), pp. 331–49, who stresses (p. 332) the "broadly humanistic direction" of Hobbes's work after 1615 and begins to trace (pp. 332–6) the relations between Hobbes's early studies and the Renaissance *studia humanitatis*.

6 The argument that follows draws heavily on ch. 6 of Quentin Skinner, *Reason and Rhetoric in the Philosophy of Hobbes* (Cambridge, 1996), although I have revised and greatly extended my earlier analysis, in particular by the use of various manuscript sources not previously exploited.

7 On the Renaissance *studia humanitatis* see P. O. Kristeller, "Humanism and Scholasticism in the Italian Renaissance," in *Renaissance Thought and its Sources*, ed. M. Mooney (New York, 1979), pp. 85–105.

8 Kenneth Charlton, *Education in Renaissance England* (London, 1965), pp. 116–19; Anthony Grafton and Lisa Jardine, *From Humanism to the Humanities: Education and the Liberal Arts in Fifteenth- and Sixteenth-century Europe* (London, 1986), pp. 143–5.

9 John Aubrey, *Brief Lives*, ed. A. Clark (2 vols., Oxford, 1898), vol. 1, p. 329.

10 *Ibid.*, vol. 1, p. 328.

11 *Ibid.*

12 *Ibid.*, vol. 1, pp. 328–9.

13 Thomas Hobbes, *Thomae Hobbes Malmesburiensis Vita Carmine Expressa*, in *Thomae Hobbes Malmesburiensis Opera Philosophica Quae Latine Scripsit, Omnia*, ed. Sir William Molesworth, vol. 1 (London, 1839), pp. lxxxvi–lxxxvii, lines 33–50.

14 Aubrey, *Brief Lives*, vol. 1, p. 330.

15 Hobbes, *Thomae Hobbes Malmesburiensis Vita Carmine Expressa*, p. lxxxvii, lines 63–5.

16 Noel Malcolm, "Biographical Register of Hobbes's Correspondents," in *The Correspondence of Thomas Hobbes* (2 vols., Oxford, 1994), pp. 855–6.

17 Charlton, *Education in Renaissance England*, pp. 142, 159; Joan Simon, *Education and Society in Tudor England* (Cambridge, 1979), pp. 203–9.

18 Chatsworth MSS, Hardwick MS 29, p. 38; cf. Malcolm, "Biographical Register of Hobbes's Correspondents," p. 856n.

19 Thomas Hobbes, *T. Hobbes Malmesburiensis Vita*, in *Opera Philosophica*, ed. Molesworth, vol. 1, p. xiii: "Anno sequente, cum domino suo in urbe perpetuo fere degens, quod didicerat linguae Graecae et Latinae, magna ex parte amiserat."

20 *Ibid.*

21 Chatsworth, Hobbes MS A.6, lines 75–6 cf. Hobbes, *Thomae Hobbes Malmesburiensis Vita Carmine Expressa*, p. lxxxviii, lines 73–4:

> Ille per hos annos mihi praebuit otia, libros
> Omnimodos studiis suppeditatque meis.

Hobbes MS A.6 (Chatsworth) is a fair copy of Hobbes's verse *Vita* in the hand of his last amanuensis, James Wheldon, with some corrections by Hobbes. Since this is in some places a better text than the one printed by Molesworth (Hobbes, *Thomae Hobbes Malmesburiensis Vita Carmine Expressa*), I have preferred to use it when quoting from the *Vita*, although I have also given references to Molesworth's edition in brackets.

22 Hobbes, *T. Hobbes Malmesburiensis Vita*, pp. xiii–xiv: "Itaque cum in Angliam reversus esset, Historicos et poetas (adhibitis grammaticorum celebrium

commentariis) versavit diligenter."

23 *Ibid.*, p. xiv: "non ut floride, sed ut Latine posset scribere, et vim verborum cogitatis congruentem invenire."

24 See Thomas Hobbes, *Leviathan, sive De Materia, Forma, & Potestate Civitatis Ecclesiasticae et Civilis* in *Thomae Hobbes Malmesburiensis Opera Philosophica Quae Latine Scripsit, Omnia* (1668), p. 346, on Lucian as "bonus author linguae Graecae."

25 Thomas Hobbes, *Critique du De Mundo de Thomas White*, ed. Jean Jacquot and Harold Whitmore Jones (Paris, 1973), p. 329.

26 Thomas Hobbes, *Lux Mathematica*, in *Opera Philosophica*, ed. Molesworth, vol. v (1845), p. 148.

27 Thomas Hobbes, *Historia Ecclesiastica*, in *Opera Philosophica*, ed. Molesworth, vol. v, p. 361, line 438.

28 Thomas Hobbes, *Leviathan, or The Matter, Forme, & Power of a Common-wealth Ecclesiasticall and Civill*, ed. Richard Tuck (Cambridge, 1996), p. 56. The reference is duly picked up by Tricaud in Thomas Hobbes, *Leviathan*, ed. and trans. François Tricaud (Paris, 1971), p. 73.

29 Hobbes, *Leviathan*, ed. Tuck, p. 147; cf. Lucian, "Heracles," in *Lucian*, ed. and trans. A. M. Harmon, vol. i (1913), p. 65.

30 The paraphrase, published in English as *A Briefe of the Art of Rhetorique*, appeared anonymously, but Hobbes's authorship has never hitherto been questioned. For some serious doubts, however, see below, note 114.

31 See for example Strauss, *Political Philosophy of Hobbes*, pp. 35, 41–2; Gary Shapiro, "Reading and Writing in the Text of Hobbes's *Leviathan*," *Journal of the History of Philosophy* 18 (1980), 148–50.

32 Thomas Hobbes, *Of the Life and History of Thucydides*, in *Hobbes's Thucydides*, ed. Richard Schlatter (New Brunswick, NJ, 1975), pp. 10, 18–19, 26–7. As Lessay points out in Thomas Hobbes, *Textes sur l'hérésie et sur l'histoire*, ed. Franck Lessay (Paris, 1993), p. 139n., Hobbes's reference to the *De Oratore* is inaccurate. The passage he cites comes from *De Oratore*, ix.32.

33 See the allusions in Thomas Hobbes, *The Answer of Mr. Hobbes to Sir Will. D'Avenant's Preface before Gondibert*, in *Sir William Davenant's Gondibert*, ed. David F. Gladish (Oxford, 1971), especially pp. 49–51; various references in Hobbes, *Leviathan*, ed. Tuck (e.g., p. 176) and the invocation of Quintilian's judgment on Lucian in Thomas Hobbes, *Concerning the Virtues of an Heroic Poem*, Preface to *The Iliads and Odysseys of Homer*, in *The English Works*, vol. x, ed. Molesworth (London, 1844), p. viii.

34 Hobbes, *Thomae Hobbes Malmesburiensis Vita Carmine Expressa*, p. lxxxviii, lines 77–8.

35 Aubrey, *Brief Lives*, vol. i, p. 349.

36 See, respectively, Hobbes, *Critique du De Mundo de Thomas White*, ed. Jacquot and Whitmore Jones, p. 121 and note; Hobbes, *Leviathan*, ed. Tuck, p. 312; Thomas Hobbes, *De Corpore*, in *Opera Philosophica*, ed. Molesworth, vol. i, p. 414: "Densum ergo idem est quod frequens, ut densa caterva; rarum idem quod infrequens, ut rara acies, rara tecta." Virgil, *Aeneid*, ed. and

trans. H. Rushton Fairclough (2 vols., London, 1916–18), VIII, lines 98–9 has "rara domorum/ tecta vident" while IX, line 508 has "rara est acies." See Virgil, *Aeneid*, ed. Rushton Fairclough, vol. II, pp. 66 and 146.

37 Hobbes, *Thomae Hobbes Malmesburiensis Vita Carmine Expressa*, ed. Molesworth, p. lxxxviii, line 79.

38 Duly noted by Tricaud in Hobbes, *Leviathan*, ed. Tricaud, p. 105 and note.

39 Hobbes, *De Cive: the Latin Version*, ed. Howard Warrender (2 vols., Oxford, 1983), XV.XV, vol. II, p. 227; cf. Martial, *Epigrams*, ed. and trans. Walter C. A. Ker (2 vols., London, 1919–20), VIII. XXIV, vol. II, p. 18.

40 Hobbes, *Concerning the Virtues of an Heroic Poem*, in *English Works*, vol. X, ed. Molesworth, p. vii; cf. Hobbes, *Answer to D'Avenant's Preface Before Gondibert*, ed. Gladish, p. 46.

41 Hobbes not only imitates Ovid's elegiac couplets but even echoes some turns of phrase. For details see Skinner, *Reason and Rhetoric in the Philosophy of Hobbes*, p. 233, n. 145.

42 In *The Elements of Law* the reference to "an *oderunt peccare* in the unjust" alludes to Horace, *Satires, Epistles and Ars Poetica*, ed. and trans. H. Rushton Fairclough (revised edn., London, 1929), I.XVI, line 52. See p. 354, and cf. Thomas Hobbes, *The Elements of Law Natural and Politic*, ed. Ferdinand Tönnies (2nd edn., intro. M. M. Goldsmith, London, 1969), p. 83. In Hobbes, *De Cive*, ed. Warrender, the line "qui consulta patrum, qui leges iuraque servant" is quoted (except that *servant* should read *servat*) from Horace, *Epistles*, I.XVI, line 41. See Horace, *Satires, Epistles and Ars Poetica*, ed. Rushton Fairclough, p. 354 and cf. Hobbes, *De Cive*, ed. Warrender, XIII.XII, vol. II, p. 200. (The quotation recurs in *Leviathan*. See Hobbes, *Leviathan*, ed. Tuck, p. 26.) In the *Critique* of Thomas White's *De Mundo* the phrase "quis vir bonus" alludes to Horace, *Epistles*, i.xvi, line 40. See Horace, *Satires, Epistles and Ars Poetica*, ed. Rushton Fairclough, p. 354 and cf. Hobbes, *Critique du De Mundo de Thomas White*, ed. Jacquot and Whitmore Jones, p. 414. (In *De Corpore* Hobbes converts the allusion into a quotation. See Hobbes, *De Corpore*, ed. Molesworth, p. 26.) A further allusion to Horace's *Epistles* occurs in chapter 42 of *Leviathan*. See Horace, *Satires, Epistles and Ars Poetica*, ed. Rushton Fairclough, I.XVIII, line 15, p. 368 and cf. Hobbes, *Leviathan*, ed. Tuck, p. 339.

43 Hobbes, *T. Hobbes Malmesburiensis Vita*, ed. Molesworth, p. xx: "Natura sua, et primis annis, ferebatur ad lectionem historiarum et poetarum."

44 Hobbes MS (Chatsworth) A.6, lines 77–8 (cf. Hobbes, *Thomae Hobbes Malmesburiensis Vita Carmine Expressa*, ed. Molesworth, p. lxxxviii, lines 75–6):
   Vertor et ad nostras, ad Graecas, atque Latinas
      Historias.

45 Hobbes, *T. Hobbes Malmesburiensis*, ed. Molesworth, p. xiv; see also Hobbes MS A.6, line 82 (cf. Hobbes, *Thomae Hobbes Malmesburiensis Vita Carmine Expressa*, ed. Molesworth, p. lxxxviii, line 80): "Sed mihi prae reliquis Thucidides placuit."

46 Aubrey, *Brief Lives*, vol. I, p. 331. But if this was so, it seems strange that

Hobbes never makes any reference or even (so far as I am aware) any allusion to the *Commentarii* in his later works.

47 *Ibid.*, p. 349.

48 For *The Elements* see Hobbes, *Elements of Law*, ed. Tönnies, pp. 175–6. For *De Cive* see Hobbes, *De Cive*, ed. Warrender, XII.XII, pp. 192–3. Hobbes also quotes Sallust in his *Critique* of Thomas White's *De Mundo*. See Hobbes, *Critique du De Mundo de Thomas White*, ed. Jacquot and Whitmore Jones, p. 424.

49 Duly noted by Tricaud in Hobbes, *Leviathan*, ed. Tricaud, p. 18 and note. Several anecdotes in *De Cive* also appear to be taken from Plutarch. See for example Hobbes, *De Cive*, ed. Warrender, V.V, p. 133; VII.XVI, p. 157; X.XV, p. 179.

50 The discussion of cobweb laws in chapter 27 of *Leviathan* is taken from Plutarch's life of Solon, evidently in North's translation. See Hobbes, *Leviathan*, ed. Tuck, p. 204 and cf. Plutarch, *The Lives of the Noble Grecians and Romanes, Compared Together,* trans. Thomas North (1579), p. 89. That Hobbes read Plutarch at an early stage is clear from the fact that he already refers to this passage in the *Discourse* on Tacitus published in *Horae Subsecivae* in 1620. See [William Cavendish and Thomas Hobbes], *Horae Subsecivae. Observations and Discourses* (1620), p. 272. For Hobbes's authorship of this *Discourse* (and of two others) see below, notes 76 and 77.

51 See Thomas Hobbes, *Eight Bookes of the Peloponnesian Warre Written by Thucydides ... Interpreted ... By Thomas Hobbes* (1629), in which "The Mappe of Antient Greece" is tipped in after Sig. c, 4^v.

52 *Hobbes's Thucydides*, ed. Schlatter, p. 9.

53 See for example Hobbes, *Eight Bookes of the Peloponnesian Warre Written by Thucydides*, Sig. b, 2^v.

54 *Ibid.*, Sig. c, 1^r; Sig. c, 2^r; Sig. c, 3^r.

55 For full detail see Skinner, *Reason and Rhetoric in the Philosophy of Hobbes*, p. 236, n. 167. Hobbes later alludes to Livy's history at several points in *Leviathan*. See for example Hobbes, *Leviathan*, ed. Tuck, p. 82 (the story of Numa) and p. 99 (the example of an oath). He also refers to Livy by name on two occasions. See Hobbes, *Leviathan*, ed. Tuck, pp. 49, 261.

56 Hobbes, *Of the Life and History of Thucydides,* in *Hobbes's Thucydides*, ed. Schlatter, p. 27.

57 See below, notes 103 and 104.

58 Hobbes, *Elements of Law*, ed. Tönnies, pp. 30, 172. Hobbes had earlier mentioned *Utopia* in *A Discourse of Lawes*, one of his anonymous contributions to *Horae Subsecivae* in 1620. See [Cavendish and Hobbes], *Horae Subsecivae*, p. 509, and for Hobbes's contributions to the *Horae* see below, notes 76 and 77.

59 Letter 18 in Thomas Hobbes, *The Correspondence*, ed. Noel Malcolm (2 vols., Oxford, 1994), p. 32. Hobbes and Selden were fellow members of Magdalen Hall Oxford, and became friends toward the end of Selden's life. Aubrey, *Brief Lives*, vol. I, p. 369.

60 Hobbes, *Elements of Law*, ed. Tönnies, pp. 170, 174, 177.

61 William Jaggard, *A Catalogue of such English Bookes, as lately have bene, and now are in Printing for Publication*, ed. Oliver M. Willard, in *Stanford Studies in Language and Literature* (Stanford, CA, 1941), p. 169.

62 [Cavendish, William], *A Discourse Against Flatterie* (1611), Sig. A, 2^r.

63 See, most recently, John T. Harwood, *Introduction* to *The Rhetorics of Thomas Hobbes and Bernard Lamy* (Carbondale and Edwardsville, IL, 1986), p. 26 and note.

64 One of the findings of the computer analysis reported in Noel B. Reynolds and John L. Hilton, "Thomas Hobbes and Authorship of the *Horae Subsecivae*," in *History of Political Thought* 14 (1993), 369.

65 Noel Malcolm, "Hobbes, Sandys, and the Virginia Company," *Historical Journal* 24 (1981), 321, suggests that these were probably drafted before 1610, although later revised to take account of Cavendish's foreign travels, including as they do the Discourse describing Rome.

66 Hobbes MSS (Chatsworth), MS D.3, p. vi.

67 Correctly noted in Strauss, *Political Philosophy of Hobbes*, p. xii and note, and more recently in Friedrich Wolf, *Die Neue Wissenschaft des Thomas Hobbes ... Mit Hobbes' Essayes* (Stuttgart, 1969) and Harwood, *Introduction* to *Hobbes and Lamy*, p. 26 and note.

68 Hobbes MS D.3 has corrections at pp. 5, 13, 15, 22, 48, 58, etc., and Cavendish's signature at p. vi.

69 As claimed in Wolf, *Die Neue Wissenschaft des Hobbes*, pp. 113–31.

70 For example, on the value of studying history.

71 Hobbes MS D.3, title page.

72 [Cavendish and Hobbes], *Horae Subsecivae*.

73 Edward Arber (ed.), *A Transcript of the Registers of the Company of Stationers of London, 1554–1640 AD* (5 vols., London and Birmingham, 1875–94), vol. IV, p. 362.

74 The two pieces added to the earlier collection of ten "Essayes" (Hobbes MS D.3) are entitled "Of a Country Life" and "Of Religion."

75 [Cavendish and Hobbes], *Horae Subsecivae*, pp. 223–324; 325–417; 419–503; 505–41.

76 See the computer analysis reported in Reynolds and Hilton, "Thomas Hobbes and Authorship of the *Horae Subsecivae*," pp. 366, 369, and Figure 6 in Appendix 3, p. 378.

77 Reynolds and Hilton, *ibid.*, p. 366, state the outcome of their computer analysis with precision when they conclude that what it shows is that "these texts are statistically indistinguishable from uncontested Hobbes texts." Later they state that "we conclude that Hobbes wrote" these three Discourses (p. 369). They also state (p. 369) that the analysis establishes no less firmly that Hobbes was *not* the author of the fourth Discourse – the one on flattery – which now appears almost certainly to have been written by Cavendish, though no doubt with the advice of Hobbes.

78 Malcolm, "Biographical Register of Hobbes's Correspondents," pp. 808–9.

79 *Ibid.*

80 Hobbes, *Thomae Hobbes Malmesburiensis Vita Carmine Expressa*, ed. Molesworth, p. lxxxix, line 103.

81 *Ibid.*, p. lxxxix, lines 99–101.

82 Hobbes MSS (Chatsworth), MS D.2, an exercise-book in the hand of the third Earl of Devonshire. This contains thirty geometrical proofs, twelve of which are initialed by Hobbes ("T.H."), presumably to show that he had checked them. The first ten proofs have marginal comments added by Hobbes, who also supplied corollaries in the case of 10, 13, 14, 25, 26, 27, 29, and 30.

83 Hobbes MS A.6, lines 98–9 (cf. Hobbes, *Thomae Hobbes Malmesburiensis Vita Carmine Expressa*, ed. Molesworth, p. lxxxviii, lines 95–6):

> Hunc Romanarum sensus cognoscere vocum,
> Iungere quoque decet verba Latina modo.

84 Hobbes MSS (Chatsworth) MS D.1, bound MS volume marked on spine *Latin Exercises*.

85 Hobbes MS A.6, lines 100–1 (cf. Hobbes, *Thomae Hobbes Malmesburiensis Vita Carmine Expressa*, ed. Molesworth, p. lxxxviii, lines 97–8):

> Fallere quaque solent indoctos Rhetores arte;
> Quid facit Orator . . .

86 Hobbes MS A.6, line 101 (cf. Hobbes, *Thomae Hobbes Malmesburiensis Vita Carmine Expressa*, ed. Molesworth, p. lxxxviii, line 98): "Quid facit Orator, quidque Poeta facit."

87 Hardwick MS 70 (Chatsworth), exercise-book in hand of third Earl of Devonshire, 53 fos., unpaginated, signed "William Cavendysshe" on inside front and back covers, "William Devoshier" on inside back cover. All the translations in this manuscript are taken from a single source, a selection from Valerius Maximus entitled *Factorum et Dictorum Memorabilium Libri Novem*. I am deeply indebted to Karl Schuhmann for establishing this point.

88 Cf. also Hobbes MS D.1, the exercise-book containing the Latin version of Aristotle's *Rhetoric* at pp. 1–143. This also contains (at pp. 160–54 *rev.*) some Latin prose extracts, including notes on Tarquin and Brutus (p. 157), Camillus (p. 156) and Romulus (p. 155). Karl Schuhmann has identified the source as Florus's epitome of Livy's history.

89 Hardwick MS 70, *sub* "Of the elder Cato."

90 Hardwick MS 70, *sub* "Of Publius Rutilius and Gaius Mallius [*sic*] Consuls" and *sub* "Of the Uses of the Velites first found out."

91 Sir Thomas Elyot, *The Book Named the Governor*, ed. S. E. Lehmberg (London, 1962), p. 39.

92 Hobbes MSS (Chatsworth) MS A.8, bound folio volume marked on spine *Three Digests*. The *Parva Moralia* manuscript, thirty-nine fos., is marked MS A.8 (1). Due to a modern misbinding, it no longer appears as the first in order in the bound volume. I have followed Beal in assuming that the manuscript was "probably made by Hobbes for his pupil, the third Earl of Devonshire." Peter Beal, ed., *Index of English Literary Manuscripts*, vol. II,

1625–1700, Part 1, *Behn–King* (London, 1987), p. 582. However, Karl Schuhmann has expressed some doubts (private communication) as to whether this manuscript is likely to have been commissioned by Hobbes in connection with his teaching duties. It is certainly true that some of the philological points made in the manuscript are so detailed that it is hard to think of them as part of an elementary course of instruction in moral science. The manuscript has been little studied, and many puzzles about its provenance and character remain to be solved.

93 Aubrey, *Brief Lives*, vol. 1, p. 357.
94 Hobbes MS A.8 (1). These chapters are preceded by a longer discussion entitled *De Virtute Generatim Spectata* (pp. 1–11) and occupy pp. 12–32.
95 Hobbes MS A.8 (1), p. 33: *De Virtutibus Improprie Dictis et Primo de Verecundia*. The other four chapters occupy pp. 34–9.
96 Hardwick MS 70, *sub* "Of Cornelia." Cavendish himself notes that the story comes from Pomponius Rufus, although he is referring to it at second hand. On this point see above, note 87.
97 Hardwick MS 70, *sub* "Of Simonides." The story is preserved in Cicero, *De Oratore*, ed. and trans. E. W. Sutton and H. Rackham (2 vols., London, 1942), II.LXXXVI.353, vol. 1, p. 464. Cavendish is translating and commenting on this passage, although again doing so at second hand.
98 Hardwick MS 70, *sub* "Of Solon."
99 Hardwick MS 70, *sub* "Of Diogenes."
100 Hardwick MS 70, *sub* "Of Socrates a Philosopher."
101 Hardwick MS 70, *sub* "Of Carneades a Philosopher."
102 Cicero, *De Oratore*, ed. Sutton and Rackham, II.IX.36, vol. 1, p. 224. On history and "the light of truth" in Renaissance England see D. R. Woolf, *The Idea of History in Early Stuart England: Erudition, Ideology and "The Light of Truth" from the Accession of James I to the Civil War* (London, 1990).
103 R. Blackbourne, "Vitae Hobbianae Auctarium," in *Opera Philosophica*, ed. Molesworth, vol. 1, p. xxv. On Bacon and the Cavendishes see also Vittorio Gabrieli, "Bacone, La Riforma e Roma nella Versione Hobbesiana d'un Carteggio di Fulgenzio Micanzio," *English Miscellany* 8 (1957), and Noel Malcolm, *De Dominis (1560–1624): Venetian, Anglican, Ecumenist and Relapsed Heretic* (London, 1984), pp. 47–54.
104 Aubrey, *Brief Lives*, vol. 1, p. 331.
105 Henry Seile, the publisher, entered the book in the Stationers' Register on March 18, 1628 (i.e., 1629 our style). Arber, *Stationers' Register*, vol. III, p. 161.
106 *Hobbes's Thucydides*, ed. Schlatter, p. 8; and cf. Schlatter, "Introduction" to *Hobbes's Thucydides*, pp. xi–xii.
107 *Ibid.*, pp. xi–xii.
108 Not Porta, the form in which the name mistakenly appears in Schlatter's edition. See Hobbes, *Of the Life and History of Thucydides*, in *Hobbes's Thucydides*, ed. Schlatter, p. 8, but cf. Karl Schuhmann, "Francis Bacon und Hobbes' Widmungsbrief zu *De Cive*," *Zeitschrift für Philosophische Forschung* 38 (1984), 177n. Portus's edition was published at Frankfurt in 1594.

109 *Hobbes's Thucydides*, ed. Schlatter, p. 8.
110 *Ibid.*, p. 8.
111 Susan M. Kingsbury, ed., *The Records of the Virginia Company of London* (4 vols., Washington, DC, 1906–35), vol. II, pp. 340–1, 533–4.
112 For the evidence that Hobbes used Goulston's text see Harwood, *Introduction* to *Hobbes and Lamy*, pp. 21–2, 50, 99–100.
113 It was G. C. Robertson who first identified as the third earl's dictation-book the volume containing the Latin version of the *Briefe* of Aristotle's *Rhetoric* eventually published in English in 1637. See George Croom Robertson, *Hobbes* (Edinburgh, 1886), p. 29 and note and cf. Harwood, *Introduction* to *Hobbes and Lamy*, pp. 1–2, and Malcolm, "Biographical Register of Hobbes's Correspondents," p. 815. The dictation book (Hobbes MS D.1) is signed "W. Devonshire" twice on the inside covers and frequently elsewhere. It is also signed "Thomas Hobbes" inside the back cover, although not in Hobbes's hand. The book is in the third earl's handwriting, with headings, corrections, and additions by Hobbes.
114 On Hobbes's authorship see above, note 30. However, a number of anomalies and misunderstandings in the translation have led Karl Schuhmann to the dramatic but convincing conclusion that, while in substance the *Briefe* is Hobbes's work, the English translation is not.
115 On these changes see Harwood, *Introduction* to *Hobbes and Lamy*, especially pp. 7, 13, 17, 19–20; Jeremy Rayner, "Hobbes and the Rhetoricians," *Hobbes Studies* 4 (1991), 87–91.
116 The MS copy at Chatsworth (Hobbes MS A.1) is partly in Hobbes's hand (most of p. 7, all of p. 8, top half of p. 9).
117 Anthony à Wood, *Athenae Oxoniensis* (2 vols., London, 1691–2), p. 479 states that the poem was "printed at *Lond.* about 1636."
118 Thomas Hobbes, *De Mirabilibus Pecci, Carmen*, in *Opera Philosophica*, ed. Molesworth, vol. V (London, 1845), p. 325, line 16.
119 *Ibid.*, p. 326, line 31.
120 *Ibid.*, p. 334, lincs 298–9.
121 *Ibid.*, p. 339, lines 503–4.
122 *Hobbes's Thucydides*, ed. Schlatter, pp. 576, 577, 578, 581, 583.
123 *Ibid.*, p. 6.
124 Hobbes, *Of the Life and History of Thucydides*, in *Hobbes's Thucydides*, ed. Schlatter, p. 13.
125 *Ibid.*, p. 13.
126 See [Cavendish and Hobbes], *Horae Subsecivae*, in which this theme is first taken up at p. 252 and thereafter occupies the whole of the *Discourse*.
127 *Ibid.*, p. 224.
128 *Ibid.*, p. 273.
129 *Ibid.*, p. 260.
130 *Ibid.*, p. 316.
131 Niccolò Machiavelli, *Il Principe e Discorsi*, ed. Sergio Bertelli (Milan, 1960), ch. V, p. 29.

132 [Cavendish and Hobbes], *Horae Subsecivae*, pp. 255, 257.

133 *Ibid.*, p. 320.

134 Hobbes added this *Praefatio ad Lectores* when he reissued *De Cive* in 1647. See Howard Warrender, "Editor's Introduction" to *De Cive*, ed. Warrender, vol. I, pp. 8–13.

135 Hobbes, *De Cive*, ed. Warrender, *Praefatio*, p. 82: "patriam meam, ante annos aliquot quam bellum civile exardesceret, quaestionibus de iure Imperii, & debita civium obedientia."

136 This is the form in which the title appears in the two best MSS. See B. L. Harl. MS 4235 and cf. Hobbes MSS (Chatsworth) MS A.2.B (except that the latter reads "Elementes").

137 The Epistle dedicatory to *The Elements* is signed "May the 9th. 1640." See B. L. Harl. MS 4235, fo. 2ᵛ and cf. Hobbes, *Elements of Law*, ed. Tönnies, p. xvi. As Tönnies recognized, this was the work described by Hobbes in his *Considerations* of 1662 as the "little treatise in English," of which "though not printed, many gentlemen had copies." Tönnies, "The Editor's Preface" to *Elements of Law*, pp. v–viii; cf. Thomas Hobbes, *Considerations upon the Reputation, Loyalty, Manners, and Religion, of Thomas Hobbes of Malmesbury*, in *English Works*, ed. Molesworth, vol. IV (London, 1840), p. 414.

138 Warrender, "Editor's Introduction" to *De Cive*, vol. I, pp. 5–8.

139 [Cavendish and Hobbes], *Horae Subsecivae*, p. 531.

140 *Ibid.*, p. 506.

141 *Ibid.*, p. 507.

142 Quintilian, *Institutio Oratoria*, ed. and trans. H. E. Butler (4 vols., London, 1920–2), III. IV. 1, vol. I, p. 390.

143 Harwood, *Introduction* to *Hobbes and Lamy*, p. 41.

144 *Ad C. Herennium de ratione dicendi*, ed. and trans. Harry Caplan (London, 1954), I.II.2, p. 4: "tria genera sunt causarum ... demonstrativum, deliberativum, iudiciale."

145 Quintilian, *Institutio Oratoria*, ed. Butler, II. XXI. 23, vol. I, p. 366: "Aristoteles tres faciendo partes orationis, iudicialem, deliberativam, demonstrativam."

146 Harwood, *Introduction* to *Hobbes and Lamy*, p. 41.

147 *Ibid.*, p. 53.

148 *Ibid.*, p. 54.

149 Quintilian, *Institutio Oratoria*, ed. Butler, III. VII. 6, vol. I, p. 466; III. VII. 26–7, vol. I, p. 476; and III. VII. 27, vol. I, p. 478 on "rerum omnis modi."

150 *Ibid.*, III. VII. 26, vol. I, p. 476: "multum auctoritatis adfert vetustas."

151 *Ibid.*, II. VII. 27, vol. I, p. 476 on "honor, utilitas, pulchritudo."

152 On this development see Quentin Skinner, "Machiavelli's *Discorsi* and the Pre-humanist Origins of Republican Ideas," in *Machiavelli and Republicanism*, ed. Gisela Bock, Quentin Skinner, and Maurizio Viroli (Cambridge, 1990), pp. 125–6. On epideictic oratory in the Renaissance see O. B. Hardison, Jr., *The Enduring Monument: a Study of the Idea of Praise in Renaissance Literary Theory and Practice* (Chapel Hill, NC, 1962), and John M.

McManamon, *Funeral Oratory and the Cultural Ideals of Italian Humanism* (Chapel Hill, NC, 1989).

153 For an edition see Hans Baron, *From Petrarch to Leonardo Bruni* (Chicago, 1968), pp. 217–63.

154 For an edition see G. Waitz, "De Laude Civitatis Laudae," in *Monumenta Germaniae Historica*, vol. xxii (Hanover, 1872), pp. 372–3. For the suggested date see J. K. Hyde, "Medieval Descriptions of Cities," *Bulletin of the John Rylands Library* 48 (1965), 340.

155 For an edition see Bonvesin della Riva, *De Magnalibus Mediolani*, ed. M. Corti (Milan, 1974). For a similar though later celebration of Milan (dated *c.* 1316 in Hyde, "Medieval Descriptions of Cities," p. 340) see Benzo d'Alessandria, *De Mediolano Civitate*, ed. L. A. Ferrai, *Bollettino dell'istituto storico italiano* 9 (1890), 15–36.

156 Charlton, *Education in Renaissance England*, pp. 111–12.

157 Richard Rainolde, *A Booke called the Foundacion of Rhetorike* (London, 1563), fo. xxxvii^r.

158 Harwood, *Introduction* to *Hobbes and Lamy*, p. 41.

159 See for example *Ad C. Herennium*, ed. Caplan, iii.ii.2–3, pp. 158–60.

160 *Ibid.*, i.ii.2, p. 4. Cf. Cicero, *De Inventione*, ed. and trans. H. M. Hubbell (London, 1949), ii.iv.12, p. 176 and Quintilian, *Institutio Oratoria*, ed. Butler, iii. viii. 6, vol. i, pp. 480–2.

161 Cicero, *De Inventione*, ed. Hubbell, ii.li.156, p. 324: "In deliberativo autem Aristoteli placet utilitatem, nobis honestatem et utilitatem." Cf. *ibid.*, ii. lv. 166, p. 332 and Quintilian, *Institutio Oratoria*, ed. Butler, iii.viii. 22, vol. i, p. 490. The author of the *Ad C. Herennium* reverts to a more Aristotelian position. See *Ad C. Herennium*, ed. Caplan, iii. ii.3, p. 160.

162 Harwood, *Introduction* to *Hobbes and Lamy*, p. 41.

163 *Ibid.*, p. 54.

164 Cicero, *De Inventione*, ed. Hubbell, i.v.7, p. 16.

165 *Ibid.*, ii.iv.12, p. 176: "quid aequum sit quaeritur."

166 Hobbes, *De Mirabilibus Pecci, Carmen*, ed. Molesworth, p. 325, lines 4–5.

167 *Ibid.*, p. 330, lines 179, 183.

168 *Ibid.*, p. 332, line 238.

169 *Ibid.*, p. 339, line 472: "dignissima visu."

170 [Cavendish and Hobbes], *Horae Subsecivae*, p. 395. Page references to Hobbes's *Discourses* from the *Horae Subsecivae* are hereafter given in brackets in the text.

171 For a detailed attempt to establish this point, see Skinner, *Reason and Rhetoric in the Philosophy of Hobbes*, pp. 244–9.

172 Hobbes, *Of the Life and History of Thucydides*, in *Hobbes's Thucydides*, ed. Schlatter, pp. 17, 18–19.

5 CASUISTRY AND ALLEGIANCE IN THE ENGLISH CIVIL WAR

1 [Edward Symmons], *A loyall subjects beliefe, expressed in a letter to Master Stephen*

Marshall (1643), "To my Reverend Brethren of the Ministry," p. 2v.

2 "Memoirs of Captain John Hodgson," in *Original memoirs written during the Great Civil War; being the life of Sir Henry Slingsby, and memoirs of Capt. Hodgson* (Edinburgh, 1806), p. 89.

3 East Sussex Record Office, Danny MS 64.

4 John M. Wallace, *Destiny his Choice: the Loyalism of Andrew Marvell* (Cambridge, 1968), pp. 10, 2.

5 Hodgson, "Memoirs," pp. 91–3.

6 East Sussex Record Office, Danny MS 64.

7 Quoted in William M. Lamont, *Richard Baxter and the Millennium. Protestant Imperialism and the English Revolution* (London, 1979), p. 108.

8 Ferne, *Conscience satisfied. That there is no warrant for the armes now taken up by subjects* (1643), "To the Conscientious Readers among the People," p. 3; East Sussex Record Office, Danny MS 94, 97.

9 John Morrill, *The Nature of the English Revolution* (London, 1993), p. 305. Active participation in the Civil War could of course be either civil or military; my concern here is with the choice actually to take up arms rather than to support or run the war in a civilian capacity, and hence I shall look primarily although not exclusively at work addressed to soldiers and military action.

10 *Ibid.*, pp. 47, 49, and see pp. 285–306. Cf. Richard Tuck, "'The Ancient Law of Freedom': John Selden and the Civil War," in *Reactions to the English Civil War 1642–1649*, ed. John Morrill (London, 1982), pp. 144—5, and see pp. 158–9.

11 *Memoirs of the Life of Colonel Hutchinson*, ed. James Sutherland (London, 1973), pp. 53, 62, 70, 76.

12 See Michael Mendle, *Henry Parker and the English Civil War. The Political Thought of the Public's "Privado"* (Cambridge, 1995), especially chs. 4 and 5; B. H. G. Wormald, *Clarendon. Politics, History & Religion 1640–1660* (Cambridge, 1951), pp. 11–12, 150–4, 189–90, 221–7 (on Hyde as a moderate, consensus-seeking parliamentary royalist). Cf. Glenn Burgess, *The Politics of the Ancient Constitution* (London, 1992), pp. 221–5, on the transformation of "political discourse" in the 1640s as royalists and parliamentarians diverged from consensual prewar discourse dominated by the "common law mind."

13 Wallace, *Destiny his Choice*, pp. 9–11; Keith Thomas, "Cases of Conscience in Seventeenth-century England," in *Public Duty and Private Conscience in Seventeenth-century England*, ed. John Morrill, Paul Slack, and Daniel Woolf (Oxford, 1993), pp. 29–56; Alan Donagan, "Moral Dilemmas Genuine and Spurious: a Comparative Anatomy," in *The Philosophical Papers of Alan Donagan* (2 vols., Chicago, 1994), vol. II, pp. 154, 167–8; see also Margaret Sampson, "Laxity and Liberty in Seventeenth-century English Political Thought," and Johann P. Sommerville, "'The New Art of Lying': Equivocation, Mental Reservation, and Casuistry," in *Conscience and Casuistry in Early Modern Europe*, ed. Edmund Leites (Cambridge, 1988), pp. 72–118, 159–84; B. Donagan, "Godly Choice: Puritan Decision-making in Seven-

teenth-century England," *Harvard Theological Review* 76 (1983), 322–6.

14 See Sampson, "Laxity and Liberty," pp. 99–102.

15 Hodgson, "Memoirs," p. 91; for prewar guides to good conscience, see e.g. Arthur Dent, *The plain man's path-way to heaven; wherein every man may clearly see whether he shall be saved or damned. Set forth dialogue-ways, for the better understanding of the simple* (1734); William Ames, *Conscience with the power and cases thereof* (1639). Dent, first published in 1601, was in his twenty-sixth edition by 1643 and was still valued in the eighteenth century. Ames was translated from Latin "for more publique benefit," and reissued twice in 1643.

16 *Orders and institutions of war, made and ordained by His Maiesty, and by him delivered to ... the Earle of Newcastle* (1642), p. 8.

17 Compare Conrad Russell, "Divine Rights in the Early Seventeenth Century," in *Public Duty and Private Conscience*, ed. Morrill, Slack, and Woolf, p. 104, on "the belief that God was the only source of legitimacy: either authority existed by divine right, or it was no authority."

18 I owe this last point to Derek Hirst.

19 *A sermon concerning unity and agreement. Preached at Carfax Church in Oxford, August 9. 1646* (1646), p. 44.

20 *Ibid.*, p. 24; and see Jasper Maine, *A sermon against false prophets. Preached in S. Maryes Church in Oxford* (1646), see e.g. pp. 20, 27–9.

21 J. Willis Bund, ed., *Diary of Henry Townshend of Elmley Lovett. 1640–1663* (2 vols., Worcestershire Historical Society, 1915–20), vol. I, p. 132. The text, significantly, was Psalm 3, verses 1–2, "Being David's flying from Absalom his son upon his rebellion."

22 Ed[ward] Symmons, *Scripture vindicated, from the misapprehensions misinterpretations and misapplications of Mr. Stephen Marshall* (1644), pp. 28, 85–86; Stephen Marshall, *A copy of a letter written by Mr. Stephen Marshall to a friend of his in the City* (1643), pp. A2–2.

23 Edward Symmons, *A military sermon, wherein by the word of God, the nature and disposition of a rebell is discovered, and the Kings true souldier described and characterized* (1644), pp. 15–17.

24 Richard Bernard, *The faithfull shepherd ... with precepts and examples, to further young divines in the studie of divinitie, with the shepherd's practise* (1621), pp. 28, 36–8; Thomas Gataker, *A discours apologetical* (1654), p. 87.

25 Ric[hard] Newcourt, *Repertorium ecclesiasticum parochiale Londinense* (2 vols., 1708–10), vol. II, p. 265; *Sermon concerning unity & agreement ... at Carfax*, p. 37.

26 Surviving royalist sermons probably represent a more highly selected set of preachers than the parliamentarian multitude that crowded into print. Published royalists tended to be at the top end of the preaching scale, men chosen to preach on special occasions or those whose message seemed particularly telling.

27 William Chillingworth, *A sermon preached at the publike fast before his Maiesty at Christ-church in Oxford* (1644), pp. 1–2, 5, 7–10, 13, 25. This sermon may have been preached at Reading in November 1642. The version cited here is a "spurious" but undoctored edition published in London.

28 Edmund Staunton, *Phinehas's zeal in execution of iudgement* (1645), pp. 14–15; [H. Ferne], *The camp at Gilgal. Or, a view of the King's army, and spirituall provision made for it* (1643), pp. 15, 18, 20–1, and see pp. 9, 13–14; Will[iam] Meeke, *The faithfull scout: giving an alarme to Yorkeshire* (1647), pp. 42–3. See also H. Ferne, *A sermon preached before his Majesty at Newport . . . November the 29. 1648* (1649), p. 16. For other examples of royalist moral reformism, including attacks on swearing (once thought to be a peculiarly puritan obsession), see e.g. Symmons, *Military sermon*, p. 44; BL Harl. MSS 6802, fo. 215, and 6804, fos. 75–75v., 81–81v (drafts of the royalist proclamation against swearing); and see *His Maiesties declaration and manifestation to all his souldiers* (1642), p. 5, for the king's moral prescription for his soldiers.

29 One exception to this generalization was royalist attention to quarreling and duels. See [Ferne], *The camp at Gilgal*, p. 35, on "a false opinion of honour and reputation [that] thrusts men into *Duells*," and on the connection between drunkenness and "a Valour that deserves not to be armed with swords but drinking pots."

30 Hoard, the rector of Moreton from 1626 until 1658, was "a zealous Calvinist in the beginning, but a greater Arminian afterwards." Anthony Wood, *Athenae Oxonienses* (2 vols. in one, 1721), vol. II, cols. 221–2.

31 John Berkenhead, *A sermon preached before his Majestie at Christ-Church in Oxford. On the 3. of Novemb. 1644, after his returne from Cornwall* (1644). It was delivered a few days after the second Battle of Newbury which, though hardly decisive, counted as a royalist success. It followed parliamentary defeat at Cropredy Bridge in June and disaster at Lostwithiel in Cornwall in August; thus, despite defeat at Marston Moor, the occasion lent itself to an upbeat and unconciliatory statement of the royalist position.

32 *Ibid.*, p. 13. Romans 13:5 reads: "ye must needs be subject, not only for wrath, but also for conscience sake."

33 Berkenhead, *Sermon*, pp. 1, 4–6.

34 *Ibid.*, pp. 20–1.

35 *Ibid.*, p. 16.

36 Chillingworth, *Sermon*, p. 11.

37 Conrad Russell, *The Causes of the English Civil War* (Oxford, 1990), pp. 132–6; J. P. Sommerville, *Politics and Ideology in England, 1603–1640* (London, 1986), pp. 44–5; Glenn Burgess, *Absolute Monarchy and the Stuart Constitution* (New Haven, CT, 1996), pp. 23–5.

38 See e.g. discussion in John Sym, *Lifes preservative against self-killing. Or, an useful treatise concerning life and self-murder* (1637), pp. 142–9 (on justified and unjustified martyrdom), and E. S. Shuckburgh, ed., *Two Biographies of William Bedell Bishop of Kilmore* (Cambridge, 1902), pp. 215–18; Cf. Sampson, "Laxity and Liberty," in *Conscience and Casuistry*, ed. Leites, pp 106–7; John Morrill, "Introduction," in *Reactions to the English Civil War*, ed. Morrill, pp. 5–7; and see B. Donagan, "The York House Conference Revisited: Laymen, Calvinism and Arminianism," *Historical Research* 64 (1991), 323–4, on one way in which acceptance of a doctrine of royal supremacy could

evolve, without need for theoretical U-turns, to belief in the need for resistance.

39 On the evolution of Roman Catholic theories of resistance, and the ultimate convergence of Catholic and Calvinist theory, see Quentin Skinner, *The Foundations of Modern Political Thought* (2 vols., Cambridge, 1978), vol. II, pp. 122–3, 126–9, 177–8, 320–1, 345–8. Skinner observes (vol. II, p. 321) that "we may say with very little exaggeration that the main foundations of the Calvinist theory of revolution were in fact constructed entirely by their Catholic adversaries."

40 William Sheils, "Provincial Preaching on the Eve of the Civil War: Some West Riding Fast Sermons," in *Religion, Culture and Society in Early Modern Britain. Essays in Honour of Patrick Collinson*, ed. Anthony Fletcher and Peter Roberts (Cambridge, 1994), p. 309, and see pp. 300–9.

41 *A letter from Mercurius Civicus to Mercurius Rusticus: or, Londons confession but not repentance* (1643), pp. 8–9; Newcourt, *Repertorium ecclesiasticum*, vol. II, p. 265; Calybute Downing, *A Sermon preached to the renowned Company of the Artillery, 1 September, 1640* (1641). The other Smectymnuans were Edmund Calamy, Thomas Young, Matthew Newcomen, and William Spurstow – collectively, Smectymnuus.

42 C[alybute] D[owning], *A discourse of the state ecclesiasticall of this Kingdome, in relation to the Civill* (2nd edn., 1634), pp. 2, 104. On the "subtle" and "consensual" position of Downing before 1640 and the "guarded" quality of the Artillery Garden sermon of 1640, see Burgess, *Absolute Monarchy*, pp. 112–13; cf. Sommerville, *Politics and Ideology*, pp. 37, 68, 74, 80, on Downing's progression from "earlier absolutism" to an argument for resistance.

43 Symmons, *Scripture vindicated*, p. 87; Marshall, *Copy of a letter*, p. 3.

44 Most royalists acknowledged the potential legitimacy of other forms of government elsewhere, although they denied it in England. See e.g. the 1640 sermon by Henry King, the future Bishop of Chichester, which insisted that monarchy was by so far the best form of government that a king was as necessary "as Aire to our Breath"; yet although other forms were inferior in theory and practice he did not suggest that they were *per se* illegitimate. Mary Hobbs, ed., *The sermons of Henry King (1592–1669), Bishop of Chichester* (Cranbury, NJ, 1992), p. 223. Compare Clarendon in 1646: "I believe monarchy is not held such an institution *iure divino*, that all other forms of government are concluded anti-Christian. Nonetheless, to abolish ... monarchy in England would be such a sin, as no honest man can consent to it." Bodl. Libr., MS Clarendon, v. 29, fo. 5.

45 Morrill, *Nature of the English Revolution*, pp. 49–50, and see pp. 285–306, on the freedom with which charges of tyranny were bandied about when they were little more than "abusive rhetoric," and the cautious muting of such charges when, in 1641–2, they threatened to assume practical political applicability.

46 Marshall, *Copy of a letter*, p. 22.

47 Francis Cheynell, *Chillingworthi Novissima. Or, the sicknesse, heresy, death, and buriall of William Chillingworth* (1644), p. D. Compare the view of a lay theorist

in 1647: "whether Tyranny or abused Authority shall be said to be the Ordinance of God, and so not to be disobeyed ... I take it cleare they shall not." Robert Derham, *A manuell or brief treatise of some particular rights and priviledges belonging to the high court of Parliament* (1647), p. 100. This argument was to return to haunt the victors in the Civil War when, as the new wielders of "lawfull power" in the state, they were held to use it tyrannically. Cf. Ferne, *Conscience satisfied*, p. 58.

48 William Beech, *More sulphure for Basing* (1645), p. 23. Beech was virulently anti-popish, but the grievances that he picked on here as justifying parliament's taking arms were as much chauvinist and constitutional as religious.

49 Marshall, *Copy of a letter*, p. 25; compare Ferne, *Conscience satisfied*, pp. 5–6.

50 Beech, *Sulphure*, pp. 26–7; and see Burgess, *Politics of the Ancient Constitution*, pp. 229–30; Mendle, *Henry Parker*, pp. 43–8, 82–8.

51 Bodl. Libr., MS Add. c. 132, fo. 36.

52 *A most worthy speech, spoken by the right honourable Robert Earle of Warwick; in the head of his army* (1642), p. 4. Compare Beech, *Sulphure*, p. 23: "shall wee touch the Lords Anoynted?"

53 Marshall, *Copy of a letter*, pp. 2, 22–5. The Irish rebellion was of course seen as a popish attack, but its religious character rapidly merged with racial, military, and political considerations.

54 Derham, *Manuell*, p. 70, and see p. 71 for Derham's catalogue of the king's threatening actions.

55 Cheynell, *Chillingworthi Novissima*, pp. A3v.–[A3(2)], H2v.; *Evangelium armatum. A specimen: or short collection of several doctrines and positions destructive to our government both civil and ecclesiastical* (1663), p. 48: "none can deny it, but it is lawful to take up arms, to maintain that civil right we have to our Religion ... For we have not onely a right to our religion, by the Law of God, but we have a Civil right to this our Religion, that other Christians have not had."

56 Cheynell, *Chillingworthi novissima*, p. A3v.

57 Marshall, *Copy of a letter*, pp. 22, 25; Symmons, *Scripture vindicated*, pp. 26–7: "M. *Marshall* ... doth fancy his *Parliament* to be *infallible* ... [We] may conjecture, that [he] will never hence forth finde fault with the *Popish* Collyer for blindly beleeving as the *Church beleeves*." Compare Michael Mendle, "Henry Parker: the Public's Privado," in *Religion, Resistance, and Civil War*, ed. Gordon Schochet (Washington, DC, 1990), p. 161, on the theorist Henry Parker's infallible parliament, "ever reverenced as the *vox dei*."

58 *Most worthy speech ... by ... Warwick*, p. 4; Marshall, *Copy of a letter*, pp. 22–3.

59 Cheynell, *Chillingworthi novissima*, pp. C2, A3.

60 This speech was regarded as sufficiently noteworthy to be excerpted in a Restoration collection recalling "destructive" doctrines of the past. See *Evangelium armatum*, p. 49.

61 Symmons, *Scripture vindicated*, p. 60.

62 See Ernst H. Kantorowicz, *The King's Two Bodies* (Princeton, NJ, 1957), ch. 2,

especially pp. 40–1.

63 Cheynell, *Chillingworthi novissima*, p. A3v.

64 Derham, *Manuell*, pp. 99–100.

65 *Lords' Journals*, vol. 5, p. 606; *The Weekly Account*, June 18–24 (1645), Cc. Such incidents foreshadowed popular reaction to the king's execution. The distinction between power. and person was not confined to parliamentarians. For royalists it provided a way to admit past faults of policy on the king's part – that is, in exercise of power – which had now been corrected and which in no way weakened the obligation of loyalty to his person.

66 See e.g. Ferne, *Conscience satisfied*, pp. 2–3.

67 Wilde declared that "*Warres well grounded are nought else . . . but sutes of Appeale to the great Consistory of Heaven.*" Metaphors and biblical reference familiar from puritan writings reappear: "Incense at the Altar burnes the sweeter for the Gunpowder in the field," he said; gunpowder employed in a bad cause was a "stench" in the nostrils of the Almighty, but when used in defense of religion it was like "the precious Oyntment on *Aarons* Head." [George Wilde], *A sermon preached upon Sunday the third of March in St. Maries Oxford, before the great assembly of the members, of the honourable House of Commons there assembled* (1643), pp. 1–3, 5, 9–10.

68 Which privileges of parliament were "just" could of course be a matter of opinion. *His Majesties declaration and manifestation to all his souldiers* (1642). pp. 1–2.

69 Ferne, *Conscience satisfied*, pp. 6, and "To the conscientious Readers among the People," p. 3. See also [Ferne] *The camp at Gilgal*, p. 8: "you are assured it is for the established Religion, for the Freedome of Parliament, for the Liberty of Subjects that you bare Armes."

70 *Ibid.*, p. 3; Ferne, *Conscience satisfied*, p. 6.

71 [Wilde], *Sermon*, p. 20.

72 *Ibid.*, p. 17.

73 See the full title to Ferne's *Conscience satisfied*, n. 8.

74 Gr[iffith] Williams, *Vindiciae Regum; or, the grand rebellion that is, a looking-glasse for rebels* (1643), title page.

75 *Ibid.*, p. 38.

76 Ferne, *Conscience satisfied*, pp. 56–7.

77 *Ibid.*, p. 58.

78 *Ibid.*

79 *Ibid.*, p. 59.

80 [Samuel Hoard], *Gods love to mankind. Manifested by dis-proving his absolute decree for their damnation* (1633), p. 1; Shuckburgh, ed., *Two biographies of . . . Bedell*, pp. 364–5; Wood, *Athenae Oxonienses*, vol. II, cols. 221–2.

81 *Dictionary of National Biography*, "Featley, or Fairclough, Daniel"; Robert S. Paul, *The Assembly of the Lord. Politics and Religion in the Westminster Assembly and the "Grand Debate"* (Edinburgh, 1985), pp. 79, 85, 101, 105, 381; *Mercurius Rusticus* (1646), pp. 166–7; *Lords' Journals*, vol. 4, 30, 37, 483, and vol. 7, 343; *Commons' Journals*, vol. 3, 44, 644–5; *To the right honourable the House of Lords . . .*

The humble petition of the inhabitants of Lambeth. presented February 20, 1642 (1643) n.p.; Daniel Featley, *Roma ruens, Romes ruine: being a succinct answer to a popish challenge, concerning the antiquity, unity, universality, succession, and perpetuall visibility of the true Church, even in the most obscure times* (1644) n.p.

82 [Symmons], *Loyall subjects beliefe*; the first phrase quoted is part of the extended title.

83 Symmons, *Scripture vindicated*, pp. 26–8, 60, 62–3; *Loyall subjects beliefe*, "To my Reverend Brethren of the Ministry," pp. 2–3.

84 *Ibid.*, p. 2. Principle and consistency were his downfall, said Symmons: "What I am, you know; and what my Doctrine and conversation hath beene." As an honest man, he was told, he did more harm than a hundred knaves. *Ibid.*, p. 2v. His implied distinction between war and rebellion had important legal and practical consequences; B. Donagan, "Atrocity, War Crime, and Treason in the English Civil War," *American Historical Review* 99 (1994), 1140–1.

85 [Symmons] *Loyall subjects beliefe*, "To my Reverend Brethren of the Ministry", p. 2.

86 *Ibid.*, p. 2v.

87 For Symmons on conquest and usurpation, see *Scripture vindicated*, p. 60.

88 Symmons, *Military Sermon*, p. 3.

89 *Ibid.*, pp. 4, 15–16, 22–3, 33.

90 *Ibid.*, p. 23.

91 *Ibid.*, pp. 4, 22–4. Cf. Dudley Digges's conclusion in 1626 that kings could not command "ill or unlawful Things. When they speak even by Letters Patents, if the Thing be evil, those Letters Patents are void. And whatsoever ill Event succeeds, the Executioner of such Commands must answer for them." *Lords' Journals*, vol. 3, 596. Army discipline and private conscience co-existed uncomfortably then as now.

92 Symmons, *Scripture vindicated*, p. 87.

93 Henry Palmer, *Scripture and reason pleaded for defensive armes* (1643), quoted in Sampson, "Laxity and Liberty," in *Conscience and Casuistry*, ed. Leites, p. 110.

94 Sheils, "Provincial Preaching," in *Religion, Culture and Society*, ed. Fletcher and Roberts, pp. 301–2.

95 Symmons, *Scripture vindicated*, "Preface to the Reader," n.p. That the soldiers were now prisoners of the royalists may be further evidence that response to casuist argument varied according to circumstance.

96 Wallace, *Destiny his Choice*, pp. 229–31.

97 G. A. Starr, "From Casuistry to Fiction: the Importance of *The Athenian Mercury*," *Journal of the History of Ideas* 28 (1967), 20–1: Thomas, "Cases of Conscience," in *Public Duty and Private Conscience*, ed. Morrill, Slack, and Woolf, pp. 51–5.

98 Wallace, *Destiny his Choice*, p. 10.

99 As John Wallace observed, "Charles and Lilburne could have shaken hands on the fact that all power was of God: the quarrel was about its distribution, not its origin." *Ibid.*, pp. 11–12.

6   THOMAS MAY AND THE NARRATIVE OF CIVIL WAR

1 The only monograph to review May's life and letters as a whole seems to be
   that of A. G. Chester, *Thomas May: Man of Letters, 1595–1650* (Philadelphia,
   1932); originally a doctoral dissertation submitted to the University of
   Pennsylvania.
2 The attribution is as old as John Aubrey; see *Brief Lives*, "Thomas May."
   One would rather like to reject it, but there are difficulties in doing so.
   There is a comment on the poem as Marvell's in John M. Wallace, *Destiny
   his Choice: the Loyalism of Andrew Marvell* (Cambridge, 1968), pp. 103–4.
3 The opinion of David Norbrook, "Lucan, Thomas May, and the Creation
   of a Republican Literary Culture," in *Culture and Politics in Early Stuart
   England*, ed. Kevin Sharpe and Peter Lake (London, 1994), pp. 45–66,
   331–6. Norbrook's highly important *Writing the English Republic: Poetry, Rhetoric and Politics, 1627–1660* (Cambridge, 1999) reached me when this chapter
   had gone to press. Our readings of May differ, but are perhaps not
   incompatible.
4 Wallace, *Destiny his Choice*.
5 *The history of the Parliament of England which began November the third, MDCXL.
   With a short and necessary view of some precedent yeares. Written by Thomas May,
   Esquire, Secretary for the Parliament, Published by Authority. . . . Imprinted at London
   by Moses Bell for George Thomason ... MDCXLVII.* Preface (unpaginated),
   A3v–A4.
6 Chester, *Thomas May*, pp. 66–7.
7 Preface to *History*, A4–4v.
8 *Ibid.*, A4v.
9 *Ibid.*, A4v–B1.
10 Franciscus Haraeus, *Annales ducum seu principum Brabantiae totiusque Belgii*
   (Antwerp, 1623). Emanuel van Meteren, *Historia belgica nostri potissimum
   temporis Belgii sub quatuor burgundis et totidem austriacis principibus coniunctionem et
   gubernationem ...* (n.p., 1598). An English translation by Thomas Churchyard
   and Richard Robinson had appeared in 1602.
11 Preface to *History*, B1–B1iv.
12 "That I have written more concerning the actions of reformers and patriots
   than of those done by the contrary party is not to be wondered at, since I
   have had greater conversation and familiarity with the former. If the
   contrary party will set forth and publish the same with the like honesty,
   posterity will be able to read all that was done, and know it thoroughly and
   with great profit."
13 Preface to *History*, B2–B2v.
14 *Ibid.*, B2v.
15 Edward Hyde, Earl of Clarendon, *The History of the Rebellion and Civil Wars in
   England* (1732), vol. 1, p. 3. The reference in full does not point directly at
   May, but at a conspiracy thesis suggesting that the rebellion was "contriving
   from (if not before) the death of queen *Elizabeth*, and fomented by several

Princes, and great Ministers of State in *Christendom*, to the time that it broke out." This is not May's contention, and its author must be sought elsewhere.

16 J. G. A. Pocock, ed., *The Political Works of James Harrington* (Cambridge, 1977); *James Harrington: The Commonwealth of Oceana and a System of Politics* (Cambridge, 1992). Also Pocock, *The Ancient Constitution and the Feudal Law: English Historical Thought in the Seventeenth Century* (Cambridge, 1957, 1987), ch. vi; *The Machiavellian Moment: Florentine Political Thought and the Atlantic Republican Tradition* (Princeton, NJ, 1975), ch. xi.

17 See above, p. 114.

18 Henri, duc de Rohan, *De l'interest des princes et estats de la Chrestiente* (1638). English translation by Henry Hunt (1641). For this work's place in the literature of interest of state, see Friedrich Meinecke, trans. Douglas Scott, *Machiavellism: the Doctrine of Raison d'Etat and its Place in Modern History* (London, 1957), pp. 162ff.; William F. Church, *Richelieu and Reason of State* (Princeton, NJ, 1972), pp. 352–4.

19 *History of the Parliament of England*, Book i, p. 2. The *History* is divided into three books, separately paginated in the 1647 edition. All references are to the 1647 edition.

20 *Ibid.*, p. 3.

21 *Ibid.*, p. 6.

22 *Ibid.*, pp. 11–12.

23 *Ibid.*, p. 19. The historian quoted is Livy, I, 9.

24 *History*, Book i, p. 22.

25 *Ibid.*, p. 25.

26 *Ibid.*, p. 27.

27 *Ibid.*, p. 28.

28 *Ibid.* The same verdict is passed on the Laudian bishops Cosin and Wren; *ibid.*, pp. 82–3.

29 *Ibid.*, p. 26, for a Venetian distinction of English religious groups into papists, Protestants, and puritans.

30 *Ibid.*, pp. 46–8.

31 *History*, Introduction, B3.

32 *History*, Book ii, pp. 19–20.

33 *History*, Book i, pp, 69, 72. For a modern account of these speeches, see Conrad Russell, *Fall of the British Monarchies, 1637–1642* (Oxford, 1991), pp. 104–10 (the Short Parliament), 214–21 (the Long).

34 *History*, Book i, pp. 72–8.

35 *Ibid.*, pp. 87–8.

36 *Ibid.*, pp. 95–6.

37 *Ibid.*, p. 102.

38 *Ibid.*, p. 113.

39 Above, p. 000.

40 *Brief Lives*, "Thomas May."

41 *History*, Book i, pp. 115–16.

42 I am indebted to Michael Mendle for pointing this out.

43 *History*, Book I, p. 117.

44 This seems to indicate the works of Henry Ferne, Charles Herle, Dudley Digges, and Philip Hunton, perhaps carrying the date of the passage into 1643. For the debate over resistance in the first year of civil war, see Andrew Sharp, *Political Ideas of the English Civil Wars, 1641–1649* (London, 1983), and even now, J. W. Allen, *English Political Thought, 1603–1660: vol. I, 1603–1644* (London, 1938).

45 *History*, Book I, pp. 117–18.

46 *History*, Book II, p. 2.

47 *Ibid.*, p. 18.

48 *Ibid.*, pp. 4–16. See, however, pp. 34–7, where the mutual suspicions are set forth and the king's slow reply given in full.

49 He is mentioned at Book I, p. 96 and II, pp. 48–9, as alienated from the parliament by the House's burning his printed speech at the time of Strafford's trial. The account of the attempt on the five members does not mention him; Book II, pp. 21–9.

50 *History*, Book II, p. 45.

51 B. H. G. Wormald, *Clarendon: Politics, History and Religion, 1640–1660* (Cambridge, 1951).

52 *History*, Book II, p. 46.

53 *Ibid.*, pp. 53–4.

54 Mendle (see note 42) and "Parliamentary Sovereignty: a Very English Absolutism," in *Political Discourse in Early Modern Britain*, eds. Nicholas Phillipson and Quentin Skinner (Cambridge, 1993), pp. 97, 119.

55 *History*, Book II, pp. 58–9.

56 *History*, Book III, p. 92.

57 *History*, Book II, p. 63.

58 *Ibid.*, p. 64.

59 *Ibid.*, p. 96.

60 *Ibid.*, pp. 99–100. The survey by counties occupies pp. 101–14.

61 *Ibid.*, pp. 115–22, 122–8.

62 *History*, Book III, p. 6.

63 *Ibid.*, pp. 1–4.

64 *Ibid.*, p. 13; cf. p. 12.

65 *Ibid.*, pp. 29–30.

66 *Ibid.*, p. 47.

67 *Ibid.*

68 *Ibid.*, p. 48.

69 *Ibid.*, pp. 52–3.

70 *Ibid.*, p. 108.

71 *Ibid.*, p. 115.

72 *Ibid.* The text has "Nations."

73 *Historiae parliamenti angliae breviarium tribus partibus explicitum ... authore T.M. Londoni: typis Caroli Sumptner; prostant venales officina Thomae Brusteri*, 1650, 1651.

74 *A Breviary of the History of the Parliament of England. Expressed in three Parts ...*

(1650), pp. 1–2.

75 *Ibid.*
76 *History*, Book I, p. 54.
77 *Breviary*, p. 19.
78 *Ibid.*, pp. 31–2.
79 Above, p. 138 and *History*, Book I, p. 102.
80 *Breviary*, p. 47.
81 *Ibid.*, pp. 59–61.
82 *Ibid.*, pp. 70–1.
83 *Ibid.*, pp. 85–6. The pagination is continuous throughout.
84 *Ibid.*, pp. 108–10, 127–9.
85 *Ibid.*, p. 137.
86 *Ibid.*, p. 142.
87 *Ibid.*, p. 146.
88 *Ibid.*, pp. 156–7.
89 Above, p. 113.
90 *Breviary*, p. 158.
91 *Ibid.*, p. 159.
92 *Ibid.*, p. 186.
93 *Ibid.*, pp. 186–7.
94 *Ibid.*, p. 190.
95 *Ibid.*, pp. 201–2.
96 *Ibid.*, p. 203.
97 *Ibid.*, p. 209.
98 *Ibid.*, pp. 209–10; continued without a break from the previous quotation.
99 *Ibid.*, pp. 211–12.
100 *Ibid.*, p. 215.
101 *Brief Lives*, "Thomas May." Aubrey further says that May "would, *inter pocula*, speake slightingly of the Trinity." His religion is not investigated here.
102 Above, p. 114.

7 SAMUEL PARKER, ANDREW MARVELL, AND POLITICAL
CULTURE, 1667–73

I am indebted to Richard Strier and Steven Zwicker for their comments on drafts of this chapter.

1 N. H. Keeble, *The Literary Culture of Nonconformity* (Leicester, 1987), especially p. 146.
2 See for example the admirable discussions of the late 1660s controversy over conscience in John M. Wallace, *Destiny his Choice: the Loyalism of Andrew Marvell* (Cambridge, 1968), pp. 184–207; Richard Ashcraft, *Revolutionary Politics and Locke's Two Treatises of Government* (Princeton, NJ, 1986), pp. 41–74; and Gary De Krey, "Rethinking the Restoration: Dissenting Cases for Conscience, 1667–1672," *Historical Journal* 38 (1995), 53–83.

3 See T. Harris, *Politics under the Later Stuarts* (London, 1993).
4 For the terminology, see Gary De Krey, "The First Restoration Crisis: Conscience and Coercion in London, 1667–73," *Albion* 25 (1993), 565–80.
5 The sufferings of the dissenters under these measures have been amply chronicled; less known is Hobbes's growing sense of the danger of the stake, and the decision of Gerard Winstanley, one-time Digger and soon-to-be Quaker, to leave his Latitudinarian home in the Church of England of the earlier 1660s: P. Milton, "Hobbes, Heresy and Lord Arlington," *History of Political Thought* 14 (1993), 501–46; J. D. Alsop, "John Wilkins and Winstanley," *Notes and Queries* n.s. 36 (1989), 46–8.
6 The key text in this campaign was John Owen, *A Peace-Offering in an Apology and Humble Plea for Indulgence* (1667); see also John Corbet, *A Discourse of the Religion of England* (1667).
7 Roger Thomas, "Comprehension and Indulgence," in *From Uniformity to Unity 1662–1962*, eds. Geoffrey F. Nuttall and Owen Chadwick (London, 1962), pp. 195–206.
8 Quoted in Wallace, *Destiny his Choice*, p. 186.
9 For some reflections on the cultural milieu of the godly sermon, see Patrick Collinson, "Elizabethan and Jacobean Puritanism as Forms of Popular Religious Culture," in *The Culture of English Puritanism, 1560–1700*, eds. Christopher Durston and Jacqueline Eales (London, 1996), pp. 46–8. Keeble has noted the way establishment sermons by 1660 found the hallmarks of "enthusiasm'" and "fanaticism" in homespun metaphor and allegory: *The Literary Culture of Nonconformity*, pp. 243–4. For charges of "cant," see below; for an instance of impatience with the posturing of the "pious and pretious as they phrase it out with a full mouth,'" see D. Hirst, "The Fracturing of the Cromwellian Alliance: Leeds and Adam Baynes," *English Historical Review* 108 (1993), 880.
10 W. Penn, *No Cross, No Crown* (1669), epistle dedicatory.
11 See William C. Diamond, "Public Identity in Restoration England: From Prophetic to Economic," unpublished PhD dissertation, Johns Hopkins University, 1982.
12 Patrick, *A Friendly Debate* (1669), especially pp. 2–3, 21.
13 *Ibid.*, especially pp. 4–5. He was soon joined in this judgment by Samuel Parker; as an enemy noted, one of Parker's (Hobbesian) phobias was "Praying by the Spirit, which he chargeth at the highest rate, as that which will destroy all Government in the world." *An Expostulatory Letter to the Author of the Late Slanderous Libel Against Dr. O.* (1671), p. 26.
14 Patrick, *Friendly Debate*, pp. 5–9; Hobbes, *Leviathan* (1651), chs. 5 and 8.
15 Patrick, *Friendly Debate*, p. 15. Patrick's charge found some support from the other side when Robert Ferguson (the future "plotter") conceded that dissenters used metaphor "for the most part in Popular Discourses, where less accuracy and propriety in expression is required..." Robert Ferguson, *The Interest of Reason in Religion; with the Import and Use of Scripture-Metaphors* (1675), p. 291, also pp. 295–7, 360.

16 Collinson, "Puritanism as Popular Religious Culture," p. 47.

17 See J. A. Barish, *The Anti-Theatrical Prejudice* (Berkeley, CA, 1981). I am indebted to Richard Strier for this reference, and for discussions on this theme.

18 Samuel Rolle, *A Sober Answer to the Friendly Debate* (1669), p. 20.

19 John Owen, *Truth and Innocence Vindicated* (1669), especially pp. 17, 45–52, 61–5; [John Humfrey], *A Case of Conscience* (1670), p. 9. For Humfrey as thinker, see Gary De Krey, "Rethinking the Restoration," 53–83.

20 Samuel Parker, *Discourse of Ecclesiastical Politie* (1670), esp. pp. xxxiii–xxxiv, and see below.

21 *Ibid.*, p. 338.

22 Owen, *Truth and Innocence Vindicated*, p. 71; [Humfrey], *A Case of Conscience*, p. 31.

23 Rolle, *A Sober Answer*, p. 12.

24 I am indebted to Richard Strier for pointing out to me the echo of *Eikonoklastes*.

25 Ashcraft, *Revolutionary Politics*, p. 54.

26 For the complaints of Eachard's instructively bipartisan assailants, including Barnabas Oley, publisher of the 1671 edition of Herbert's *Country Parson*, and another Anglican who saw Eachard as a "Fanatical skip-jack,'" see John Eachard, *Mr. Hobbs's State of Nature Considered; in a Dialogue between Philautus and Timothy* (2nd edn., 1672), pp. 166–286, especially p. 197. For modern confusions, see Peter Harrison, *"Religion" and the Religions in the English Enlightenment* (Cambridge, 1990), pp. 78, 81; John Spurr, *The Restoration Church of England* (New Haven and London, 1991), pp. 220–2.

27 Llewellyn Powys, *The Life and Times of Anthony à Wood* (London, 1932), p. 169.

28 Ferguson, *The Interest of Reason in Religion*.

29 Keeble, *The Literary Culture of Nonconformity*, pp. 244, 247–50.

30 *An Expostulatory Letter*, pp. 16–17; for other examples, see [Humfrey], *A Case of Conscience*, pp. 9, 18, 31; Owen, *Truth and Innocence Vindicated*, pp. 17, 18–20, 71; *Insolence and Impudence Triumphant* (1669), p. 7.

31 Samuel Parker, *A Defence and Continuation* (1671), pp. 157–81.

32 Keeble, *The Literary Culture of Nonconformity*, p. 115. Keeble's claim appears to be the most sustained attempt to explain a gesture of Marvell's that all scholars have of course noted, but otherwise ignored.

33 Andrew Marvell, "On Mr Milton's Paradise Lost": I am grateful to Steven Zwicker for stressing this point to me.

34 Marvell, *The Rehearsal Transpros'd* (1672), p. 127.

35 *Loyalty and Nonconformity; or, a Loyal Nonconformist decently Interr'd* (1669), p. 20.

36 [Humfrey], *A Case of Conscience*, p. 9. John Lacy acted the part of the tyrant in *Tyrannick Love*, which opened in 1669 and was published in 1670. By an irony Marvell would surely have appreciated, Lacy was himself to emerge as a dissenting controversialist: Lacy, *The Arraignment of Thomas Howard* (1685).

37 *Rehearsal Transpros'd*, p. 10. Lacy had also, to be sure, just played Bayes.

38 See for example Ashcraft, *Revolutionary Politics*, pp. 39–74; Justin Champion, *The Pillars of Priestcraft Shaken. The Church of England and its Enemies, 1660–1730* (Cambridge, 1992), and Harrison, *"Religion" and the Religions*, pp. 77–85.

39 [Anon.] *The Famous Battel of the Catts in the Province of Ulster. June 25. 1668* (1668), p. 11: the copy microfilmed by University Microfilms International carries a manuscript attribution to Sir John Denham. I am grateful to Rob Hermann for the reference.

40 See John Morrill, Paul Slack, and Daniel Woolf, eds., *Public Duty and Private Conscience in Seventeenth-Century England* (Oxford, 1993).

41 For reflections on some of these issues, see P. Zagorin, *Ways of Lying: Dissimulation, Persecution, and Conformity in Early-Modern Europe* (Cambridge, MA, 1990), pp. 186–254.

42 See Derek Hirst and Steven Zwicker, "Fatherhood and Longing: Andrew Marvell and the Toils of Patriarchy," *English Literary History* (1999).

43 Gordon J. Schochet, "Between Lambeth and Leviathan: Samuel Parker, Church of England and Political Order," in *Political Discourse in Early Modern Britain*, eds. Quentin Skinner and Nicholas Philipson (Cambridge, 1993), pp. 189–208. That Parker's ambivalence about Hobbes extended beyond the immediate political moment is made clear by J. G. A. Pocock, "Thomas Hobbes: Atheist or Enthusiast? His Place in a Restoration Debate," *History of Political Thought* 11 (1990), 737–49.

44 See Milton, "Hobbes, Heresy and Lord Arlington," 502–46.

45 Parker, *Discourse*, p. 118; James A. Wynn, *Dryden and his World* (New Haven, CT, 1987), pp. 216, 218.

46 A point seized on by some of the Rota critics: *The Friendly Vindication of Mr. Dryden* (1673), especially p. 12; *The Censure of the Rota* (1673), pp. 15–16 (both anon.).

47 Oddly enough, the latest work on this theme, Champion's *The Pillars of Priestcraft Shaken*, contains no reference to Parker, to Patrick, to Eachard, or indeed any of the protagonists in this story other than Hobbes.

48 See for example Eachard, *The Grounds and Occasions of the Contempt of the Clergy and Religion* (8th edn., 1672); Parker, *Discourse*, pp. xxxvii–xli, 35–6, and *Defence and Continuation*, pp. 724–50. Among the non-conformists, see for example Robert Wild, *A Letter from Mr. Wild to his Friend Mr. J.J. Upon Occasion of his Majesty's Declaration for Liberty of Conscience* (1672), p. 14; Sir Charles Wolseley, *The Reasonablenes of Scripture-Beleif* (1672), sig. A3v.–A4; Thomas Watson, *The Mischief of Sinne* (1671), sig. A2v.–A3; [John Humfrey], *A Case of Conscience*, p. 9; William Penn, *No Cross, No Crown*, preface, sig. A3.

49 Parker, *Discourse*, p. vi; cf. his *Defence*, pp. 171–6.

50 The great example of this complaint is Eachard's *Grounds and Occasions*; see Parker, *Discourse*, pp. xxxvii–xl, for another.

51 See especially the preface to *Discourse*, pp. xxxiii–xli.

52 Spurr, *Restoration Church of England*, p. 222.

53 Richard Allestree, *A Sermon Preached before The King … Nov. 17. 1667*, pp. 8ff. Allestree's analysis was shared by Anthony à Wood, who concluded gloom-

ily as he looked back, "This folly of laughing at [things worthwhile] continued worse and worse until 1679" – the year of course of renewed political crisis: quoted in Spurr, *Restoration Church of England*, p. 221.

54 Parker, *Discourse*, p. 30. Eachard betrayed his sensitivities by opening his *Grounds and Occasions*, sig. A3–A3v., with jibes at Milton.

55 Parker, *Discourse*, pp. xxi–xxii, xliii–xliv.

56 Thus, Parker closed his "Preface" to John Bramhall, *Bishop Bramhall's Vindication of Himself* (1672) with a long denunciation of Machiavellianism: sig. e4ff.

57 Parker, *Discourse*, pp. 135, 137.

58 Spurr thus mistakes the nature of Restoration polemical strategies when he takes at face value Eachard's approval of Patrick's "pleasant" style, and assumes that the "lightness of touch" found in the latter and in Parker meant that they were "aimed at Dissent." *Restoration Church of England*, p. 227 and n.

59 The tactic was not dissimilar to that of Richard Hooker as he preached to a select audience of lawyers and gentlemen at the Temple.

60 Parker, *Discourse*, preface, p. xii.

61 Thomas, "Comprehension and Indulgence," pp. 200–1; *A Letter from Mr. Wild*, p. 10.

62 Parker, *Discourse*, pp. xliii–xliv, 149–50; "Preface" to Bramhall, *Bishop Bramhall*, sig. e3v.–e4.

63 Spurr, *Restoration Church of England*, pp. 116–18, 129–32.

64 See Derek Hirst and Steven Zwicker, "High Summer at Nun Appleton 1651," *Historical Journal* 36 (1993), 265–6; for Marvell's continuing attachment to the duke, see Conal Condren, "Andrew Marvell as Polemicist," in *The Political Identity of Andrew Marvell*, ed. Conal Condren and A. D. Cousins (Aldershot, 1990), p. 165.

65 *The Rehearsal Transpros'd*, pp. xiii, 9–10.

66 *Ibid.*, p. 47. Marvell's "Nonconformists" of 1672 had of course been in power in 1650, and therefore scarcely non-conforming; but in the eyes of the churchmen, and of Hobbesians, their spiritual character had not changed.

67 Sir William Davenant's *Preface* to *Gondibert* is accessibly printed, with Hobbes's *Answer*, in J. Spingarn, ed., *Critical Essays of the Seventeenth Century* (3 vols., Oxford, 1908–9), vol. II, pp. 1–67, especially pp. 4, 9–10, 25.

68 *The Rehearsal Transpros'd*, pp. 10–12: the quotation is to be found at p. 11.

69 See Hirst and Zwicker, "High Summer at Nun Appleton," 265–6.

70 Spingarn, *Critical Essays*, vol. II, p. 12.

71 See above all Wallace, *Destiny his Choice*, pp. 189–93, for the subtlety of Marvell's argument here.

72 Davenant had in 1650 dedicated the *Preface* to *Gondibert* to Hobbes, and Hobbes's *Answer* shows his appreciation of the message as well as the compliment: for the texts of these, see Spingarn, *Critical Essays*, vol. II, pp. 1–67. In a revealing aside in his 1672 essay *Of Heroic Plays*, Dryden

asserted that "the poet is then to endeavour an absolute dominion over the minds of the spectators": *The Essays of John Dryden*, ed. W. P. Ker (2 vols., Oxford, 1900), vol. I, p. 155.

73 Robert M. Bliss, *Revolution and Empire. English Politics and the American Colonies in the Seventeenth Century* (Manchester, 1990), p. 175.

74 With its claim that there was a separate culture of dissent, Keeble's *Literary Culture of Nonconformity* generally accords with such assumptions. For the beginnings of a corrective, see E. Duffy, "The Godly and the Multitude in Stuart England," *The Seventeenth Century* 1 (1986), 31–55. Christopher Hill may have gone a trifle too far, in *Milton and the English Revolution* (London and New York, 1978), in locating the poet firmly in the culture of the alehouse.

75 Ashcraft, *Revolutionary Politics*.

76 For the last, see *Insolence and Impudence triumphant; Envy and Fury enthron'd: the Mirrour of Malice and Madness, In a late Treatise, Entituled, A Discourse of Ecclesiastical Polity, &c. or, The Lively Portraiture of Mr. S. P. Limn'd and drawn by his own hand* (1669).

77 *Loyalty and Nonconformity*.

78 *The Censure of the Rota* (1673), pp. 2–3, 13–14, 19; cf. *The Friendly Vindication of Mr. Dryden* (1673), pp. 12, 15.

79 *A Description of the Academy of the Athenian Virtuosi* (1673), pp. 11, 15: the identification of the Censurer is fixed not only by the references to Wild but also by the account of the Censurer's wife with a herring's tail between her teeth – a description borrowed from Wild himself: *A Letter from Mr. Wild*.

80 Dryden's essay is accessibly reprinted in *Essays of John Dryden*, ed. Ker, vol. I, pp. 21–108; the discussion of Wild is to be found at pp. 31–3.

81 Steps in the career can be traced in Robert Wild, *Iter Boreale* (1660); for Wild's presbyterian versifying, see the poems appended to the 1665 edition of *Iter Boreale*, his lament in *Upon the Rebuilding of the City* (1669) at the barriers to non-conformist church-building after the Fire, and "Poetica Licentia" in *A Letter from Mr. Wild*, pp. 25–36.

82 *A Letter from Mr. Wild*, pp. 14–15. The monkey in question was John Eachard, *Mr. Hobbs's State of Nature Considered*.

83 Parker, *Reproof to the Rehearsal Transpros'd* (1673), pp. 250–1.

84 *The Famous Battel of the Catts*, p. 11: I am indebted to Rob Hermann for this reference; *A Letter from Mr. Wild*, pp. 14–15.

85 Eamonn Duffy, "The Godly and the Multitude in Stuart England," *The Seventeenth Century* 1 (1986), 42, and, more generally, 31–55. I am grateful to Richard Strier for reminding me of the connections to Marprelate.

86 See Steven Zwicker, "Milton, Dryden, and the Politics of Literary Controversy," in *Culture and Society in the Stuart Restoration*, ed. Gerald MacLean (Cambridge, 1995), pp. 137–58.

87 And so a challenge to a duel could pass in 1669 between two of the king's ministers when one threatened to vilify the other on the stage: Wynn, *Dryden and his World*, p. 201.

88 Tessa Watt, *Cheap Print and Popular Piety, 1560–1650* (Cambridge, 1991);

Eamonn Duffy, "The Godly and the Multitude in Stuart England," 31–55; Peter Lake, "Deeds against Nature: Cheap Print, Protestantism and Murder in Early Seventeenth Century England," in *Culture and Politics in Early Stuart England*, ed. Kevin Sharpe and Peter Lake (London, 1993), pp. 257–83. To be fair, the editors of the latter volume provide a more nuanced version in their introduction: pp. 9–12.

89 Samuel Parker, *A demonstration of the Divine Authority of the Law of Nature* (1681), preface, pp. iii–iv: quoted in Pocock, "Thomas Hobbes: Atheist or Enthusiast?" 741.

8 SYDNEY'S *DISCOURSES* ON POLITICAL IMAGOES AND ROYALIST ICONOGRAPHY

1 This is the conclusion of Jonathan Scott in his exceptional biography, *Algernon Sidney and the English Republic, 1623–1677* (Cambridge, 1988), and *Algernon Sidney and the Restoration Crisis* (Cambridge, 1991). I am indebted to Scott and to Alan Huston's *Algernon Sidney and the Republican Heritage in England and America* (Princeton, NJ, 1991): their discussions of Sidney's self-representation (Scott) and model of rational autonomy (Huston) raised the issue I address here – the *Discourses'* conception of political iconography in its criticism of Filmer. I am grateful to Jayne Lewis, Richard Kroll, Richard Strier, and Derek Hirst for their considerable help with this essay.

2 See Peter Laslett, ed. *Patriarcha and Other Political Works of Sir Robert Filmer* (1949; rpt. New York, 1984); John Locke, *Two Treatises of Government*, ed. Peter Laslett (1963; rpt. New York, 1965); Gordon J. Schochet, *Patriarchalism in Political Thought* (Oxford, 1975); Sommerville, ed., *Patriarcha and Other Writings / Sir Robert Filmer* (Cambridge, 1991); Richard Ashcraft, *Revolutionary Politics and Locke's Two Treatises of Government* (Princeton, NJ, 1986); J. G. A. Pocock, *The Machiavellian Moment* (Princeton, NJ, 1975), especially pp. 333–506; and Blair Worden, "The Commonwealth Kidney of Algernon Sidney," *Journal of British Studies* 24 (1985), 1–40. In the last decade, there has been a burst of interest in Sidney, largely owing to Worden and Scott, and culminating in the recent publication of *The Court Maxims*, ed. Hans W. Blom, Eco Haitsma Mulier and Ronald Janse (Cambridge, 1996), which Worden himself unearthed in the Warwickshire County Record Office in the 1970s.

3 Laslett, ed., *Patriarcha*, pp. 37–9.

4 *Ibid.*, 39.

5 David Cannadine, *Aspects of Aristocracy* (New Haven, CT, 1994), pp. 130–62.

6 Algernon Sidney, *Discourses concerning government*, ed. Thomas G. West (Indianapolis, 1990), p. 82. All subsequent references to this edition appear in the text.

7 Compare *Court Maxims*, Third and Fourth Dialogues, pp. 24–65.

8 Laslett, ed., *Patriarcha*, p. 31. Laslett refers to "the principle of consent. This

to Filmer was an obvious contradiction of the social reality around him ... If authority could be exercised without consent, if in fact it was perpetually being so exercised, then there must be some other source of obligation. This other sort of obligation could only be by nature ...”

9 This is a point continually reaffirmed, for example, by James J. Murphy in his work on medieval rhetorical theory (see *Rhetoric in the Middle Ages* [Berkeley, CA, 1974], pp. 99–101). For Hobbes's use of Aristotle, see my “Hobbes on Rhetoric,” in *The Cambridge Companion to Hobbes*, ed. Tom Sorrell (Cambridge, 1996), pp. 329–45. On the rhetorical and discursive dimensions of Machiavelli's politics, see Victoria Kahn, *Machiavellian Rhetoric from the Counter-Reformation to Milton* (Princeton, NJ, 1994), pp. 243–8.

10 Compare *Court Maxims*, Ninth Dialogue, pp. 127–33.

11 Sidney makes these suggestive comments about the moral use of self-portraiture in his essay *Of Love*, in *A Collection of Scarce and Valuable Tracts ... of the Late Lord Somers*, ed. Sir Walter Scott (9 vols., 2nd edn., London, 1809–15), vol. VIII, pp. 612–19. See Huston's account of this essay as contributing to Sidney's model of rational autonomy, *Republican Heritage*, pp. 130–6.

12 Sidney, *Of Love, Somers Tracts*, vol. VIII, p. 612.

13 Compare *Court Maxims*, Fifth and Seventh Dialogues, pp. 66–70, 81–6.

14 The ubiquity of these topoi in the sixteenth and seventeenth centuries is nicely illustrated by Ben Jonson's *Explorata, or Discoveries*, which not only rehearse Sidney's same complaints about courtiers but also construe political turpitude as an imagistic as well as moral degeneracy. See George Parfitt, ed., *Ben Jonson: The Complete Poems* (New Haven, CT, 1982), especially pp. 394–8, 403–20.

15 Michel Foucault, *The History of Sexuality* (3 vols., New York, 1990), vol. II, p. 85. Again, Ben Jonson draws the same moral equation between “effeminacy” and sensual incontinence, and assigns the “effeminate” a particular order of self-expression.

16 The *Court Maxims* treats this popular degeneration as the calculated effect of royalist strategy. See the Sixth Dialogue, pp. 73, 78–80.

17 The classic study is Ernst Kantorowicz, *The King's Two Bodies: A Study in Medieval Political Theology* (Princeton, NJ, 1981). For accounts of royalist iconography in France and England at the time, see for example, Peter Burke, *The Fabrication of Louis XIV* (New Haven, CT, 1992); David Howarth, *Images of Rule: Art and Politics in the English Renaissance, 1485–1649* (Berkeley, CA, 1997); Louis Marin, *Portrait of the King* (Minneapolis, MN, 1988); Richard Ollard, *The Image of the King: Charles I and Charles II* (London, 1993); Roy Strong, *The Cult of Elizabeth* (Berkeley, CA, 1977), and *Van Dyck: Charles I on Horseback* (New York, 1972).

18 It has frequently been remarked – not least by the Romantic poets who always paired them admiringly – that Sidney's brand of republicanism seems most completely to resemble Milton's, especially in its distinctive emphasis on the subject principle in government – on the exercise of civic consent and civic virtue however conceived – as a significant means to the

common good. In short, for both Sidney and Milton, justice entails acknowledging the subjective crux to civic order, if only because they each insist upon the moral dignity of those who represent a people as their magistrates. Liberty is not just of body or possessions but of understanding and choice, a freedom both regard as natural and innate to every human being. Moreover, like Sidney, Milton analyzes the assumptions and practice of what he too condemns as royalist iconolatry, a pathology he most completely exemplifies in the Satans of *Paradise Lost* and *Paradise Regained*. But precisely because Milton and Sidney observe the contingency of political forms or expressions, they differ markedly from each other in polemical idiom, with the single exception of a discursiveness shared with many of their contemporaries. For an account of the relationship between Milton's politics and his iconography, see my *Predicament of Milton's Irony* (Princeton, NJ, forthcoming).

19 Carol Pateman, *The Sexual Contract* (Stanford, 1988).
20 Robert Filmer, *Patriarcha and Other Writings*, ed. Johann P. Sommerville (Cambridge, 1991), p. 4.
21 John Dunn, *The Political Thought of John Locke: An Historical Account of the Argument of the Two Treatises of Government* (Cambridge, 1969), p. 76.
22 This is Foucault's account of Renaissance culture in *The Order of Things* (New York, 1973), pp. 17–45.
23 On the conceptual and moral impact of absurdity, see Thomas Nagel's *Mortal Questions* (Cambridge, 1991), p. 20.
24 James Sutherland, *English Literature of the Late Seventeenth Century* (Oxford, 1969), p. 360. Scott cites this remark and the passage from Keats's letters in *The English Republic*, p. 8 and n. Further examples abound.
25 See the appendix of Violet A. Rowe's *Sir Henry Vane the Younger: A Study in Political and Administrative History* (London, 1970), pp. 275–83, especially p. 281.
26 Ruth Kelso, *The Doctrine of the English Gentleman in the Sixteenth Century* (Urbana, IL, 1929; rpt. New York, 1964), p. 39.
27 These memorabilia are cited in *Folklore, Myths and Legends of Britain* (London, 1973), pp. 160, 208, 224. Bram Stoker's tale, "The Judge's House," is collected in *The Oxford Book of English Ghost Stories*, ed. Michael Cox and R. A. Gilbert (Oxford, 1989), pp. 109–24.
28 For Sidney's unprecedented composure, see Scott, *Sidney and the Restoration Crisis*, pp. 320–59; see also Alan Huston's discussion of the autobiographical impulse behind Sidney's theory of rational autonomy, *Republican Heritage*, pp. 130–6.
29 Joseph Wittreich, Jr., ed., *The Romantics on Milton* (Cleveland, OH, 1970), pp. 552–3. See also pp. 120–1, for similar remarks from Wordsworth in the context of Bonapartism.
30 See *A Complete Collection of State Trials*, ed. T. B. Howell (33 vols., London, 1811), vol. IX, pp. 817–1022, especially pp. 902–3.
31 *Ibid.*, vol. IX, pp. 867–8.

32 Jeffrey Reiman, *Justice and Modern Moral Philosophy* (New Haven, CT, 1990),
   p. 113. Reiman's emphasis on the subjective as the proper dimension of
   justice is not unlike Sidney's.
33 *State Trials*, vol. IX, p. 916.

Index

Abbott, Archbishop George, 151
Ad Herennium, 84–5
Abraham (in Genesis), 178–9
Allestree, Richard, 155
Althusser, Louis, 3
Ames, William, 111
Andrewes, Lancelot, 93
Appian, 73
Aquinas, Saint Thomas, 111
Ariès, Philippe, 52, 53, 64, 68
Aristophanes, 72
Aristotle, 72, 74, 76, 77–8, 80, 83, 84, 85, 86, 168–9
Arlington, Henry Bennett, Earl of, 156
Arminians (and Arminianism), 3, 91, 93, 96, 107, 118, 121
Ascham, Roger, 2, 71
Ashcraft, Richard, 149, 160, 166
Assembly, Westminister, 107, 134, 140
Aubrey, John, 56, 57, 58, 61, 62, 70, 72, 73, 79, 126, 130, 143
Augustus (Emperor), 82

Bacon, Sir Francis, 2, 17, 25, 41, 74, 79
Bagshaw, Edward, 123
Baxter, Richard, 90
Bellarmine, Cardinal, 86
Bentham, Jeremy, 44
Berger, Harry, 22, 28
Berkenhead, John, 96–7, 105
Bligh, E. W., 62
Blount, Edward, 75
Bodin, Jean, 74
Bourdieu, Pierre, 29
Bradshaw, John, 184
Braganza, Catherine of (Queen of England), 152
Bramhall, Bishop John, 157, 158
Broughton, Elizabeth, 56
Breda, Declaration of, 146
Breight, Curt, 26, 27

Brown, Paul, 26
Bruni, Leonardo, 84
Buchanan, George, 14
Buckingham, George Villiers, 1st Duke of, 119
Buckingham, George Villiers, 2nd Duke of, 149, 156, 157, 158, 163
Bunyan, John, 160
Burroughs, Jeremiah, 102, 106

Caesar, Julius, 73
Caligula, 177
Calvinism, 3, 96, 107, 118–19
Campion, Sir William, 89, 90, 107, 110
Cannadine, David, 167
Carey, Sir George, 18
Castiglione, Baldesar, 15
Catherine, Saint (of Siena), 152
Cavendish, William, 1st Earl of Devonshire, 70
Cavendish, William, 2nd Earl of Devonshire, 2, 5, 70–1, 74–5
Cavendish, William, 3rd Earl of Devonshire, 75–6
Cavendish, William, Earl of Newcastle, 74 and 188n.
Césaire, Aimé, 10, 11, 17, 25, 27
Charles I (King of England), 4, 52, 69, 99–105, 118, 119–20, 125–6, 128, 129–30, 131–3, 137–8, 141, 143, 144, 184
Charles II (King of England), 141, 146, 150, 152, 153
Cheke, Sir John, 71
Cheshire, Bishop Joseph, 37
Chillingworth, William, 95, 105
Cheynell, Francis, 99, 101, 102
Churchill, Sir Winston, 167
Cicero (and Ciceronianism), 2, 72, 74, 78, 85, 168
Clarendon, Edward Hyde, Earl of, 56, 90, 117, 128, 145, 155, 160
Clifford, Thomas Lord, 156
Clotworthy, Sir John, 123

233

Printed in the United Kingdom
by Lightning Source UK Ltd.
135791UK00001B/270/P